PROCEDURAL AUTONOMY ACROSS EUROPE

PROCEDURAL AUTONOMY ACROSS EUROPE

Edited by
Bart Krans
Anna Nylund

INTERSENTIA

Intersentia Ltd
8 Wellington Mews
Wellington Street | Cambridge
CB1 1HW | United Kingdom
Tel.: +44 1223 736 170
Email: mail@intersentia.co.uk
www.intersentia.com | www.intersentia.co.uk

Distribution for the UK and Ireland:
NBN International
Airport Business Centre, 10 Thornbury Road
Plymouth, PL6 7PP
United Kingdom
Tel.: +44 1752 202 301 | Fax: +44 1752 202 331
Email: orders@nbninternational.com

Distribution for Europe and all other countries:
Intersentia Publishing nv
Groenstraat 31
2640 Mortsel
Belgium
Tel.: +32 3 680 15 50 | Fax: +32 3 658 71 21
Email: mail@intersentia.be

Distribution for the USA and Canada:
Independent Publishers Group
Order Department
814 North Franklin Street
Chicago, IL 60610
USA
Tel.: +1 800 888 4741 (toll free) | Fax: +1 312 337 5985
Email: orders@ipgbook.com

Artwork on cover: Tatiana Korchemkina – Alamy Stock Photo

ISBN 978-1-78068-906-7
D/2020/7849/4
NUR 822

British Library Cataloguing in Publication Data. A catalogue record for this book is available from the British Library.

PREFACE

This book is the result of a great collaboration with colleagues from various EU Member States. The idea for this book crystallised during a seminar in Leiden in November 2018, where each of the contributors presented their initial findings on Procedural Autonomy in their respective Member State. The outcomes were discussed at great length and, following the conclusion of the seminar, each of the authors involved in this volume continued to work on developing their presentation into the final book chapters submitted for publication in this richly analytical and comparative collection.

We are happy to have been able to work with Intersentia once more on this book, building on the strong working relationship established during previous collaboration on earlier titles in this field. The cooperation with Intersentia has been, as always, a pleasure.

As editors of this book and organisers of the abovementioned seminar, we look back on both the dynamic discussions enjoyed in Leiden and the production of Procedural Autonomy Across Europe fondly, both were thoroughly inspiring experiences.

Lastly, we are grateful for the valuable comments and suggestions that our peer reviewers provided, and to Leiden Law School for its financial contribution to this project.

Bart Krans and Anna Nylund
Leiden/Tromsø, January 2020

CONTENTS

TABLE OF CASES

SUPRANATIONAL

THE COURT OF JUSTICE OF THE EUROPEAN UNION

THE EFTA COURT

EUROPEAN COURT OF HUMAN RIGHTS

NATIONAL

BELGIUM

ENGLAND AND WALES

FINLAND

THE NETHERLANDS

NORWAY

POLAND

SLOVENIA

LIST OF AUTHORS

Laura Ervo is a professor at Örebro University, Sweden. She is also an adjunct professor (docent) in procedural law at the University of Turku, the University of Helsinki and the University of Eastern Finland. Her field of special interest is procedural law, especially human rights within the field of procedural law.

Aleš Galič is full professor at the University of Ljubljana Faculty of Law, Slovenia. His major interests in teaching and research are civil procedure, international private law, arbitration and ADR.

Wolfgang Hau is full professor of private law and German, international and comparative civil procedure at Ludwig-Maximilians-University Munich, Germany. He is also a judge at the *Oberlandesgericht* (Higher Regional Court) Munich.

Bart Krans is full professor at the University of Leiden, the Netherlands, where he holds the chair of private law and civil procedure law. His research mainly concerns civil procedure law and contract law. Among his publications are books on the influence of EU law on Dutch civil procedure law, on the law of evidence and on the law of obligations.

Jordi Nieva-Fenoll is full professor (chair) of procedural law at the University of Barcelona, Spain. His research interests include the law of evidence, *res iudicata*, cassation, artificial intelligence, neuroscience and procedure, among other topics. He holds five doctorates *honoris causa* from universities in South America and has been a panelist in over 100 international congresses across almost 20 countries.

Anna Nylund is a professor at the University of Tromsø – The Arctic University of Tromsø, Norway. Her research and teaching mainly concern national, comparative and European civil procedure and alternative dispute resolution. She is the chair of the research group of procedural law and dispute resolution.

Anna Piszcz is a professor at the University of Bialystok, Poland. Her research and teaching mainly concern economic law, competition law in particular, and civil law.

John Sorabji is a senior teaching fellow at University College London and the principal legal adviser to the Lord Chief Justice of England and Wales and the Master of the Rolls. He is the author of, amongst other publications, *English Civil Justice after Woolf and Jackson.*

Piet Taelman is senior full professor at Ghent University Law School, Belgium. He teaches courses on civil procedure and has written on a wide variety of topics on civil procedural law in national and international publications. He has previously practised as a lawyer and arbitrator as a member of the Ghent Bar and served as dean of the Ghent Law School between 2008-2014.

Anna Wallerman Ghavanini is an associate professor at the University of Gothenburg, Sweden, and a Ragnar Söderberg Postdoctoral Fellow in law. She has previously held positions at the European University Institute and the University of Zurich. Her research interests include EU law and civil procedure.

Jarich Werbrouck is a doctoral candidate at Ghent University, Belgium, funded by the Research Foundation Flanders. His work focuses on the impact of EU consumer law on the procedural autonomy of the Member States. He has published in both national and international journals on several topics, including his doctoral topic, European product liability and the EAPO-regulation.

ASPECTS OF PROCEDURAL AUTONOMY

Bart Krans and Anna Nylund

1. INTRODUCTION

Procedural autonomy plays an important role in the relation between EU law and national civil procedural law. It has traditionally been recognised that Member States are, in the absence of EU procedural law, free to set up the procedural system as they deem fit. Up until the early 2000s the main limitation to procedural autonomy was the requirement of equal and effective protection of rights arising from EU law. Since the early 2000s, Member States have been confronted with a growing body of EU legislation and case law on procedural topics.

Considering that 'Europe is in a period of increasing Europeanisation of civil procedure',[1] it is topical to question whether the term 'procedural autonomy' still accurately describes the power of national lawmakers.

---

1 A. Nylund and B. Krans, 'The European Union and National Civil Procedure – A Rocky Road or a Smooth Process' in A. Nylund and B. Krans (eds), *European Union and National Civil Procedure*, Intersentia, Antwerp-Cambridge 2016, p. 1.

Perhaps the room for manoeuvre is limited in such a way that procedural autonomy is misleading, and Member States are no longer able to construct their procedural system as they deem fit. The process of Europeanisation of national civil procedure has not come to an end. On the contrary: the influence of Europe on national civil procedure of the Member States is ongoing.

The nature of procedural autonomy has been debated. In EU law, it sometimes refers primarily to ECJ case law where the principles of effective and equivalent protection of rights arising from EU law have been developed and refined. In other settings, procedural autonomy encompasses the wider context of EU law with civil procedural implications. It could also be interpreted as a principle requiring EU law to respect national idiosyncrasies of national law as long as these do not significantly hamper the enforcement of EU law.

Moreover, the perception of procedural autonomy and the manner and intensity to which it limits national civil procedure law may vary among the Member States. These variations could, in turn, have implications for the implementation of EU procedural law. Hence, exploring perceptions of procedural autonomy in the Member States puts the term in a wider context and enables us to assess what procedural autonomy, understood broadly, is today and whether the term procedural autonomy is appropriate today.

2. A BRIEF HISTORICAL OVERVIEW OF PROCEDURAL AUTONOMY

2.1. AUTONOMY, EFFICIENCY, EQUIVALENCE AND JUDICIAL PROTECTION

Although procedural autonomy is a widely used concept, the exact nature and tenets of it are unclear.

The history of the concept of procedural autonomy can be traced back to the seminal ECJ rulings in the *Rewe*[2] and *Comet*[3] cases in 1976. The ECJ ruled that

> in the absence of Community rules on this subject, it is for the domestic legal system of each Member State … to determine the procedural conditions

2 Case 33–76, *Rewe-Zentralfinanz eG and Rewe-Zentral AG v. Landwirtschaftskammer für das Saarland*, ECLI:EU:C:1976:188.

3 Case 45–76, *Comet BV v. Produktschap voor Siergewassen*, ECLI:EU:C:1976:191.

> governing actions at law intended to ensure the protection of the rights which citizens have from the direct effect of Community law, it being understood that such conditions cannot be less favourable than those relating to similar actions of a domestic nature …
>
> In the absence of such measures of harmonization the right conferred by Community law must be exercised before the national courts in accordance with the conditions laid down by national rules.[4]

The rulings set out the requirements of equal and efficient enforcement of rights deriving from EU law, i.e. the principles of effectiveness and equivalence. These have been reiterated in numerous cases.[5] In the landmark *Factortame I*[6] ruling, the ECJ found that any rule or practice that prevents courts from 'do[ing] everything necessary … to set aside national legislative provisions which might prevent, even temporarily, Community rules from having full force and effect' is incompatible with the very essence of Community law, thus extending the test of the *Rewe* ruling.

In *van Schijndel*, the ECJ refined the test to an analysis of whether 'a national procedural provision renders application of Community law impossible or excessively difficult' viewed as a whole and in its context in the light of 'the basic principles of the domestic judicial system, such as protection of the rights of the defence, the principle of legal certainty and the proper conduct of procedure'.[7] This entails balancing the aims of national rules with the requirements of EU law. The ECJ also stated that 'national legislation must be applied in a manner which is not discriminatory as

4 Case 33–76, *Rewe*, above note 2, at [5] and Case 45–76, *Comet*, above note 3, at [13]–[16].

5 E.g. Joined cases C-430/93 and C-431/93, *Jeroen van Schijndel and Johannes Nicolaas Cornelis van Veen v. Stichting Pensioenfonds voor Fysiotherapeuten*, ECLI:EU:C:1995:441; Case C-312/93, *Peterbroeck, Van Campenhout & Cie SCS v. Belgian State*, ECLI:EU:C:1995:437; Case C-126/97, *Eco Swiss China Time Ltd v. Benetton International NV*, ECLI:EU:C:1999:269; Joined cases C-240/98 to C-244/98, *Océano Grupo Editorial SA and others v. Roció Murciano Quintero and others*, ECLI:EU:C:2000:346; Case C-453/99, *Courage Ltd v. Bernard Crehan and Bernard Crehan v. Courage Ltd and Others*, ECLI:EU:C:2001:465; Joined cases C-295/04 to C-298/04, *Vincenzo Manfredi and others v. Lloyd Adriatico Assicurazioni SpA and others*, ECLI:EU:C:2006:461.

6 Case C-213/89, *The Queen v. Secretary of State for Transport, ex parte: Factortame Ltd and others*, ECLI:EU:C:1990:257 at [20].

7 Joined cases C-430/93 and C-431/93, *Jeroen van Schijndel and Johannes Nicolaas Cornelis van Veen v. Stichting Pensioenfonds voor Fysiotherapeuten*, ECLI:EU:C:1995:441 at [19] and Case C-312/93, *Peterbroek, Van Campenhout & Cie SCS v. Belgian State*, ECLI:EU:C:1995:437 at [14].

compared to procedures for deciding national disputes of the same type'.[8] This development could be described as the Court stepping back from the doctrine in *Factortame I* to allow more autonomy for the Member States.[9] It could also be characterised as a pendulum swing between more intense and more lenient tests.

In addition to the principles of effectiveness and equivalence, the ECJ has applied the principle of judicial protection that obliges national courts to:

> interpret the procedural rules governing actions brought before them ... in such a way as to enable those rules, wherever possible, to be implemented in such a manner as to contribute to the attainment of the objective ... of ensuring effective judicial protection of an individual's rights under Community law.[10]

Effective judicial protection is a general principle of EU law and has a far more overreaching and intrusive approach than the principles of effectiveness and equivalence, as it constitutes a fundamental right with a constitutional status.[11] Although the principle of effective judicial protection could, and should, be separated from the principles of effectiveness and equivalence due to differences in scope, scrutiny, legal basis and purpose,[12] from the perspective of the Member States all three principles limit the 'discretion'

---

8 E.g. Joined cases 205/82 to 215/82, *Deutsche Milchkontor GmbH and others v. Federal Republic of Germany*, ECLI:EU:C:1983:233, at [19]- [23].

9 E.g. E. Storskrubb, *Civil Procedure and EU Law. A Policy Area Uncovered*, Oxford University Press, Oxford 2008, p. 15; M. Dougan, *National Remedies Before the Court of Justice. Issues of Harmonisation and Differentiation*, Hart Publishing, Oxford and Portland Oregon 2004, pp. 28–34 and 227ff. For a criticism of this line of argumentation, see M. Bobek, 'Why There Is No Principle of "Procedural Autonomy" of the Member States' in B. de Witte and H. Micklitz (eds), *The European Court of Justice and Autonomy of the Member States*, Intersentia, Antwerp-Cambridge 2011.

10 Case C-432/05, *Unibet (London) Ltd and Unibet (International) Ltd v. Justitiekanslern*, ECLI:EU:C:2007:163 at [36]–[37] and [43]–[44].

11 Case 222/84, *Marguerite Johnston v. Chief Constable of the Royal Ulster Constabulary*, ECLI:EU:C:1986:206 at [13]–[21]; Case C-279/09, *DEB Deutsche Energiehandels- und Beratungsgesellschaft mbH v. Bundesrepublik Deutschland*, ECLI:EU:C:2010:811. In the latter case, the Court stated explicitly that the right to effective judicial protection is enshrined in Article 47 of the EU Fundamental Rights Charter.

12 For a comparison of the principles, see S. Prechal and K. Cath, 'The European acquis of civil procedure: constitutional aspects' [2014] *Unif L Rev* 19, S. Prechal and R. Widdershoven, 'Redefining the Relationship between "Rewe-effectiveness" and Effective Judicial Protection' [2011] *Rev of Euro Adm L* 4. See also Joined cases C-317/08 to C-320/08, *Rosalba Alassini and Others v. Telecom Italia SpA and Others*, ECLI:EU:C:2010:146, where the Court discussed both principles in parallel.

to design the national civil justice system, i.e. their procedural autonomy. Over the years, the ECJ has scrutinised numerous aspects of civil procedure law, including *inter alia* rules on time limits, *locus standi*, interim measures and rules of evidence.[13]

2.2. PROCEDURAL AUTONOMY AND A GROWING BODY OF EU CIVIL PROCEDURE LAW

At the time of the *Rewe* and *Comet* cases, EU civil procedure law was virtually non-existent: there were few, if any, provisions of relevance. EU civil procedure law was nascent – the 1968 Brussels Convention on jurisdiction and the enforcement of judgments in civil and commercial matters[14] and the 1971 Luxembourg Protocol[15] conferring the power to interpret the Convention to the ECJ which in practice transferred the Convention to EU law – but no-one could foresee the transformational changes from the turn of the millennium and onwards. The rulings were logical considering the decentralised enforcement of EU law.[16] The *Rewe* and *Comet* cases could be interpreted as a manifestation of the principles of cooperation and of subsidiarity in an age where EU law had not yet exerted influence on the procedural systems of the Member States.

The legal landscape of EU civil procedure some 40 years later is completely different. It is an 'unstoppable wave'[17] (or perhaps consecutive waves) of a variety of instruments regulating procedure with increasing density: 'constitutional' protection of the right to a fair trial in Article 47 of the EU Fundamental Rights Charter; numerous directives and regulations either partly or exclusively regulating procedural matters; ECJ case law with a direct impact on national civil procedure; soft law instruments; and

[13] E.g. K. Lenaerts, I. Maselis and K. Gutman, *EU Procedural Law*, Oxford University Press, Oxford 2014, pp. 111–156.

[14] 1968 Brussels Convention on jurisdiction and the enforcement of judgments in civil and commercial matters [1972] OJ L 299/32.

[15] Protocol concerning the interpretation by the Court of Justice of the convention of 27 September 1968 on jurisdiction and the enforcement of judgments in civil and commercial matters – signed in Luxembourg on 3 June 1971 [1975] OJ L 204/28.

[16] E.g. B. Hess, *Europäisches Zivilprozessrecht*, Heidelberg, C. F. Müller 2010, pp. 617–625.

[17] E. Storskrubb, 'Civil Justice – A Newcomer and an Unstoppable Wave' in P. Craig and G. De Búrca (eds), *The Evolution of European Law*, Oxford University Press, Oxford 2011, pp. 299–322.

even international treaties fundamentally entangled with EU law.[18] The primary subject matter and aims of EU civil procedure law varies: some of it deals with topics of judicial cooperation, such as recognition and enforcement of judgments and taking of evidence; some creates European procedures, such as the small claims procedure; and some of it is sectoral, regulating only certain types of cases, such as consumer cases, intellectual property rights or competition cases.[19] As a result, two (or more) parallel procedures or sets of rules are present in national law: a national procedure for domestic cases and a European procedure for cross-border cases, or one set of rules for disclosure for cases on infringement of intellectual property rights; one set for cases on competition law, and in all other cases, a third set of rules, or none at all. All these cases, rules, regulations and recommendations restrict national procedural autonomy.

Furthermore, EU civil procedure law sometimes challenges concepts, ideas and structures of national law. Depending on the degree of difference – it could be a matter of nuances or of colliding fundamental concepts, principles and structures – and the predicaments, they might ensue a need for radical reforms with potentially momentous consequences.[20]

2.3. THE NATURE OF PROCEDURAL AUTONOMY

Based on the current state of EU law with a significant procedural impact, a narrow construction of procedural autonomy would refer primarily to ECJ case law starting from *Rewe*. This line of thought reflects the perspective of EU law. The broad conception of procedural autonomy would be based on, in addition to the above-mentioned case law, all kinds of EU law that

---

18 For more details, see e.g. A. Nylund and M. Strandberg (eds), *Civil Procedure and Harmonisation of Law*, Intersentia, Antwerp-Cambridge 2018; A. Nylund and B. Krans (eds), *European Union and National Civil Procedure*, Intersentia, Antwerp-Cambridge 2016; B. Krans, 'EU Law and National Civil Procedure Law: An Invisible Pillar' [2015] *Eur. Rev. of Priv. L.* 567; Storskrubb, above note 17.

19 For a discussion on the shifting approaches to harmonisation of civil procedure, see E. Storskrubb, 'Civil Justice: The contested nature of the scope of EU legislation' in F. Trauder and A. R. Servent (eds), *Policy Change in the Area of Freedom, Security and Justice. How EU Institutions matter*, Routledge, London and New York 2015, and B. Hess, 'Procedural Harmonisation in a European Context' in X. E. Kramer and C. H. van Rhee (eds), *Civil Litigation in a Globalising World*, Asser Press, The Hague 2012, pp. 159ff.

20 See e.g. Nylund and Strandberg, above note 18, and Nylund and Krans, above note 18.

limits the discretion of the Member State to design the civil justice system as it wishes. This perspective is procedural and is likely to coincide with the Member State perspective.

As EU civil procedure law expands in depth, coverage and methods, the nature of procedural autonomy becomes less clear, and the immanent tension between procedural autonomy and harmonisation becomes manifest.[21] Vagueness of procedural autonomy also emanates from the case-by-case approach and the fact that many of the cases concern administrative law rather than core civil procedure.[22] Is procedural autonomy a principle of law expressing national sovereignty?[23] Or, a principle for delimiting competencies,[24] or a reminder that the profound variation in the cultural underpinnings of procedural law must be respected?[25] Is it a shorthand for the line of argumentation in ECJ case law?[26] Perhaps the ECJ does not recognise the procedural autonomy of the Member States at all,[27] or procedural autonomy is 'not much more about lip service than reality',[28] a kind of 'euphemism'.[29] Residual powers might be more descriptive than procedural autonomy.

Even the word 'procedural' has been questioned, as 'enforcement autonomy' or 'remedial autonomy' could be more accurate labels.[30] The latter issue also reflects the fact that the EU appears to focus on enforcement

---

21 Storskrubb, above note 9, pp. 13ff.

22 E.g. A. P. Komninos, 'New Prospects for Private Enforcement of EC Competition Law: *Courage v. Crehan* and the Community Right to Damages' (2002) 39 *Common Market Law Review* 447ff.

23 This conclusion could be inferred from *Delena Wells*, where the Court referred to the principle of procedural autonomy three times, Case C-201/02, *Delena Wells v. Secretary of State for Transport, Local Government and the Regions*, ECLI:EU:C:2004:12 at [65], [67] and [70].

24 M. Ludwigs, 'Die Verfahrensautonomie der Mitgliedstaaten – Euphemismus oder Identitätsfaktor?' [2018] *NVwZ* 1417.

25 E.g. A. Arnull, 'The Principle of Effective Judicial Protection in EU Law: An Unruly Horse?' [2011] *EurLR* 52.

26 E.g. S. Prechal, 'Community Law in National Courts: The Lessons from van Schijndel' (1998) 35(3) *Common Market Law Review* 681–706.

27 E.g. Bobek, above note 9, p. 305, and C. N. Kakouris, 'Do the Member States Possess Judicial Procedural "Autonomy"?' (1997) 34(6) *Common Market Law Review* 1389–1412.

28 P. Haapaniemi, 'Procedural Autonomy: A Misnormer' in L. Ervo, M. Gräns and A. Jokela (eds), *Europeanization of Procedural Law and the New Challenges to Fair Trial*, Europa Law Publishing, Groningen 2009, p. 119.

29 See Ludwigs, above note 24. However, Ludwigs describes procedural autonomy as a principle, not just a description of case law.

30 S. Prechal and K. Cath, above note 12, pp. 180–181.

and remedies, whereas national law oftentimes focuses on rights[31] and treats procedural law as a coherent system, which results in differences in the perceptions depending on whether one analyses procedural autonomy from the perspective of the EU or the Member States.

Viewing procedural autonomy as a principle is appealing for Member States advocating for maximum autonomy: the principle requires the EU to respect national procedural law and administration of civil justice as long as the national rules do not hinder the functioning of the single market, have cross-border implications or in any other way be contrary to EU law and unless EU law regulates the issue at hand.[32] The principle would guarantee maximum liberty for national law and perhaps even that the main bases for enacting new EU law, TFEU[33] Articles 81 and 114, would be interpreted and applied restrictively. Considering the principle of efficiency, the focus on enforcement of community rights and the proliferation of EU procedural law, this interpretation is inaccurate and represents a romanticised long for the 'paradise lost' when their national procedural systems remained 'intact' and consider the current situation as dissatisfactory.[34] It disregards how the idiosyncrasies of each Member State sometimes impede access to justice in cross-border cases and for rights ensuing from EU law.

Regardless of how one sees the nature of procedural autonomy, one should recognise the increasing 'relativisation' of it.[35] Both the ECJ and the Commission focus on enforcement and efficient judicial protection. The Antitrust Damages Directive[36] on private enforcement of competition law serves as an example of EU law where effective enforcement appears to be the paramount rationale.[37] It requires the Member States to enact

31 M. Ruffert, 'Rights and remedies in European community law: a comparative view' (1997) 34(2) *Common Market Law Review* 307.

32 E.g. Dougan, above note 9, p. 19.

33 Consolidated version of the Treaty on the Functioning of the European Union [2002] OJ C 326/47.

34 D.-U. Galetta, *Procedural Autonomy of EU Member States: A Paradise Lost? A Study of the 'Functionalizes Procedural Competence' of EU Member States*, Springer, Heidelberg 2010, p. 5.

35 Hess, above note 16, p. 622.

36 Directive 2014/104/EU of the European Parliament and of the Council of 26 November 2014 on certain rules governing actions for damages under national law for infringements of the competition law provisions of the Member States and of the European Union (Antitrust Damages Directive) [2004] OJ L 349/1.

37 Effective and effect appear numerous times in the Directive, in both the preamble and several of the provisions, see e.g. preamble paras 3–6 and 34 and Article 1.

inter alia specific mechanisms for collective redress and disclosure of evidence, which may not be fully compatible with existing national principles and regulation, nor is it certain that these innovations resolve the most pressing hindrances to efficient enforcement of rights.

So far, the ECJ has mostly assumed a middle position by balancing considerations for the effective and equal application of EU law with the need for coherence at the national level.[38] There are, however, exceptions particularly in the field of consumer law, where it has developed a rule on *ex officio* application of consumer law.[39]

3. A BOTTOM-UP APPROACH TO PROCEDURAL AUTONOMY AND NATIONAL CIVIL PROCEDURE

From the point of view of the Member States, procedural autonomy encapsulates general principles of law, hard law, soft law and even international law that is entangled with EU law, in addition to case law. The sectoral approach of EU law, whether it is creating rules applicable only for rights based on EU law, for cross-border cases or for a certain area of law, causes incoherence and inconsistency in the procedural law of Member States.[40] For instance, different criteria to determine the identity of a case could be used in national and EU law, or the notions of the duty and powers of the court to apply consumer law on its own motion could

38 Hess, above note 16, pp. 623–626; Storskrubb, above note 9, pp. 17–18.

39 For a discussion of the relevant case law, see e.g. A. Ancery and B. Krans, 'Consumer Protection and EU-Driven Judicial Activism in the Netherlands' in A. Nylund and M. Strandberg (eds), *Civil Proecdure and Harmonisation of Law*, Intersentia, Antwerp-Cambridge 2018, pp. 131–136; I. Bach, 'The Role of the Judge in Consumer Cases – A German Perspective' in A. Nylund and M. Strandberg (eds), *Civil Proecdure and Harmonisation of Law*, Intersentia, Antwerp-Cambridge 2018, pp. 142–148; T. Andersson, '*Ex Officio* Application of the Unfair Terms Directive Cases Against Consumers – A Swedish Perspective' in A. Nylund and M. Strandberg (eds), *Civil Proecdure and Harmonisation of Law*, Intersentia, Antwerp-Cambridge 2018, pp. 155–159; and H. H. Fredriksen and M. Strandberg, '*Ex Officio* application of EU Consumer Protection Law in Norwegian Courts' in A. Nylund and M. Strandberg (eds), *Civil Proecdure and Harmonisation of Law*, Intersentia, Antwerp-Cambridge 2018.

40 For a more detailed discussion, see E. Storskrubb, 'EU Civil Justice at the Harmonisation Crossroads?' in A. Nylund and M. Strandberg (eds), *Civil Proecdure and Harmonisation of Law*, Intersentia, Antwerp-Cambridge 2018, and S. Huber, 'Koordinierung europäischer Zivilprozessrechtsinstrumente' in R. Geimer and R. A. Schütze (eds), *Recht ohne Grenzen*, Festschrift für Athanassios Kaissis, Verlag Dr. Otto Schmidt 2012.

be incompatible, necessitating reform to align national civil procedure law with the requirements of EU law.

While sectoral harmonisation is at first glance a 'soft' method of implementation since it concerns a limited category of cases, it could, in fact, be invasive. Introducing collective redress or rules of disclosure in one sector creates fragmentation at the national level and could thus result in spill-over implementation where disclosure and collective redress are extended to other types of cases as well. What at first appeared to be a minor discrepancy or change, could turn out to be a snowball setting off an avalanche of changes. From the perspective of the Member States, these types of EU law restrain procedural autonomy. Thus, one could claim that the room for manoeuvre has been significantly limited since the turn of the century.

The extent to which the room for manoeuvre is limited, and the perceived nature of the limitations, is unclear. Based on previous studies, the impact of EU law on national civil procedure law is variegated and depends on numerous factors.[41] A fundamental aspect of civil procedure system might be discordant with the principles and doctrines of EU civil procedure law, such as the brevity of grounds for rulings in French law. National courts could suddenly become aware of a specific issue in EU civil procedure law and spark a discussion nationally, and possibly a dialogue with the ECJ, such as in the case of *ex officio* application of consumer law in the Netherlands. Innovations in EU law could be an impetus for reform of national law, in particular for introducing court-connected mediation, disclosure and collective redress, as numerous examples from various Member States demonstrate.

Concomitantly, EU law could also be overlooked, or its role and potential impact could be downplayed. A lack of interest in and knowledge of EU civil procedure law is an approximate description of the general picture in several Member States. EU law is oftentimes treated as 'technicalities' relating to cross-border cases with little or no consequence for civil procedure law, as a whole, or EU law is not applied simply because the involved lawyers are not aware of its existence or relevance in the case at hand.

In some ways, one could even spot recalcitrance towards EU civil procedure law. The English have oftentimes been accused for subversion, so have Swedish and Norwegian courts been in their reluctance to refer

41 Nylund and Strandberg, above note 18, and Nylund and Krans, above note 18.

cases for preliminary rulings and advisory opinions.[42] There are numerous other examples as well.

Previous studies have, however, not been able to identify traits that would consistently explain these differences. On the contrary, differences in the relationship between EU law and national civil procedure law cannot be attributed directly to the size, geography or legal cultural traits, nor does EU-scepticism or multi-speed integration seem to have fundamental effect in this respect. On the contrary, EU civil procedure has foundational impact even on countries refraining from participation in civil justice matters, i.e. Denmark, and a non-Member State, albeit with strong ties to the single market through the EEA Agreement, i.e. Norway.

In the light of the differences and similarities among Member States, and even non-members, the paramount question is how procedural autonomy is perceived nationally, and whether and how EU law limits the national room for manoeuvre in the domain of civil procedure. The national perspectives could deviate from the EU perspective, and hence ignite controversies and result in undesired outcomes in terms of inadequate implementation of EU law, or of EU law employing unsatisfactory methods of approximation.

4. THE AIM, STRUCTURE AND METHODS OF THIS BOOK

The book explores the impact of European law on national civil procedure using case-studies for several countries.

Colleagues coming from ten countries have contributed to this book. Each of them has been asked to discuss for his or her own country the impact of EU law on national procedural law and the room for manoeuvre in national procedural law. The participating colleagues have been asked to discuss how the civil procedure system of their country has reacted to EU law. By doing so, the aim is to disseminate the reasons for why these changes are the most significant and the further implications of EU law on the civil procedure.

This book aims to contain current developments and procedural autonomy will be the core matter. The national perspective of the respective

42 N. Andrews, 'European Influences Upon English Civil Justice: Tempests or Gentle Breezes?', A. Nylund, 'Norway: An Insider Outside – or an Outsider Insider – European Civil Justice' and A. Wallerman, 'The Curious Incident of the Dog in the Night-Time: Europeanisation of Civil Procedure in Sweden' in A. Nylund and B. Krans (eds), *Civil Procedure and National Law*, Intersentia, Antwerp-Cambridge 2016.

chapters aims to provide this book with a distinctive feature. By following these lines, this current book hopes to make visible the role of procedural autonomy of the Member States and the Europeanisation of national civil procedure law. It asks how procedural autonomy, or at least the room for manoeuvre in civil procedural law, is perceived in the Member States and to discuss some of the underlying reasons for the prevailing perceptions, consequences of the prevailing perceptions, or both. Secondly, this book asks whether there is still room for manoeuvre in national civil procedure, and if so, how much.

The lesson from previous studies is that limiting this book to selected regulations, ECJ cases etc is not advisable: what sparks controversy or reforms in one Member State may be smoothly incorporated into national law in another Member State. Therefore, the authors of each chapter have chosen the topic(s) they find most interesting from the perspective of their country (and perhaps also their individual research interests). By doing so, this book will hopefully broaden the understanding of the developments of procedural autonomy on the EU level from the perspective of Member States.

Ten countries representing small and large states, old and new Member States, different geographic parts of Europe and different legal traditions (civil law, common law, Nordic and post-socialist) have been selected for this book. To study whether multi-speed integration influences procedural autonomy, England and Norway have been chosen to be included. England has an opt-out from judicial cooperation, at least until Brexit. Norway is not an EU Member State, but through the Agreement on the European Economic Area (EEA) EU law still has a significant impact on Norwegian law. Comparing the selected Member States, i.e. Belgium, Germany, Finland, the Netherlands, Poland, Slovenia, Spain and Sweden, with England (or the UK) on its way out of the EU and Norway, could illuminate how multi-speed integration works in practice.

In the concluding chapter, it is aimed to provide a more comprehensive comparison between the countries represented in the book. Which doctrines, which pieces of legislation or features in legislation pose problems for national civil procedure? Are some legal systems or topics more prone to integrate European rules, and are others more resistant to changes? Is procedural autonomy more limited in some countries than others? Are there differences in how procedural autonomy is understood and conceptualised nationally? The answer to these questions will help us assess whether procedural autonomy still accurately describes the powers of EU Member States in private law.

PROCEDURAL AUTONOMY AND BELGIAN CIVIL PROCEDURE LAW

A Turbulent Cohabitation

Piet Taelman and Jarich Werbrouck

1. INTRODUCTION

A thorough knowledge of and familiarity with each other are prerequisites for any well-balanced relationship. Cohabitation in a multi-layered legal system, with complex interrelations between its different layers, is not always a walk in the park. Member States have to learn to live with their shrinking procedural autonomy and the way this affects their national legal system, due to the varying impact of EU (case) law, fundamental legal principles and even soft law instruments.

Against this background of procedural autonomy, two topics are analysed which are particularly relevant from a Belgian viewpoint. The first reveals, in the wake of a recent CJEU judgment, the urgent need to rethink profoundly and deliberate the Belgian rules on litigation costs. The second topic confronts us with the phenomenon of spontaneous harmonisation. Transposing a rule written for cross-border litigation in the domestic context has to be applauded. But the transposition could have been done in a much more effective way.

2. THE RECOVERABILITY OF COSTS OF LAWYERS' FEES AND COSTS OF TECHNICAL ADVISERS AFTER *UNITED VIDEO PROPERTIES INC. v. TELENET NV* (C-57/15)

2.1. RECOVERABILITY OF LAWYERS' FEES AND EXPENSES IN BELGIUM: ANTECEDENTS OF THE CASE

EU regulations and directives have repercussions on a vast list of procedural topics. Litigation costs is one of them. Recent Belgian case law offers an example of serious friction with national rules, caused by Article 14 of the IP Rights Enforcement Directive.[1] This provision states:

> Member States shall ensure that reasonable and proportionate legal costs and other expenses incurred by the successful party shall, as a general rule, be borne by the unsuccessful party, unless equity does not allow this.

In its *Realchemie* judgment the CJEU reminded that this provision aims to strengthen the level of protection of intellectual property, by avoiding the situation in which an injured party is deterred from bringing legal proceedings in order to protect his rights.[2]

---

1 EP and Council Directive (EC) 2004/48 of 29 April 2004 on the enforcement of intellectual property rights [2004] OJ L195/16.

2 Case C-406/09, *Realchemie Nederland BV v. Bayer CropSience AG*, ECLI:EU:C:2011:668 at [48].

Although some have argued that also Article 14 of the Directive required implementation[3] because of the nature of IP cases, especially the complexity of the legal and technical issues at stake which makes, e.g. patent litigation quite expensive,[4] the Belgian legislator did not transpose this provision. As a result, the general rules regarding the recoverability of lawyers' fees are also applicable in IP cases. Those rules have been subject to a major statutory reform in 2007, introducing a (fixed or variable flat-rated) recoverability of lawyers' fees.[5]

Article 1022 BJC defines the expenses of a judicial procedure as a fixed compensation for the expenses and fees of the lawyer assisting the winning or successful party.[6] 'Fixed' implies that not the actual fees are recoverable: they are limited to a fixed amount, in principle related to the value of the claim. This amount is deemed to cover the lawyer's fees and costs of that party. The word 'lawyer' implies that the successful party is only entitled to expenses of a judicial procedure if this party was assisted and/or represented by a lawyer during the proceedings.

After having established the principle and scope of the recoverability of lawyers' fees and having assigned the judge a series of discretionary powers subject to specific criteria, the legislator left it to the Crown to set the amounts of the procedural indemnity in consultation with the Bar Associations. These fixed amounts were set by a Royal Decree of

---

3 Implementation of other provisions of this Directive in Belgium led to the introduction of a specific type of seizure and special rules on provisional measures in IP cases (see Articles 1369*bis*/1-1369*ter* Belgian Judicial Code, hereinafter: BJC).

4 See in this vein B. Vandermeulen and A. Schockaert, 'De verhaalbaarheid van advocatenkosten in geschillen rond intellectuele eigendom: mythe en realiteit' (2018) 1 *Cah. Jur.* 9–10, nrs 7–8. It had previously been incumbent on each party to defray its own defence costs, including its legal fees. Such expenditure was not part of the procedural costs chargeable to the losing party. The only correction had been the 'procedural indemnity' permitting the judge to order the losing party to pay an indemnity for material acts performed during proceedings by a lawyer. By judgment of 02.09.2004, the Court of Cassation accepted that lawyers' fees could be subsumed under the compensation to be paid in the context of contractual liability. This judgment prompted numerous comments, and case law split on a series of questions bound up with recoverability of costs.

5 Law of 21 April 2007 on the recoverability of fees and costs of legal representation, *Official Gazette of Belgium*, 09.11.2007. V. Sagaert and I. Samoy, 'Cost and Fee Allocation in Civil Procedure' [2010] International Academy of Comparative Law <www-personal.umich.edu/~purzel/national_reports/Belgium.pdf>.

6 Not to his lawyer (Court of Cassation 20.10.2014, C.13.526.F). All (published) decisions of Belgium's Supreme Judicial Court (*Hof van Cassatie/Cour de cassation*) are accessible in Dutch and French on their date via <juridat.be>.

26 October 2007.[7] The Decree provides for a basic amount, a maximum amount and a minimum amount. In principle, the basic amount is awarded, but the court can increase or reduce the basic amount (without exceeding the fixed minimum and maximum amounts) at the request of one of the parties, thereby taking into account (one or more of) the following criteria: the financial capacity of the losing party (in order to lower the amount of compensation), the complexity of the litigation, the contractually agreed compensation for the winning party and the manifestly unreasonable nature of the situation. No party can be obliged to pay additional compensation for the lawyer's intervention of the opposite party above the lump sum allowance awarded by the court.

The staggered scale for the amounts of procedural cost indemnity ranges from €75.00 (the minimum amount, applicable to actions where the subject has a value of up to €250.00), to €30,000.00 (the maximum amount, which is applicable to actions the value of which, evaluated in monetary terms, is more than €1,000,000.01).[8]

No similar rule exists for the fees and costs of technical experts assisting parties during legal proceedings. Belgian case law established that such fees and costs are only recoverable in the event that the losing party has committed a (contractual[9] or extra-contractual[10]) fault and the fees and costs paid to those experts are the inevitable consequence thereof.

It was strongly contested whether this approach of recoverability of lawyers' and experts' fees and costs in IP cases was compatible with Articles 3, 13 and 14 of the IP Rights Enforcement Directive.[11]

---

7 *Belgian Official Gazette*, 09.11.2007.

8 For actions in which the object cannot be evaluated in monetary terms, Article 3 of the Royal Decree of 26 October 2007 provides a basic amount of €1,200.00, a minimum amount of €75.00 and a maximum amount of €10,000.00. Article 8 of the Royal Decree of 26.10.2007 provides that these basic, minimum, and maximum amounts are linked to the consumer price index, every rise or fall of the index by 10 points leading to an increase or reduction by 10% of these sums.

9 Court of Cassation 24.04.2014, C.13.0328.N; Court of Cassation 15.11.2013, C.11.0656.F; Court of Cassation 02.09.2004, C.01.0186.F.

10 Court of Cassation 01.03.2012, C.10.0425.N; Court of Cassation 16.11.2006, C.05.0124.F.

11 The Antwerp Court of Appeal held that the Belgian rules and case law were not in compliance with the IP Rights Enforcement Directive (e.g. Antwerp Court of Appeal 15.06.2009 [2010] *IRDI* 286), whereas the Ghent Court of Appeal decided to the contrary (e.g. Ghent Court of Appeal 02.03.2009 [2009] *Jaarboek Handelspraktijken en Mededinging* 761; Ghent Court of Appeal 24.06.2013 [2014] *Ing. Cons.* 78). See for an overview of this discussion: J. Deene, 'De rechtsplegingsvergoeding in procedures

In 2015 the Antwerp Court of Appeal referred the issue in a patent dispute to the CJEU for a preliminary ruling, opposing a patentee (the US-based company United Video Properties (hereinafter: UVP)) to an alleged patent infringing party (Telenet, a major player on the Belgian telecom market). Telenet ultimately won the case but it incurred legal costs and expenses, which considerably exceeded those recoverable under Belgian law. Telenet paid €185,462.55 as fees to its lawyers and €40,400.00 as costs to its patent agent. In its contested judgment[12] the first judge considered only an amount of €11,000.00[13] to be recoverable vis-à-vis UVP under the Belgian legal expenses and cost rules of 2007.

The Antwerp Court of Appeal referred the following two questions to the CJEU:[14]

- Do the terms 'reasonable and proportionate legal costs and other expenses' in Article 14 of Directive 2004/48 preclude the Belgian legislation which offers courts the possibility of taking into account certain well-defined features specific to the case and which provides for a system of varying flat rates in respect of costs for the assistance of a lawyer?
- Do the terms 'reasonable and proportionate legal costs' and 'other expenses' in Article 14 of Directive 2004/48 preclude the case law which states that the costs of a technical adviser are recoverable only in the event of fault (contractual or extra-contractual)?

2.2. JUDGMENT OF THE CJEU OF 28 JULY 2016

The CJEU started its preliminary ruling on the first question by pointing out that the concept of 'legal costs' in Article 14 of Directive 2004/48 includes, amongst others, the lawyer's fees. Next, under reference to recital 17 of the Directive, the Court stated that the measures, procedures and remedies set out in that directive should be determined in each case in such a manner as to take due account of the specific characteristics

inzake intellectuele rechten: een *sui generis*-regime?' (2011–2012) 23 *RW* 950–952, nrs 10–18.

12 Antwerp Commercial Court 03.04.2012, no. A/11/05443 <www.eplawpatentblog.com>.

13 At that time the maximum amount that could be awarded for a non-monetary claim on the basis of the above-mentioned Belgian rules and case law.

14 Antwerp Court of Appeal 26.01.2015, AR 2490/12, unpublished.

of that case. As Article 14 requires Member States to ensure the reimbursement only of 'reasonable' legal costs and Article 3(1) of the Directive provides, *inter alia*, that the procedures laid down by the Member States must not be unnecessarily costly, the CJEU concludes that legislation – such as the Belgian one – providing for a flat-rate of reimbursement of a lawyer's fees could, in principle, be justified, on condition that it is intended to ensure the reasonableness of the costs to be reimbursed. The subject matter of the proceedings, the sum involved, the work to be carried out to represent the client concerned are, according to the Court, factors that could be taken into account in assessing the fairness of these costs.[15] However, legislation imposing a flat-rate significantly below the average rate actually charged for the services of a lawyer in the Member State concerned does not comply with the requirement of reasonableness. Moreover, such legislation would be incompatible with Article 3(2) of Directive 2004/48, prescribing that procedures and remedies must have a dissuasive effect on a (potential) infringer. It would also compromise the principal aim pursued by this legal instrument, i.e. ensuring a high level of protection of intellectual property rights in the internal market.[16]

Article 14 also provides that the legal costs to be supported by the unsuccessful party must be 'proportionate'. The CJEU takes the view that the question of whether those costs are proportionate cannot be assessed independently of the costs that the successful party actually incurred in respect of the assistance of a lawyer, provided they are reasonable. While the requirement of proportionality does not imply that the unsuccessful party must necessarily reimburse the entirety of the costs incurred by the other party, it does mean, however, that the successful party should have the right to reimbursement of, at the very least, a significant and appropriate part of the reasonable costs actually incurred by that party.

In a nutshell, the CJEU requires that a legal system such as the Belgian one, laying down absolute limits for the recoverability of costs attached

---

15 The CJEU justly underscores, with reference to the very wording of the first question, that Belgian legislation offers the (national) courts, in principle, the possibility of taking account of those features (Case C-57/15, *United Video Properties Inc. v. Telenet NV*, ECLI:EU:C:2016:611 at [28]).

16 See recital 10 to Directive 2004/48 in accordance with Article 17(2) of the Charter of Fundamental Rights of the European Union.

to the assistance of a lawyer must ensure, on the one hand, that these limits reflect the reality of the rates charged for services of lawyers in disputes on intellectual property in its jurisdiction. On the other hand, it must guarantee that at least a significant and appropriate part of the reasonable costs actually incurred by the successful party are borne by its opponent. If the applicable limit is too low, the reimbursement which the successful party is entitled to may become disproportionate or even insignificant, thus depriving Article 14 of Directive 2004/48 of its practical effect, according to the CJEU.

Concerning the second question, the CJEU first stated that the concept of 'other costs' provided for by Article 14, in principle also encompasses the costs incurred by a litigant for the services of a technical adviser. However, the Court, following an observation of its Advocate General with reference to the 'costs of identification and research' mentioned in recital 26 to the directive which in its turn refers to situations as foreseen by Article 13(1) of the directive (i.e. damages in case of an infringement by an infringer who knowingly or with reasonable grounds for knowing engaged in such an activity), points out that these costs incurred, often before judicial proceedings, do not necessarily fall within the scope of Article 14. A wide interpretation of the latter provision, without going into any detail about those costs, risks conferring excessive scope on that article and thus depriving Article 13 of its practical effect. The CJEU concludes that the concept 'other costs' needs to be interpreted narrowly. It takes the view that only costs directly and closely related to judicial proceedings fall under 'other expenses', within the meaning of Article 14.

Second, the Court emphasises that it cannot be concluded from Article 14 that the Member States may subject the reimbursement of 'other expenses', or legal costs in general, in the context of proceedings seeking to ensure the enforcement of an intellectual property right, to a condition of fault on the part of the unsuccessful party.

It concluded its ruling on the second question by deciding that Article 14 precludes national rules providing that reimbursement of the costs of a technical adviser are provided for only in the event of fault on the part of the unsuccessful party, given that those costs are directly and closely linked to a judicial action seeking to have such an intellectual property right upheld. Consequently, the Belgian case law on this point clearly conflicts with Union Law as interpreted by the CJEU.

2.3. SUBSEQUENT JUDGMENT OF THE ANTWERP COURT OF APPEAL OF 8 MAY 2017

The Antwerp Court of Appeal passed its final judgment in this case on 8 May 2017.[17] At that time, the lawyers' fees Telenet aimed to be reimbursed for had increased to €263,171.13.

The Antwerp Court commenced the reasoning in its judgment by considering that directives have no horizontal direct effect, which implies that Telenet cannot derive any rights or claims towards UVP directly from the IP Rights Enforcement Directive. Further, the Court referred to the duty of harmonious interpretation, which obliges judges to interpret their national law as much as possible to ensure that full effect is given to Union law.

Against the background of these two principles, the Court found that Article 1022 BJC, on the one hand, grants the Belgian Government the power to determine the fixed lump sum allowances and, on the other hand, forbids any additional compensation for fees and costs related to the assistance of lawyers above these fixed amounts. The Antwerp Court of Appeal concluded that it could not award any higher amounts than those provided for by the above-mentioned Royal Decree, even if these allowances would not ensure that a significant and appropriate part of the reasonable costs set out by Telenet for its legal assistance during the trial were actually refunded. The Court of Appeal granted Telenet €24,000.00 in total.[18]

It is remarkable to read the hint in the Court's judgment at the doctrine of state liability based on the incorrect or belated transposition of the IP Rights Enforcement Directive into Belgian law, in case Telenet would intend to recover any surplus of the lawyers' fees and costs it paid on the occasion of its dispute with UVP. The Court clearly suggests that Telenet should claim damages based on the doctrine of state liability. By doing so it would put pressure on the Belgian legislator to adapt the national legislation in conformity with the CJEU's judgment.

---

17 Antwerp Court of Appeal 08.05.2017 [2017] *IRDI* 16–20, note R. Lindemans.

18 At the time of the proceedings which led to the judgment of 08.05.2017, the maximum amount of compensation for lawyers' fees in non-monetary claims had been increased to a maximum of €12,000.00 per instance (due to the linking of the procedural cost indemnity to the consumer price index, provided for in Article 8 of the Royal Decree). The Court of Appeal awarded this (maximum) allowance for both instances, thus granting €24,000.00 in total.

Concerning the costs of the technical experts on whose assistance Telenet relied during the action against UVP, the Antwerp Court ruled in line with the CJEU's preliminary ruling. It held that these costs were directly and closely linked to the judicial action aiming to uphold an intellectual property right. The erasure of the fault criterion by the CJEU, led the Antwerp Court to the conclusion that the reimbursement of these costs is governed by Article 1018 BJC, which provides for a (non-exhaustive) list of litigation costs. In principle[19] (and unless parties have concluded an agreement with respect to the litigation costs), the losing party has to pay or reimburse these litigation costs[20] to the winning party.[21] Consequently, the Antwerp Court awarded the full amount of compensation related to costs of technical assistance (€ 63,804.25) claimed by Telenet.

2.4. COMMENTS

2.4.1. Procedural Autonomy

The CJEU did *not* approach the *UVP v. Telenet* case from the perspective of procedural autonomy and its well-known limitations of equivalence and effectiveness. This is not as obvious as it might seem, because the CJEU has in the past addressed cases concerning litigation costs from this perspective. For example in *Orizzonte*, the CJEU assessed national (Italian) law concerning court fees in light of the principles of equivalence and effectiveness.[22] Since both court fees and compensation for the successful party's lawyers' fees are mentioned among the costs in Article 1018 BJC, it is worth evaluating why exactly in the Italian case the CJEU evaluated the question from the viewpoint of procedural

19 Exceptions to the 'loser pays' principle are, *inter alia*, cases relating to social security law (the costs are always borne by the social security institution, even if it wins the case) or where a party has made useless or vexatious costs (such costs will remain fully at the expense of the party who has made them, even if this party wins the case).

20 Which do not fall within the scope of the fixed sum allowance of Article 1022 BJC and the Royal Decree of 26.10.2007.

21 Article 1017(1) BJC.

22 Case C-61/41, *Orizzonte Salute – Studio Infermieristico Associato v. Azienda Pubblica di Servizi alla persona San Valentino – Città di Levico Terme*, ECLI:EU:C:2015:655.

autonomy, while in the *UVP v. Telenet* case no trace of that principle can be found. The answer to this question is twofold.

First, the approach of the CJEU depends without a doubt on how a question in the request for a preliminary ruling has been worded by the referring national court. If the question explicitly or implicitly refers to (limitations of) the procedural autonomy of the Member States, one can expect that the Court will assess the question in light of this (or these) principle(s).

Second, and more important: in *Orizzonte*, the (then applicable) Public Procurement Directive[23] does not address any aspect of court fees; whereas in *UVP v. Telenet* the IP Rights Enforcement Directive does address legal costs – litigation costs more precisely. Given the classic wording of the principle of procedural autonomy – 'only in the absence of EU rules governing the matter' – it is up to the Member States to draw up detailed procedural rules governing actions for safeguarding Union rights.[24] The (non-)existence of EU rules on the matter decides whether or not the issue is to be assessed against the background of procedural autonomy. In *Orizzonte* no Union law on court fees was provided, so the Member States were allowed to rule on this matter within the limits of equivalence and effectiveness. On the contrary, Article 14 of the Directive, which was at stake in *UVP v. Telenet*, does prescribe rules on litigation costs. It was up to the Member States to elaborate this matter during the transposition of the Directive into their legal framework. Consequently, there was no question of procedural autonomy at hand. The question at hand, which was assessed by the CJEU in its decision sketched above, is one concerning the interpretation of Union law, more specifically the concepts of reasonability and proportionality as enacted in Article 14 of the IP Rights Enforcement Directive. However, the transposition of this article into Belgian national law actually affected its procedural autonomy, as will be explained below.

---

23 Council Directive 89/665/EEC of 21 December 1989 on the coordination of the laws, regulations and administrative provisions relating to the application of review procedures to the award of public supply and public works contracts [1989] OJ L 395/33 as amended by Directive 2007/66/EC of the European Parliament and of the Council of 11 December 2007 [2007] OJ L 335/31.

24 See for example Case 33/76, *Rewe-Zentralfinanz eG and Rewe-Zentral AG v. Landwirtschaftskammer für das Saarland*, ECLI:EU:C:1976:188 at [5]; Case 45/76, *Comet BV/Produktschap voor Siergewassen*, ECLI:EU:C:1976:191 at [13]; Case C-177/10, *Francisco Javier Rosado Santana v. Consejería de Justicia y Administración Pública de la Junta de Andalucía*, ECLI:EU:C:2011:557 at [87].

2.4.2. *Recoverability of Lawyers' Fees*

The CJEU interpreted the wording of Article 14 of the Directive as containing a two-prong test on the reimbursement of lawyers' fees. In para 29 of its judgment the Court considers that 'the successful party should have the right to reimbursement of, at the very least, a significant and appropriate part of the *reasonable* costs actually incurred by that party' (emphasis added).[25] This implies that (1) only reasonable costs can be taken into consideration when (2) a judge has to assess their significance and appropriateness (vis-à-vis the lawyers' fees and costs actually incurred by the winning party).

In a *first* phase, a judge has to assess whether or not the lawyers' fees and costs charged to the winning party were reasonable. This requirement does not necessarily exclude a fixed sum system as is nowadays applicable in Belgium. It does however require that the fixed lump sum allowances are not significantly below the average rate actually charged for similar services of lawyers in IP cases in the Member State concerned.

Only when these lawyers' fees and costs are considered as 'reasonable' (which has to be judged taking into consideration the non-exhaustive guidelines set out by the CJEU, see *supra*), the *second* phase comes into play. This stage aims to assure that a significant and appropriate part of these reasonable costs will be reimbursed to the successful party.

Though both stages entail certain requirements concerning the height of the fixed lump sum allowances, their playing field differs. In the first phase an *in abstracto* assessment of the fixed allowances has to be carried out in light of the average lawyers' fees in IP cases in the Member State concerned, whereas in the second phase a more *in concreto* appreciation of the legal costs incurred by the winning party in the specific case is up for discussion. Moreover, as the CJEU rightly points out, the first step can be assessed independently of the costs which the successful party actually incurred. On the contrary, the appreciation in the second stage of the significant and appropriate character of the compensation requires definitively to take into account the costs that were actually incurred by the winning party.

However, the assessment of whether or not a certain amount is proportionate *in concreto* as indemnification of lawyers' fees and costs, leads to a difficult question: what exactly *is* proportionate? As law is not

---

[25] Case C-57/15, *United Video Properties Inc. v. Telenet NV*, ECLI:EU:C:2016:611 at [29].

an exact science, it seems to be impossible to answer it in an absolute and always valid manner.[26] However, certain guidelines can be disentangled. For example, parties may conclude an agreement on the compensation the unsuccessful party will have to pay after the trial. This cannot only be derived from the general principle of freedom of contract, but also from the wording of Article 1017 BJC.[27] Rules on legal costs are not of public policy. In principle, a court has to respect such an agreement concluded between the litigating parties.[28] When no contract is signed between them, it is important to bear in mind that the duty for the unsuccessful party to compensate the lawyers' fees and costs of its opponent in an appropriate way does not necessarily imply a full reimbursement of these amounts.

One cannot neglect that the final outcome of the *UVP v. Telenet case* uncovers a significant imbalance between the lawyers' fees actually incurred by Telenet and the rather modest compensation it received for these costs by the subsequent judgment of 8 May 2017 of the Antwerp Court of Appeal which closed the dispute. Indeed, the current maximum amounts enacted in the Royal Decree implementing Article 1022 BJC turn out to be quite problematic in light of the ruling of the CJEU that a significant and appropriate part of the lawyers' costs of the successful party has to be reimbursed. Practise has shown that in some, if not most, cases on IP disputes even the applicable absolute maximum

---

26 See in this vein J.-D. Lindemans, 'Poging tot rechtzetten van een gemiste kans om in IE-geschillen redelijke advocatenkosten te verhalen' [2017] *IRDI* 23ff.

27 Article 1017 BJC prescribes that in every final judgment, the unsuccessful party has to be condemned to pay the litigation costs, *unless the parties decide otherwise*. However, it is disputed whether parties are allowed to diverge from the maxima amounts enacted in the Royal Decree. Some scholars argue that this is forbidden, as it would be contrary to Article 1023 BJC (I. Samoy and V. Sagaert, 'De wet van 21 april 2007 betreffende de verhaalbaarheid van kosten en erelonen van een advocaat' (2007–2008) 17 *RW* 692, no. 68), while another is of the opinion that such agreements are legitimate (J.-D. Lindemans, 'Poging tot rechtzetten van een gemiste kans om in IE-geschillen redelijke advocatenkosten te verhalen' [2017] *IRDI* 24). Yet, another scholar pleads that only agreements concluded before the start of the proceedings are valid (B. Van Den Bergh, 'Commentaar bij artikel 1017 Ger.W.' in D. Lindemans, J. Laenens, P. Lemmens and R. De Corte (eds), *Gerechtelijk recht: artikelsgewijze commentaar met overzicht van rechtspraak en rechtsleer*, Kluwer, Antwerpen, looseleaf (afl. 105), 30, no. 36).

28 P. Taelman and C. Van Severen, *Civil Procedure in Belgium*, Wolters Kluwer, Alphen aan den Rijn 2018, p. 27, no. 43 and B. Wylleman, 'De verplichting van de burgerlijke rechter om ambtshalve rechtsgronden op te werpen' [2017] *Jaarverslag Hof van Cassatie van België* 173–174, no. 1.

amount is not sufficient to cover a significant and appropriate part of the costs actually incurred by the successful party.[29]

In the context of IP cases, some scholars argued that these amounts should be equalised with the ones enacted in the Rules of Procedure that will be applicable in patent cases before the Unified Patent Court (hereinafter: UPC).[30] These authors substantiate their view by indicating that two years ago the Belgian Government agreed with these amounts for supranational patent disputes handled by this supranational court. Since there is no valid reason to believe that, as a rule, patent disputes dealt with at the national level are less complex and/or less expensive than the ones that will be handled at this supranational forum, applying different maxima for the reimbursement of lawyers' fees threatens to lead, in our opinion, to an unjustifiable, unequal treatment.

In this regard, judgment no. 182/2008 of 18 December 2008 of the Belgian Constitutional Court could be directional to appreciate whether our fear of an unequal treatment is justified.[31] The Court had to assess *inter alia* whether or not the Belgian rule on compensation for lawyers' fees and costs violated the principles of non-discrimination and equality, in comparison with the national rules on combating late payment in commercial transactions as a result of the transposition of Directive 2000/35/EC.[32] At that time,[33] the Belgian legislation entitled the creditor to claim reasonable compensation from his debtor for all relevant costs incurred through the latter's late payment, on condition that these costs respected the principles of transparency and proportionality as regards the debt in question. It expressly excluded the allowance provided for by Article 1022 BJC. As a consequence, Belgian courts

29 J.-B. Hubin, 'Note d'observations – la Cour de justice relance la saga de la répétibilité' [2016] *RDTI* 84, no. 20.

30 B. Vandermeulen and A. Schockaert, 'De verhaalbaarheid van advocatenkosten in geschillen rond intellectuele eigendom: mythe en realiteit' [2018] *Cah. Jur.* 11–12, nos. 17–19. See for an overview of these amounts <https://www.unified-patent-court.org/news/upc-court-fees-and-recoverable-costs>.

31 Constitutional Court of Belgium 18.12.2008, no. 182/2008.

32 Directive 2000/35/EC of the European Parliament and of the Council of 29 June 2000, [2000] OJ L 200/35, as transposed into the Belgian legal order by Act of 2 August 2002 on the combating of late payment in commercial transactions, *Belgian Official Gazette* 07.08.2002. The whole debate in Belgium on the recoverability of lawyers' fees was triggered by this Directive.

33 In the meantime, Article 6 of the Act of 02.08.2002 on the combating of late payment in commercial transactions has been adapted by law of 22 November 2013, *Belgian Official Gazette* 10.12.2013.

were allowed to grant in these matters a higher compensation for costs of legal assistance than those foreseen by the fixed lump sum allowances introduced in 2007. The Court concluded that 'specific characteristics' could justify such a divergence. It found these distinguishing features in the fact that the deviating rule was based on the duty to implement a European directive in the national legal order and that the *ratio legis* of Directive 2000/35/EC lay in the safeguarding of the internal market.[34] Exactly the same arguments can be developed with respect to the IP Rights Enforcement Directive,[35] which makes that the aforementioned decision of the Constitutional Court could function as a blueprint concerning the issue of the recoverability of legal costs in intellectual property disputes. In its judgment no. 182/2008 of 18 December 2008 the Court decided that the different treatment was compatible with the Constitution. However, it immediately warned[36] that major differences concerning the reimbursement of legal costs should be avoided.[37]

The fixed maximum amounts provided for compensation of lawyers' fees by the Belgian Royal Decree are, in the opinion of at least one scholar, in general and *in abstracto* structurally too low, independent of the field of law in which the dispute originates. This should be especially true for the lowest categories in the staggered scale for monetary claims as well as for the single maximum amount provided for non-monetary claims.[38] From 1 January 2014 onward this issue worsened as Belgian lawyers' fees became subject to 21% VAT, but none of the fixed amounts have been adapted to this major elevation of these costs. For this reason, an adjustment of the fixed amounts in

---

[34] T. De Jaeger and K. Claeyé, 'Maximale rechtsplegingsvergoeding mogelijk op de schop' [2016] *Juristenkrant* 3. See recitals 9 and 10 of Directive 2000/35/EC.

[35] See recitals 1–3 and 8–10 of Directive 2004/48/EC.

[36] See consideration no. B.12.5 of decision no. 182/2008 of the Belgian Constitutional Court.

[37] In the authors' opinion, making use of the scale provided for by the Rules of Procedure of the UPC risks creating such a major difference, which might be found incompatible with the Constitution and Article 6 of the European Convention on Human Rights. The highest possible compensation for claims with a value up to €250,000.00 amounts to €38,000.00, thus already exceeding the absolute maximum amount of the Royal Decree of 2007 (which actually comes up to €36,000.00 for claims with a value higher than €1,000,000.00). The maximum compensation according to the Rules of Procedure (€2,000,000.00) exceeds more than 55 times the actual Belgian national maximum amount.

[38] F. Petillion, 'Gepaste rechtsplegingsvergoeding is Europees recht' [2018] *RABG* 749–750.

the Royal Decree is indeed most desirable.[39] However, as is apparent from the Explanatory memorandum on the (national) legislation introducing in Belgium the principle of the recoverability of lawyers' fees,[40] preventing the obstruction of the fundamental right of access to the court for less financially endowed parties was a major concern. This explains why the legislator sought to anticipate the widely divergent cases and situations possible by introducing a basic, a minimum and a maximum amount for this compensation. A series of discretionary powers subject to specific criteria[41] were assigned to the judge for the same reason; they allow him to pursue equity by adapting the recoverability of the lawyers' fees and costs between those boundaries.

It is clear that Article 14 of the IP Rights Enforcement Directive, strengthened by its interpretation by the CJEU, intrudes on the procedural autonomy of Member States. At the very least, it puts the Belgian legislation (and thus its legislator and judiciary) as to the recoverability of lawyers' fees and costs under severe pressure. Although some authors[42] – who as it happens to be are all IP lawyers – have pleaded to increase in IP cases the maximum amounts because Article 14 prescribes that the unsuccessful party *must* bear a reasonable and proportionate part of the legal costs made by its winning opponent and because IP disputes are by nature rather complex,[43] this is undoubtedly too

---

39 J.-B. Hubin, 'Note d'observations – la Cour de justice relance la saga de la répétibilité' [2016] *RDTI* 89, no. 26.

40 Explanatory memorandum, Belgian Senate 2005–2006, no. 3-1686, 10. I. Samoy and V. Sagaert, 'De wet van 21 april 2007 betreffende de verhaalbaarheid van kosten en erelonen van een advocaat' (2007–2008) 17 *RW* 681, no. 26; P. Taelman and S. Voet, 'De verhaalbaarheid van de advocatenhonoraria: analyse van een aantal knelpunten na één jaar toepassing' in P. Van Orshoven and B. Maes (eds), *De procesrechtwetten van 2007 ... revisited!*, die Keure, Brugge 2009, p. 197, no. 78 and p. 204, no. 87.

41 Article 1022(3) BJC.

42 J. Deene, 'De rechtsplegingsvergoeding in procedures inzake intellectuele rechten: een *sui generis*-regime?' (2010–2011) 23 *RW* 948; C. Ronse, 'De andere herstelmaatregelen en in het bijzonder de schadevergoeding' in F. Brison (ed.), *Sancties en procedures in intellectuele rechten*, Larcier, Brussels 2008, pp. 251–252; A. Puts and G. Verfaillie, 'De beoordeling van het onderscheidend vermogen van een merk en de rechtsplegingsvergoeding in intellectuele eigendomsgeschillen' [2008] *TBH* 432, no. 5; B. Vandermeulen and A. Schockaert, 'De verhaalbaarheid van advocatenkosten in geschillen rond intellectuele eigendom: mythe en realiteit' [2018] *Cah. Jur.* 9, no. 3 and J.-D. Lindemans, 'Poging tot rechtzetten van een gemiste kans om in IE-geschillen redelijke advocatenkosten te verhalen' [2017] *IRDI* 25.

43 Scientific honesty compels us to underscore that these authors have not advocated a different treatment *due to the fact* that IP disputes are complex. One could, of course,

simple a solution. It requires little argument that there are no fields of law in which complex litigation is unthinkable, just as much as it is (probably) true that some IP disputes do not lead to extremely complex legal and/or technical questions. Consequently, the legislator cannot confine itself to adapt the rules for one specific kind of disputes. On the contrary, a change in the context of IP disputes will constrain the legislator to pursue similar adaptations in all other fields of law governed by civil, penal or administrative procedure rules where the recoverability of legal costs is applicable. Article 14 urges legislators who want to maintain in their legal system fixed lump sum allowances for the recovering of legal fees and costs in proceedings, to create on the one hand a system that wields sufficiently high maxima while, on the other hand, maintains a sufficiently balanced structure to guarantee access to justice for every citizen.

2.4.3. *Compensation of Costs of Technical Advisers*

Costs related to the assistance of technical advisers of a litigant were, according to case law of the Belgian Court of Cassation, only recoverable if they were made necessary by the fault of its opponent. This approach is certainly no longer tenable in light of the CJEU decision of 28 July 2016. Moreover, the requirement of an equal, non-discriminatory treatment of litigants implies that the impact of this judgment cannot be limited to IP disputes only.

At this point the CJEU judgment, by rejecting the opinion of a high national court, does certainly cause an evolution of the Belgian legal order. However, it does not cause too much friction. The 'loser pays' principle, articulated in Article 1017 BJC, urges the losing party to pay or reimburse the litigation costs to the winning party. As the enumeration of these costs in Article 1018 BJC is not exhaustive, the costs related to services of technical advisers and even party appointed expert witnesses on behalf of the winning litigant, can easily be qualified as recoverable costs to the extent they display a direct and close link to the proceedings, as has been judiciously required by the CJEU.

Propositions have been made to introduce for this type of costs a similar system as is applicable for the recoverability of legal costs.[44]

---

by way of a naughty assumption read these authors' comments as an implicit statement in this direction.

44 J.-B. Hubin, 'Note d'observations – la Cour de justice relance la saga de la répétibilité' [2016] *RDTI* 90.

This would certainly have the advantage of contributing to the foreseeability of litigation costs. But it remains highly unclear how such a scale could be judiciously drawn up as a countless number of varying knowledges, skills and competences of all kinds of technical advisers and expert witnesses should be taken in consideration. In its judgment of 18 December 2008, the Constitutional Court considered the difference in treatment between the recoverability of lawyers' fees and costs of technical advisers compatible with the Constitution. The Court concluded that the special, long-lasting relationship existing between the lawyer and his client (especially the fact that, as a rule, a lawyer assists his client during the whole course of the proceedings) differs fundamentally from the situation of an expert witness or a technical adviser whose intervention is usually limited to a specific issue.[45]

2.4.4. *Concluding Remarks*

By way of an intermediate conclusion, it flows from *UVP v. Telenet* that the Belgian system concerning the reimbursement of lawyers' fees is *in se* not contrary to Union law. As the CJEU explicitly stated in its judgment, a system based on a flat rate of reimbursement could in principle be justified. As the CJEU also pointed out, however, these rates have to be adjusted to reality, in the sense that they must suffice to compensate a reasonable part of the costs incurred for lawyers' fees. As stated above, the Belgian rates for monetary claims should thus be reassessed. Moreover, a real problem lures in non-monetary claims. Here, it is by definition not possible to base the flat-rate scheme on the value of the claim. Consequently, the question arises to which criteria could be feasible to decide the reimbursable amount. Possible factors to be taken into account could be the costs that were actually paid and/or the complexity and/or subject matter of the case. Although the Belgian legislator has recently reviewed the legal rules on the recoverability of lawyers' fees,[46] it did not touch upon the staggered scale for the amounts of procedural cost indemnity.

As to the reimbursement of costs of technical advisers, it must be concluded that the Belgian system, which until recently was based

45 Constitutional Court of Belgium 18.12.2008, no. 182/2008, paras B.11.2 ff. <http://www.const-court.be/public/n/2008/2008-182n.pdf>. An executive summary of this judgment is available in English at <http://www.const-court.be/>.

46 Royal Decree of 29.03.2019, *Belgian Official Gazette* 10.04.2019.

on whether or not the losing party had committed a fault, cannot be maintained. As the CJEU stated, there is no legal basis to demand such a requirement to be fulfilled. Consequently, the question must be asked upon what legal footing the reimbursement of costs of technical advisers should be based. Here, the actual necessity seems to be a reasonable criterion.

Lastly, and more generally, it can be concluded that the Belgian legislator usurped more procedural autonomy than it had according to the CJEU. Whereas the former designed a scheme completely at its own will,[47] the CJEU made clear that (at least in the context of the IP Enforcement Directive) certain boundaries had to be respected from a European viewpoint.

3. NEW, EAPO INSPIRED, BELGIAN RULES FOR OBTAINING THE DEBTOR'S BANK ACCOUNT INFORMATION

3.1. EAPO REGULATION 655/2014

Fragmentation of national rules on enforcement severely hampers debt collection within the EU. Creditors seeking to enforce a civil court order in other Member States are confronted with different and diverging legal systems, procedural requirements and language barriers which entail additional costs and delays. These issues create an obstacle for the proper functioning of the European single market. Moreover, they distort competition among businesses operating in EU countries and jeopardise the interests of businesses and consumers alike.[48]

A creditor seeking to recover a monetary claim in the EU will most commonly try to do so by taking enforcement actions[49] against his/her debtor's bank account. Such procedures exist in most EU countries and, if working efficiently, are powerful weapons against recalcitrant, deferring or fraudulent debtors. They prevent debtors from removing or dissipating their assets during the time it takes to obtain and enforce a

47 That is to say, without any attention being paid to Union law.

48 C. Vanleenhove, 'Europees conservatoir bankbeslag: nieuw wapen voor schuldeiser in grensoverschrijdende geschillen' [2016] *Juristenkrant* 1.

49 By way of a ((preliminary) third-party) attachment or a preservation order.

judgment on the merits. In short, they fulfil a crucial role in debt recovery proceedings.

Regulation 655/2014[50] established a European Account Preservation Order procedure (hereinafter: EAPO), which is available to the creditor in cross-border cases,[51] as an alternative to instruments existing under national law.[52] It provides common rules relating to jurisdiction, conditions and procedure for issuing an order, how it should be enforced by national courts and authorities, the remedies for the debtor and other elements of defendant protection.[53]

An EAPO procedure allows for a single order, issued on request of the creditor in an *ex parte* procedure[54] by a court of one Member State, which is capable of 'freezing' or preserving any bank account of a debtor under essentially the same conditions as in any Member State. A creditor can apply for such an order when he has already obtained a judgment, court settlement or authentic instrument requiring the debtor to pay the creditor's claim (so-called *post-judgment* order[55]). The order will be issued

---

50 Regulation (EU) 655/2014 of the European Parliament and of the Council of 15 May 2014 establishing a European Account Preservation Order procedure to facilitate cross-border debt recovery in civil and commercial matters [2014] OJ L189/59. See for an extensive discussion of the EAPO Regulation from a Belgian perspective: K. Broeckx, 'De Europese Bankbeslagverordening' in P. Taelman and B. Allemeersch (eds), *Het burgerlijk proces opnieuw hervormd*, Intersentia, Antwerp-Cambridge 2019, pp. 171–214.

51 Circumscribed under Article 3 of the EAPO Regulation.

52 Be aware that, in a particular case, making use of an EAPO order can be less advantageous than making use of the applicable national enforcement law. For example, according to Belgian enforcement law a preliminary third-party attachment (or garnishment) – ordered by a Belgian court, following its national law – makes all the assets on the account of the debtor unavailable, even if the value of the actual claim of the debtor is below the amount due by the garnishee (the bank) to the debtor (Article 1451 BJC). Using an EAPO order implies for the creditor the duty to take the necessary steps to ensure the release of any amount which, following the implementation of the order, exceeds the amount specified in it (Articles 17.4 and 27 EAPO Regulation). In case the creditor comes in concourse with other creditors of his debtor, using an EAPO order instead of the national legal instruments for preliminary attachment, may turn out less profitable for him.

53 Standard forms for the obtaining of an EOPA order were established by Commission Implementing Regulation (EU) 2016/1823 of 10 October 2016, [2016] OJ L283/1.

54 I.e. without the debtor's knowledge (Article 11 of the EAPO Regulation). For the effectiveness of the order, this 'surprise effect' is essential. If the debtor would be warned or heard prior to the issuing of the order, chances are that assets in bank account(s) will have gone elsewhere by the time the order is issued and implemented. K. Raffelsieper, 'Le nouveau règlement n 655/2014 portant création d'une procédure d'ordonnance européenne de saisie conservatoire des comptes bancaires' [2016] *TBH* (7) 9.

55 Article 7.1 of the EAPO Regulation.

when the creditor has submitted sufficient evidence to satisfy the court that there is an urgent need for such a protective measure because there is a real risk that, without such an order, the subsequent enforcement of the creditor's claim against the debtor will be impeded or made substantially more difficult.[56] However, the Regulation also accepts an application for an EAPO order prior to obtaining a judgment on the merits of the case or another kind of enforceable title (so-called *pre-judgment* order[57]). Besides his aforementioned burden of proof, the creditor will have to submit sufficient evidence to satisfy the court that he is likely to succeed on the substance of his claim against the debtor.[58] Regardless, the EAPO procedure makes it less cumbersome, lengthy and costly for creditors to obtain provisional measures to preserve assets in bank accounts of their debtor(s) located in other Member States.

An important and innovative element of the Regulation, at least from a Belgian perspective,[59] is the access to information about bank accounts provided for by Article 14 in order to make it easier for creditors to recover their claims. It will prevent dishonest debtors from being able to hide their assets.[60] If a creditor[61] has reasons to believe that the

56 Ch. Claeys, 'Grensoverschrijdende inning' [2015] *NjW* 511–512. Compare Article 1413 of the BJC.

57 Article 7.2 of the EAPO Regulation.

58 Article 10 of the EAPO Regulation provides for an (extendible) time period within which the creditor has to initiate proceedings on the substance of the matter and to inform the court issuing the order of this step. If the court has not received this proof in due time, the order shall be revoked or shall be terminated, and the parties shall be informed accordingly.

59 Some Member States provide rules offering a lot more transparency and information upon (the assets on) a debtor's bank accounts than Belgium; see for an overview: B. Hess, *Study No. JAI/A3/2002/02 on making more efficient enforcement of judicial decisions within the European Union*, 2004, <http://www2.ipr.uni-heidelberg.de/studie/>, 20–60.

60 B. Volders and K. Schulpen, *Capita selecta nationaal en internationaal beslagrecht*, Intersentia, Antwerp-Cambridge 2018, p. 15, no. 26.

61 As a rule, this special procedure can only be used by creditors disposing over an *enforceable* judgment, court settlement or authentic instrument which requires the debtor to pay the creditor's claim (Article 14.1(1) of the EAPO Regulation). If the title at the disposal of the creditor is *not yet enforceable*, a similar request to obtain information about the account of the debtor can be made by the creditor on condition that (i) the amount to be preserved is substantial taking into account the relevant circumstances and (ii) the creditor has submitted sufficient evidence to satisfy the court that there is an urgent need for account information because there is a risk that, without such information, the subsequent enforcement of the creditor's claim against the debtor is likely to be jeopardised and that this could consequently lead to a substantial deterioration of the creditor's financial situation (Article 14.1(2) of the EAPO Regulation). See also Recital 20 to the Regulation.

debtor holds one or more accounts with a bank in a specific Member State, but knows neither the name and/or address of the bank nor the IBAN, BIC or another bank number allowing the bank to be identified, he may request the court with which the application for the EAPO is lodged to request that the information authority of the Member State of enforcement obtains the information necessary to allow the bank or banks and the debtor's account or accounts to be identified.[62] If the court considers the creditor's request to be well substantiated and to meet all the conditions and requirements for issuing the EAPO, it shall transmit the request for information to the information authority of the Member State of enforcement.[63] As soon as this information authority has obtained the relevant account information, it shall transmit it to the requesting court by any appropriate means.[64] Subsequently, this court will make this information available to the requesting creditor.

It is very likely that this provision will substantially decrease the number of fruitless attempts to seize assets due to the ignorance of the creditor as to with which bank the debtor holds an account in a certain Member State.[65] This newly created mechanism for getting reliable information about funds held in bank accounts not only feels just, given the fact that it is a valuable addition to the swift execution of a judgment. It has also to be cheered from an economic viewpoint.

3.2. TRANSPOSITION OF THE INFORMATION MECHANISM ON BANK ACCOUNTS INTO BELGIAN NATIONAL LAW

In the wake of the EAPO Regulation, the Belgian legislator has recently provided a similar information mechanism as the one enacted in Article 14

---

62 G. Cuniberti and S. Migliorini, *The European Account Preservation Order Regulation – A Commentary*, Cambridge University Press, Cambridge 2018, pp. 174–186.

63 Article 14.3 of the EAPO Regulation. Each Member State has to appoint an information authority competent for the purposes of obtaining the necessary information on the debtor's account or accounts pursuant to Article 14. In Belgium, the National Chamber of Bailiffs has been designated as information authority (Article 555/1, §2 BJC). This Chamber is also responsible for the development and the maintenance of a data base (Central Register EAPO), in which all relevant information on EAPO procedures will be stored for six months (Articles 1391/1-1391/6 BJC).

64 Articles 14.6 *juncto* 29 of the EAPO Regulation.

65 R. Lindemans, 'Actuele ontwikkelingen en tendensen inzake beslagrecht (2015–2018)' in M.E. Storme (ed), *Themis 107 – Insolventie- en beslagrecht*, die Keure, Brugge 2018, p. (45) 49, no. 9.

of the EAPO for 'Belgian' cases, i.e. cases in which bank accounts are held at a financial institution situated on Belgian territory and in which the prior authorisation for a preliminary third-party attachment has been requested by the creditor at a Belgian judge of attachments, according to Belgian law.[66] In what Krans has circumscribed as 'spontaneous harmonisation'[67] – i.e. at the national level, rules or instruments initiated by the EU are applied to topics that do not fall within the scope of the rules on implementation – the legislator introduced the brand new Articles 1447/1 and 1447/2 in the BJC.[68] These provisions offer to creditors a means for more transparency about the financial instruments belonging to their debtors, which is most welcome. Previously, an uninformed creditor had to seize at random banking institutions in the hope of finding one day the right one(s). The National Bank counted 87 licensed banks in Belgium.[69] The average cost of each – potentially unfruitful – preliminary seizure on bank assets is estimated at €600.00. Creditors thus often found themselves in a hopeless plight.

Consequently, spontaneous harmonisation was a smart thing to do. It avoids discriminatory treatment as creditors searching relief in a domestic case will soon find themselves in the same, more comfortable position than creditors in cross-border cases where the EAPO Regulation is applicable. It is incomprehensible and regrettable, however, that the Belgian legislator did not provide for a similar information mechanism in the national context when the creditor already has an enforceable title at his disposal and wants to be informed about with which bank his debtor holds an account. This lacuna forces the creditor to obtain a preservation order,[70] whereas he fulfils all the legal requirements for

66 Irrelevant is the country where creditor and debtor are domiciled. Of course, the creditor needs to dispose over a (foreign) judgment, court settlement or authentic instrument, which is enforceable on Belgian territory.

67 B. Krans, 'EU Law and National Civil Procedure Law: An Invisible Pillar' (2015) 23 *ERPL* 567, 588.

68 Introduced in the BJC by Articles 193 and 194 of a Law of 18.06.2018 (*Official Gazette of Belgium* 02.07.2018). Initially, these Articles should enter into force on 01.01.2019. As at that time the indispensable database was not available at Belgium's National Bank, the entering into force has been postponed by Article 192 of a Law of 21.12.2018 (*Official Gazette of Belgium* 31.12.2018). The system was further developed by means of Royal Decree of 22.04.2019, (*Official Gazette of Belgium* 30.04.2019), laying down the allowance for processing the request for account information.

69 <http://stat.nbb.be/Index.aspx?ThemeTreeId=51&lang=nl>.

70 It is in our opinion very unlikely that in such circumstances the creditor ever will make use of this preservation order. Once he is in possession of the whereabouts of the financial belongings of his debtor, nothing will stop him from executing a third-party attachment in the hands of the bank because this is the efficient and swift way to act.

the immediate enforcement of his title on money, shares, securities, etc. belonging to his debtor, e.g. by means of a garnishment. A more efficient way of transposing this information mechanism was certainly conceivable.

The reason why the Belgian legislator did not transpose Article 14 of the EAPO regulation in such a sense is not explained in the Explanatory Memorandum to the Law but is nevertheless clear to us: it did not make use of its (procedural) autonomy. It seems to be hindered by the fact that at EU level a European Account Enforcement Order was, for several reasons, not attainable and was thus not adopted. In short, these consist of (i) considerations of state sovereignty, (ii) considerations of competence of the EU to interfere with this aspect of enforcement proceedings, which is deeply embedded in the structures of enforcement in the Member States, and (iii) the considerable divergences that exist between the national systems on this matter.[71] In the authors' opinion, however, there is absolutely no justification for this reluctance, since none of the reasons mentioned matter in a purely domestic context.

3.3. CONCLUDING REMARKS

At the end of this chapter, it can be positively concluded that the Belgian system is in conformity with Union law. This is however not that much of a surprising statement since the European legislator opted to use a regulation to deal with the Account Preservation Order. Consequently, no national implementation was required, except on those points where the regulation left room for the national legislator (e.g. the appointment of the national information and competent authority). More interesting and sketching for the willingness with which the Belgian legislator sometimes acts is that a similar system to the EAPO and its information request has been introduced in 'Belgian cases' concerning preliminary seizure. It is clear that it was by no means obliged to do so.

---

71 B. Hess, *Study No. JAI/A3/2002/02 on making more efficient enforcement of judicial decisions within the European Union*, 2004, pp. 10–12, 83 and 88 <http://www2.ipr.uni-heidelberg.de/studie/>. See also B. Hess, 'Die Europäische Kontenpfändung aus der Perspektive eines Europäischen Vollstreckungsrechts' in D. Baetge, J. von Hein and M. von Hinden (eds), *Die richtige Ordnung: Festschrift für Jan Kropholler zum 70. Geburtstag*, Mohr Siebeck, Tubingen 2008, pp. 795 and 797, where he wrote about the traditional reluctance of Member States towards the intrusion of any aspect of other national, international or supranational law. W.A. Kennett, *Enforcement of judgments in Europe*, Oxford University Press, Oxford 2000, pp. 263–265.

Less positive, however, is that the Belgian legislator 'stopped' at the preliminary seizure. In our opinion, it was perfectly feasible to carry through the initiative of providing for such an information request in the context of executive seizure (more specifically garnishment). The reticence apparent from the decision not to do so was by no means justified.

More generally, it can be noted that the Belgian legislator did exactly the contrary in this context than its approach in the context of the reimbursement of costs of lawyers' fees and technical advisers: it did not make full use of its procedural autonomy, unfortunately to the detriment of legal coherence.

4. GENERAL CONCLUSION

As a general conclusion, we are of the opinion that the cohabitation between the principle of procedural autonomy and the Belgian legal system is one with ups and downs. Whereas in certain fields (e.g. the reimbursement of legal costs) the Belgian legislator appropriates more room for manoeuvre than it actually has according to the CJEU, in other areas of law it stays perfectly within the boundaries of Union law without even getting close to exploring them (e.g. the preservation of bank accounts with accompanying request for information).

It is our feeling that the Belgian legislator simply has no – at least not much – attention for the principle of procedural autonomy during the legislative process. *A fortiori* the question should be asked to what extent this principle is actually known to it. In none of the preparatory works concerning the above-treated topics' national legislation special attention has been paid to its relationship with Union law. The principle of procedural autonomy seems to be, at least from a Belgian perspective, sitting in a dark corner.

THE ENGLISH APPROACH TO PROCEDURAL AUTONOMY

John Sorabji

This chapter considers the approach taken to civil procedural harmonisation in England and Wales (England) in the light of procedural developments from EU law. It does so in the broad context of the UK's departure from the EU. It considers two approaches to EU procedural developments by English rule-makers. First, it looks at an approach which has seen the effect of EU procedural developments minimised within English civil procedure. This is an approach that treats EU developments as *lex specialis*, rather than as the basis for broader reform of English procedure. Secondly, it looks at an approach which sees English rule-makers reject EU developments to the maximum extent possible. Underpinning both approaches is a general standard, which sees the English rule-maker draw on procedural developments in common law and civilian jurisdictions where they are perceived to be best practice. The extent to which EU developments have influenced the English rule-maker thus depend on the extent to which they satisfy a pragmatic best practice test. Finally, the chapter considers two possible ways in which EU procedural developments may continue to influence English civil procedure following the UK's departure from the EU.

1. INTRODUCTION

On 29 March 2019, the United Kingdom was scheduled to leave the EU.[1] That date passed without departure taking place, as the United Kingdom and EU agreed an extension of time to put in place the basis on which withdrawal would take effect. The two agreed that withdrawal would take place on 31 October 2019. From that date, assuming withdrawal occurs, the influence of EU law on procedural developments in England and Wales (England) will, in one sense, alter fundamentally. While the EU may continue, as Krans and Nylund have described it, a trend towards an 'increasing Europeanisation of civil procedure',[2] England will no longer formally be part of that process. Whatever that trend may have been and whatever its interrelation with the principle of procedural autonomy,[3] the freedom to develop civil procedure as English policymakers chose, there was in principle prior to the UK's withdrawal from the EU, it will cease to apply thereafter. There will, it is reasonable to assume, be far more room to manoeuvre for England than there was previously. Accordingly, it can be assumed that any previous move towards harmonisation will thus reduce. That assumption rests, however, on the idea that while the UK was a member of the EU it was subject to an increasing amount of influence in terms of procedural design and development. That is not, however, the case. To a significant degree English civil procedure has, throughout the UK's membership of the EU and its predecessors, been broadly resistant to EU developments that could have been a spur to procedural harmonisation, i.e. to draw its domestic civil procedure into closer alignment with EU developments. This has not manifested itself through outright rejection, although in one case concerning the reform of collective redress, which is discussed below, that did occur. On the contrary, the general approach taken has been to minimise harmonising influences by maintaining a distinction between English and EU procedure: the latter being incorporated into its procedural rules, the Civil Procedure Rules (CPR), by way of an exception

1 European Union (Withdrawal) Act 2018, ss.1 and 20(2); The European Union (Withdrawal) Act 2018 (Exit Day) (Amendment) (No. 2) Regulations 2019 (SI 2019/859). This chapter assumes that the UK will, in fact, exit the EU.

2 A. Nylund and B. Krans, *The European Union and National Civil Procedure*, Intersentia, Antwerp-Cambridge 2016.

3 For a discussion see, for instance, M. Bobek, *Why there is no principle of 'Procedural Autonomy' of the Member States* in B. de Witte and H. Micklitz (eds), *The European Court of Justice and Autonomy of the Member States*, Intersentia, Antwerp-Cambridge 2011.

to the general rule or by way of a *lex specialis*. Examples of this would be the approach taken to EU developments relating to small claims or the European Order for Payment.[4]

The English approach to the influence of European developments on its civil procedure is both historically anomalous and, yet, not unique. It is historically anomalous due to the significant influence that European procedure has had on the development of English procedure. To give two short examples, both the privilege against self-incrimination as a feature of English procedure and documentary disclosure (historically known as discovery), in which parties to litigation can be compelled from an opposing party in litigation, are both products of European influence. As Langbein has noted, the former's place in English procedure was no more than 'the common law's repackaging of the Canon law doctrine of nemo tenetur seipsum accusare during the development of the adversarial criminal trial in the 18th and 19th centuries.'[5] Disclosure was a development of the common law, or more accurately the equity courts such as the High Court of Chancery, owed to the influence of a specific form of procedure drawn, again, from canon law: the *Denunciatio Evangelica*.[6]

English procedure can thus be seen to have been open to European influence in its early period of development. Its resistance to influence from other jurisdictions is anomalous for another reason. It has historically, and remains to this day, open to influence from other common law jurisdictions as well as from specific European jurisdictions. As Lord Parker CJ put it in the 1960s, it was 'important that the common law, and the development of the common law, should be homogeneous in the various sections of the Commonwealth';[7] a point most recently reiterated by Sir Geoffrey Vos,

4 See, for instance, CPR Pt 6 and Pt 78 prior to amendments to be affected on 29.03.2019, see G. Vos (ed), *Civil Procedure 2018*, Thomson Reuters, London 2018. Other examples would include the approach to Regulation (EC) No. 1393/2007 of the European Parliament and of the Council of 13 November 2007 on the service in the Member States of judicial and extrajudicial documents in civil or commercial matters (service of documents), and repealing Council Regulation (EC) No. 1348/2000, which saw limited amendments made to CPR Pt 6, amongst other parts of the CPR, to introduce discrete rules relating to cross-border service rather than a general revision of the approach to service of process.

5 J. Langbein, 'The Historical Origins of the Privilege against Self-Incrimination at Common Law' (1994) *92 Michigan Law Review* 1047.

6 H. Coing, 'English Equity and the Denunciatio Evangelica of the Canon Law' (1955) 71 *Law Quarterly Review* 223, 235.

7 *Smith v. Leech Brain & Co Ltd* [1962] 2 QB 405 at [415]; also see Lord Denning MR cited in J. Jacob (ed), *The Supreme Court Practice 1999*, Sweet & Maxwell, London 1999, Vol. 1, p. 1480.

Chancellor of the High Court, when commenting in *Serious Fraud Office (SFO) v. Eurasian Natural Resources Corp. Ltd* [2018] EWCA Civ 2006, [2019] 1 WLR 791 on the need to develop the law on legal professional privilege consistently with developments internationally, and particularly in other common law jurisdictions. Recent examples where that influence has been embraced on the basis that developments in other common law jurisdictions offered better ways to carry out the civil procedural process are, for instance: the influence of New Zealand's approach to the disclosure process by the Jackson Costs reforms' adoption of the so-called 'menu' option approach to disclosure;[8] the willingness to learn from docketing proceedings drawn from the United States and Australia;[9] or, the willingness to adopt the process by which expert witnesses give evidence concurrently from Australia.[10] Its willingness to be influenced by specific European jurisdictions can equally be seen from the long struggle to incorporate a general fixed recoverable litigation cost regime into English procedure. First recommended by Lord Woolf in the 1990s, such a scheme was again recommended by Lord Justice Jackson in 2009.[11] The impetus for such a development was largely taken from the successful operation of such an approach to litigation costs in Germany.[12] The English rule-maker has thus neither historically nor generally been averse to harmonisation per se. It has adopted approaches that harmonised its procedural law with that of other jurisdictions where their procedures have been seen to have a specific advantage over that already in place in England.

Notwithstanding these historic and continuing examples of English procedure's willingness to draw influence from other jurisdictions, its approach to EU developments is equally not unique. It can rather be seen as a broader resistance to general harmonisation attempts, particularly

---

8 R. Jackson, *Controlling the Costs of Disclosure (7th Implementation Lecture)* <https://www.judiciary.uk/wp-content/uploads/JCO/Documents/Speeches/controlling-costs-disclosure.pdf>.

9 Lord Neuberger MR, *Docketing: Completing Case Management's Unfinished Revolution (9th Implementation Lecture)* <https://www.judiciary.uk/wp-content/uploads/JCO/Documents/Speeches/mor-speech-solicitors-cost-conference-lecture-feb2012.pdf>.

10 An idea originally canvased by Sir Anthony Clarke MR, in A. Clarke, 'The Role of the Expert After Woolf' (2008) 14(3) *Clinical Risk* 85, and adopted by the Jackson Costs Review, see, R. Jackson, *Review of Civil Litigation Costs: Final Report*, TSO, London 2009, p. 385.

11 H. Woolf, *Access to Justice: Final Report to the Lord Chancellor on the Civil Justice System in England and Wales*, HMSO, London 1996, Ch. 7; R. Jackson, *Review of Civil Litigation Costs: Preliminary Report*, TSO, London 2009, Vol. 1 Ch. 21, Vol. 2 Ch. 55.

12 For an account see, Lord Browne-Wilkinson, *The UK Access To Justice Report: A Sheep In Woolf's Clothing*, (1999) 28 *Western Australian Law Review* 181.

which draw on traditions from outside the common law. For instance, the ALI-UNIDROIT Transnational Principles of Civil Procedure were met with scepticism as to their potential influence on English procedure. As Glasser put it, when those Principles were published, their importance and utility was minimised. The specific response to them was to set them aside as there were simply 'no pressing reasons why "English procedure" should abandon [its] own newly established code [the Civil Procedure Rules] for a different set of rules and principles for which there is no perceived demand or need.'[13] There was no need for harmonisation, and what need there was, as he put it, could be accommodated through the discrete incorporation of issue-specific instruments such as those emanating from the, then, EC on service of process, for instance.[14] And, those such instruments could then be incorporated, as noted above, in ways to minimise any potentially broader influence on procedural design they might otherwise have had. Such resistance to broader attempts at harmonisation may well prove to limit, or at the least foreshadow, the possible future influence of the ELI-UNIDROIT model European rules on civil procedure on English procedure.[15]

Two approaches to procedural harmonisation or integration can thus be seen in outline: first, a willingness to draw on specific, predominantly but not exclusively, national procedural developments; and, secondly, a scepticism to generic harmonisation, which manifests itself in either the rejection of such attempts or the minimisation of their effects. In terms of procedural design autonomy, the position would appear to be one where English procedure voluntarily draws on influences it deems beneficial or an improvement to its own approaches, while it limits the impact of other influences which replicate its own process but do so in the field of cross-border EU law. This chapter explores the nature of these distinctive approaches. First, it examines the approach taken to EU harmonisation, where the scope for procedural design autonomy is restricted. It looks at the English response to legislation relating to service of process and small claims and how the rule-maker has adopted an approach that has

---

13 C. Glasser, 'Do we need a Transnational Civil Procedure Code? A critical comment' in M. Adenas et al (eds), *The Future of Transnational Civil Litigation*, BIICL, London 2004, p. 13.

14 Ibid, p. 14.

15 For a discussion of these rules see, J. Sorabji, 'The ELI-UNIDROIT Project: An Introduction and an English Perspective' in A. Nylund and M. Strandberg (eds), *Civil Procedure and Harmonisation of Law*, Intersentia, Antwerp-Cambridge 2019.

minimised any possibility of a broader influence of EU procedural law in domestic procedure. Secondly, it examines the approach taken to EU harmonisation, where a substantive degree of procedural design autonomy is left to the national legislator. It does so by consideration of the English approach to collective redress reform. Finally, it considers the future for harmonisation following the UK's exit from the EU. In this, two possible trends are considered. First, the potential effect that competition between courts, and particularly common law courts, may have on autonomy in procedural design and thus on the ability of the English rule-maker to minimise the influence of procedural developments across the EU: competition may reduce the scope to choose to ignore or minimise developments in other jurisdictions. Secondly, the potential continuing, albeit indirect, effect that EU law may have on English procedural design autonomy; a development that could be described as 'we learn, as we leave.' Underpinning each of these various approaches one common theme will be evident: English procedural reform operates on the basis of a pragmatic approach. It seeks and accepts influence where that is viewed as providing the basis to improve its procedure. It rejects or minimises influence, including mandatory influence, where it sees it as providing no basis for improvement. Autonomy in procedural design remains and will otherwise remain paramount.

2. PROCEDURAL DESIGN AUTONOMY AND MINIMUM DISCRETION

The English approach to developments in EU procedural law where the scope for procedural design autonomy is at a minimum and harmonisation at a maximum can best be illustrated through the approach taken to two EU instruments: the European Order for Payment Regulation (EOP);[16] and the European Small Claims Procedure Regulation (ESCP).[17] Both Regulations were implemented in English civil procedure in 2008 through the same amendment to the CPR.[18] It introduced a new Part to the CPR,

16 Regulation (EC) 1896/2006 of the European Parliament and of the Council of 12 December 2006 creating a European Order for Payment procedure.

17 Regulation (EC) 861/2007) of the European Parliament and of the European Commission of 11 July 2007 establishing a European Small Claims Procedure.

18 Civil Procedure (Amendment) Rules 2008 (SI 2008/2178).

which contained provision for the operation of both the EOP and ESCP: CPR Pt 78, which only applies to cross-border disputes.[19]

In both cases the CPR contained longstanding provisions governing both small claims and uncontested debt claims. Both procedures have their origins in the mid-19th century. A dedicated small claims procedure was first introduced in 1846.[20] It was revised in the early 1970s, when it was transformed into a consent-based process that involved informal arbitration. It was further revised as a consequence of the Woolf reforms in the 1990s, when the arbitral aspect was removed. By 2008 it was a well-run, easily accessible, straightforward and inexpensive form of procedure applicable to the majority of claims with a value up to £5,000. In 2013 the general value limit was increased to £10,000.[21] The English procedure for dealing with uncontested debt claims was introduced slightly later than its small claims process. It was introduced in 1855, at which time it was a truncated statutory procedure through which a creditor could seek payment from a debtor where it was believed there was no defence to the claim.[22] Assuming no defence was entered, judgment would be given. The direct procedural descendent of that process is now contained in CPR Pt 12, which sets out a paper-based process, and Money Claims Online or MCOL, which provides a streamlined online process through which the payment of debts up to £100,000 can be secured.

For both small claims and uncontested debt enforcement, the European legislator introduced via the ESCP and the EOP procedures that were long and well established in English procedure. Additionally, both national procedures were well used and worked well. In such circumstances, the question posed by Glasser concerned the ALI-UNIDROIT Transnational rules, noted earlier, comes to the fore: in the light of a well-functioning national process what perceived need was there for the European developments to form a basis for national harmonisation? If there is no perceived need, then the likelihood was that harmonisation would either not

---

19 See Vos, above note 4, CPR Pt 78.

20 County Courts (England) Act 1846, s. 57.

21 For a discussion of the development of the small claims procedure, see J. Sorabji, 'An Examination of the Influence of European Union Law on English Civil Procedure' in A. Nylund and M. Strandberg (eds), *Civil Procedure and Harmonisation of Law*, Intersentia, Antwerp-Cambridge 2019.

22 Summary Procedure on Bills of Exchange Act (1855); for a discussion see Sorabji, above note 21.

occur or would be minimised. The English rule-maker, the Civil Procedure Rule Committee, took the latter approach. It minimised the European legislator's influence. It did so through introducing both the ESCP and the EOP as a *lex specialis*; a discrete European-only applicable Part of the CPR. In this way it secured compliance with the need to introduce a procedural mechanism to give effect to the two EU Regulations in English procedural law. It did so, however, in a way that ensured that it was an exception to the *lex generalis* contained in CPR Pt 27 (the small claims procedure) and CPR Pt 12 (the default judgment procedure), both of which would continue to apply to domestic-only cases unamended and unrevised, i.e. the EU legislation had no impact on domestic-only procedural design. As such there was no real possibility for harmonisation arising from those EU procedural developments. Procedural design autonomy was maintained through taking a minimalist approach to implementation.

There are a number of reasons that can explain why this minimalist approach was taken. They revolve around the question of perceived need. As English civil procedure knows all too well, the main spur for reform are perceived defects in the operation of its procedure. For English procedure that has historically been excess litigation cost, procedural complexity and delay.[23] Where the ESCP and EOP were concerned there were no perceived defects in the existing national procedure that would justify their principled reappraisal and potential replacement or amendment in the light of the European legislation. Perhaps more importantly, for the ESCP and EOP to have formed the basis of a reappraisal of the national procedure, they would have had to differ in important ways from it and do so in ways that suggested it offered improvements over it. Neither the ESCP nor the EOP did so. The ESCP process was broadly similar to that of the English small claims procedure, except that it operated a paper-based process with an option for an oral hearing while the English procedure was, in common with the standard English approach, one which took an oral final hearing as the default subject to an option to waive that right and have the claim determined on the papers.[24] It thus offered nothing innovative, nor did it offer any form of process that was capable of being perceived to be an improvement over that already in place.

23 N. Andrews, 'A New Civil Procedural Code For England: Party-Control "Going, Going, Gone"' (2000) 19(Jan) C.J.Q. 19–38, 20.

24 CPR r. 27.10.

On the contrary, the fact that the ESCP has had lower financial limits, initially €2,000 and then €5,000, than the English small claims procedure, put it at a distinct disadvantage in terms of its general utility. General harmonisation based on the ESCP would have introduced a form of small claims process no better and arguably of less utility to that which was already in place. The same points can be made concerning the EOP. In essence it did no more than provide a comparable form of debt collection procedure to that which already existed in the CPR. As with the ESCP it provided no novel feature or features, and no procedural improvement over the established national procedure. As such there was little, if any, incentive for their implementation other than as discrete, self-contained instruments. There was nothing in them to spur a reconsideration of the national procedure. They demonstrated no advantage over it that could justify anything other than a minimalist approach to harmonisation.

That a minimalist approach to harmonisation, one which maintained maximum procedural autonomy through the way it resulted in the marginalisation of the European legislation, was taken in respect of the ESCP and EOP should not be understood to arise from what could be referred to as 'English exceptionalism'; the supposed view that English civil procedure is superior to other forms of civil process. If that were an operative factor it would militate against English procedure being willing to reform in the light of procedural approaches taken in other jurisdictions, whether European or elsewhere. If that were the case it would not, as noted above, have drawn so heavily on the German approach to fixed recoverable costs as an inspiration for procedural reform. In both the EU and German cases, the question of influence and harmonisation, or resistance to influence, was and is a matter of utility: does the approach from the EU or the other jurisdiction provide the basis for practical improvement of the present system? If so, as in the case of German fixed recoverable costs, the answer was positive, and integration of that approach has been a consistent aim of policymakers since the 1990s. If not, as in the case of the ESCP and EOP, the answer was negative. The test whether to integrate and the extent of integration, and from there harmonisation, is essentially pragmatic rather than doctrinal. It looks to what works. If the ESCP and EOP had worked well and better than the English procedures, the real likelihood is, based on the approach taken to German fixed recoverable costs, is that they would have replaced both the small claims and default judgment procedures: they would have become the new English *lex generalis* and produced a substantial degree of procedural harmonisation.

3. PROCEDURAL DESIGN AUTONOMY AND MAXIMUM DISCRETION

The pragmatic approach to procedural autonomy and influence can be seen in the way in which English procedure has developed in an area where the European legislator has adopted a maximum flexibility approach to EU Member States' procedural design.[25] That area is collective redress reform; an area where both in England and the EU, and its predecessors, reform efforts have been ongoing since the 1980s.[26] In neither jurisdiction have substantive reforms been enacted, albeit in England a sector-specific reform was introduced via the Consumer Rights Act 2015 and in 2018, the European Commission issued a draft sector-specific Directive.[27] Both have as their focus the enforcement of consumer rights. In both jurisdictions, however, the majority of reform-focused work took place from 2005 to 2015. During this period the English pragmatism-based approach to procedural design can be seen in three ways: first, through an attempt to influence the EU reform process; secondly, through a rejection of EU influence; and, finally, through its search for influence from other and primarily common law jurisdictions.

The first issue, the attempt by English procedural policymakers to influence EU developments, occurred from 2005 to 2008. It was carried out primarily by the Civil Justice Council (CJC), a statutory advisory body which is required to provide advice to the government and judiciary, including as a consequence the Civil Procedure Rule Committee, on procedural reform.[28] During this period it took the central role in developing policy advice on collective redress reform, ultimately in 2008 recommending

---

25 It could be said that a maximum flexibility approach is one where the EU chooses not to legislate, leaving matters entirely to the EU Member State. The distinction drawn here between maximum discretion and minimum discretion concerns the situation where the EU has determined that EU Member States have to take steps, and the choice is simply over the way in which the EU determines that positive decision is to be implemented.

26 For an outline of EU developments, see, C. Hodges, 'Collective Redress: A breakthrough or a Damp Squib?' [2013] *Journal of Consumer Policy* DOI (2014) 37:67–89. For a history of developments, or the lack of them, in England see, J. Sorabji, 'Collective Action Reform in England and Wales' in D. Fairgrieve and E. Lein (eds), *Extraterritoriality and Collective Redress*, Oxford University Press, Oxford 2012.

27 Proposal for a Directive of the European Parliament and of the Council on representative actions for the protection of the collective interests of consumers, and repealing Directive 2009/22/EC (COM(2018) 184 final).

28 Civil Procedure Act 1997, s. 6; and see <https://www.judiciary.uk/related-offices-and-bodies/advisory-bodies/cjc/>.

the introduction of a generic, i.e. horizontal, collective action mechanism be introduced into the CPR.[29] While that recommendation was rejected by the government, it did accept that where evidence supported the need for their introduction sector-specific collective action mechanisms which would incorporate all of the other procedural design recommendations made by the CJC, could be introduced.[30] During this period, the European Commission was also developing its own policy framework for collective action reform via Green Papers issued by DG Comp and DG Sanco in 2005 and 2008, respectively. Both approaches considered the merits and nature of sector specific collective action mechanisms.[31]

The approach taken by the CJC between 2005–2008 was focused not on what it could learn from the DG Comp and DG Sanco. Its approach was more focused on how it might influence the design of European legislative proposals. This was an approach that took as its starting point that its own work set out the optimum approach to reform. As it put it, in its response to DG Sanco's consultation on its 2008 Green Paper,

> … While it is not appropriate within the framework of an EU mechanism setting out minimum standards as is envisaged in the present consultation to prescribe how the aim of ensuring effective and proportionate means of redress could properly be implemented as it would be a matter for member states as to what measures they incorporate into any collective redress mechanism developed as a consequence of EU reform arising out of DG Sanco's initiatives, the CJC submits that the optimum means by which this could be incorporated are those set out in the draft rules of court set out in the CJC's report …[32]

---

[29] J. Sorabji, M. Napier and R. Musgrove (eds), '*Improving Access to Justice through Collective Actions' – Developing a More Efficient and Effective Procedure to Collective Actions: Final Report*, Civil Justice Council of England and Wales, London November 2008 <https://www.judiciary.uk/wp-content/uploads/JCO/Documents/CJC/Publications/CJC+papers/CJC+Improving+Access+to+Justice+through+Collective+Actions.pdf>.

[30] Ministry of Justice, The Government's Response to the Civil Justice Council's Report: 'Improving Access to Justice through Collective Actions, Ministry of Justice, London July 2009. The CJC had made 11 design recommendations. The government accepted ten of them, see Sorabji, Napier and Musgrove, above note 29, pp. 5–6.

[31] DG Comp, *Green Paper – Damages actions for breach of the EC antitrust rules* (COM (2005) 672); DG Comp, *White Paper on Damages Actions for Breach of the EC antitrust rules* (COM (2008) 165); DG Sanco, *Green Paper on consumer collective redress*, (COM (2008) 794); DG Sanco, *Follow-up to the Green Paper on consumer collective redress* (2009).

[32] Civil Justice Council, *Response to the Commission (DG-Sanco) Green Paper on Consumer Collective Redress*, at [7], published as an Annex to Civil Justice Council, *Response to European Commission Public Consultation: Towards a Coherent European*

The CJC maintained this approach when, in 2011, the EU Commission continued its reform work in this area through a consultation (the 2011 consultation) on what steps might be taken following the failure of DG Comp and DG Sanco's initiatives to effect the introduction of an EU collective action mechanism. As it put it, for instance, the approach the Commission should take to the relationship between public and private enforcement mechanisms in this area should follow that it recommended in its 2008 Report on collective action reform.[33] More broadly, it advocated the adoption of its 2008 reform recommendations, again in 2011, as the basis for European reform.[34]

The rationale underpinning the CJC's approach was straightforward. It had examined the issues concerning collective action reform. It had done so from both a principled and theoretical basis, from an empirical basis, and from a comparative law basis. Its theoretical approach examined alternatives to court-based collective actions, e.g. ombudsman schemes, regulatory mechanisms.[35] It has also considered the proper relationship between court-based actions and alternative dispute resolution,[36] while discussing the different approaches that could be taken to court-based action, e.g. whether a collective action mechanism should be opt-in or opt-out, whether aggregate damages should be permitted.[37] Its empirical work was based on a detailed study of collective action mechanisms in England and other jurisdictions.[38] The latter point being taken further in its comparative work, which looked at such mechanisms in the United States, Australia and across Europe.[39] The first two issue are considered in this section, the final one in the final section, below.

Approach to Collective Redress (SEC (2011) 173 Final) <https://www.judiciary.uk/wp-content/uploads/JCO/Documents/CJC/Publications/consultation+responses/CJC+response+to+Commission+EU+Coll+action+consulation+2011+Final.doc>.

33 Civil Justice Council, *Response to European Commission Public Consultation: Towards a Coherent European Approach to Collective Redress (SEC (2011) 173 Final)* at [23].

34 Civil Justice Council, above note 22, at [44] and following, 'The CJC is firmly of the view that an effective, efficient, proportionate and fair system of collective redress is one which incorporates the features which it advocated in its 2008 report, operated according to procedural rules akin to those which it subsequently developed.'

35 Sorabji, Napier and Musgrove, above note 29, p. 67.

36 Ibid, p. 152.

37 Ibid, p. 145.

38 R. Mulheron, *Reform of Collective Redress in England And Wales: A Perspective of Need*, Civil Justice Council, 2008 <https://www.judiciary.uk/wp-content/uploads/JCO/Documents/CJC/Publications/Other+papers/reform-of-collective-redress.pdf>.

39 Sorabji, Napier and Musgrove, above note 29, p. 37.

In the light of its work, it drew its conclusion that its recommendations represented the best approach to take to reform. Whether it was correct in drawing that conclusion is beside the point for present purposes. The point to take here is that its conclusions, both in respect of English procedural reform and EU reform, was that the approach to take was the one that worked best. It applied the pragmatic test. From the perspective of procedural design autonomy this has an important consequence. In so far as EU recommendations were concerned, such as those that were to arise from the 2011 consultation when it issued its 2013 Recommendation on Collective Redress Reform (the 2013 Recommendations),[40] they would be rejected where they differed from those the CJC had itself recommended. They would be rejected because they would be, in its view and by implication the UK government's view – it having accepted the CJC's recommendations except that of their being a horizontal collective redress mechanism – sub-optimal.

The CJC's approach was that of an advisory body. It was not that of the English rule-making body or the government. Its approach can, however, be seen in that of the government in its rejection of the EU's 2013 Recommendation. From 2012 the UK government was considering reforms to the sector specific opt-in collective action mechanism that was operative in the UK's Competition Appeals Tribunal, a specialist civil tribunal where actions seeking damages for competition law breaches can be pursued.[41] The outcome of its deliberations was to endorse reform that mirrored the CJC's 2008 recommendations.[42] Its conclusions were enacted via section 81 and schedule 8 of the Consumer Rights Act 2015. The UK government's consultation and reform process ran in tandem with that of the EU's 2013 Recommendations. The latter offered detailed guidance on how the EU Commission desired EU Member States to introduce and, where there were existing mechanisms, reform their collective action procedures. While it was not prescriptive in its approach, an attempt to introduce a

40 Commission Recommendation, *On Common Principles for Collective Redress Mechanisms in the Member States for Injunctions against and Claims on Damages caused by violations of EU rights*, COM (2013) 3539 (11.06.2013); and see, Commission Communication, Towards a European Horizontal Framework for Collective Redress, COM (2013) 401/2 (11.06.2013).

41 Department of Business, Innovation and Science, *Private Actions in competition Law: A Consultation on options for Reform* (April 2012).

42 Department of Business, Innovation and Science, *Private Actions in competition Law: A Consultation on options for Reform – government response* (January 2013).

draft Directive having come to nothing in 2009,[43] it was intended to be highly persuasive. The EU Member States were left with a wide margin of procedural design autonomy, but to promote harmonisation the intention was that reforms were to be consistent with the recommendations, i.e. that Member States would make similar design choices. As is now apparent the idea that such recommendations would yield harmonisation was entirely misplaced.[44] Harmonisation does not arise where maximum discretion is provided.

The UK government's approach to the 2013 Recommendations was consistent with the approach taken to the ESCP and EOP. It assessed the recommendations and found them wanting. They offered no advantage or benefit over and above that contained in the work done by, and recommendations of the CJC in 2008.[45] As such the UK government adopted those recommendations, even where they were not consistent with those of the EU Commission. This approach can readily be seen from the treatment of the question whether the UK's reformed procedure should operate on an opt-out basis. The 2013 Recommendations considered such an approach to be justified in exceptional circumstances.[46] The CJC had concluded an opt-out form of collective action was essential for such a procedure to be properly effective.[47] It could not be the exception, but the rule. The UK government rejected the 2013 Recommendation's approach. It adopted the CJC's noting that its work justified the adoption of an opt-out approach, i.e. the CJC demonstrated that the 2013 Recommendation's exceptional circumstances existed. As the then Minister responsible for the reforms put it:

> There has however been extensive research carried out by the Office of Fair Trading and the Civil Justice Council, which supports that [sic] a more effective

---

43 M. Ioannidou, 'Enhancing the Consumers' Role in EU Private Competition Law Enforcement: A normative and practical approach' (2011) 8(1) *Comp. L. Rev.* 59.

44 A conclusion evident from, Report from the Commission to the European Parliament, the Council and the European Economic and Social Committee on the implementation of the Commission Recommendation of 11 June 2013 on common principles for injunctive and compensatory collective redress mechanisms in Member States concerning violations of rights granted under Union law (2013/396/EU) (COM(2018) 40 final).

45 This is not to assume that the UK government accepted the CJC's recommendations on a parochial basis. If the EU Recommendation had provided an approach to procedural design that was perceived to be superior to that recommended by the CJC, it would undoubtedly have accepted the former and rejected the latter.

46 2013 Recommendations, above note 44, at [21].

47 Sorabji, Napier and Musgrove, above note 29, p. 145.

> means to redress for parties affected by an infringement of competition law comes through an 'opt-out' approach. This is backed up by evidence gathered through the Government's own Impact Assessment and consultation on the draft Bill. An efficient means to redress within a competition regime is essential for making markets work. The Government believes this does provide the necessary justification 'on grounds of sound administration of justice' and therefore, sufficient leeway to take advantage of the Commission's exception.[48]

In other words, the UK government looked to the evidence just as was the case when it had limited room to manoeuvre with the implementation of the ESCP and EOP: what worked best and, as a consequence, to what extent might the EU approach form a basis for general reform of the relevant domestic approach. It concluded that the evidence base was such that it would act in a way that minimised any potential scope for harmonisation. Just as the CJC had concluded five years earlier, it concluded that its approach was optimal and was so, even where it diverged from the generally applicable approach to procedural reform advocated by the EU. As the CJC had proselytised in 2008 and 2011, the UK government understood its approach, based on the research by the former body and by the Office for Fair Trading, to be the better one. As the 2013 Recommendations were viewed as offering no improvement over that work and its evidence-base, the maximum scope for procedural design autonomy provided by the 2013 Recommendations was exercised as far as it possibly could be. It was because the test was, again, what was perceived to work. Resistance to EU harmonisation was, again, not a matter of principle, but pragmatism. And in this case, it was a possibility that the 2013 Recommendations facilitated through their central weakness as a vehicle for harmonisation: their optionality and provision for Member States to find exceptions to the general rules they provided. Where maximum discretion is provided to implement EU procedural design choices, the greater the limit on harmonisation exists and is likely to be taken by domestic rule-makers.

48 See J. Swinson MP (Minister of State), Letter to Lord Boswell (09.11.2013) previously published at <http://europeanmemoranda.cabinetoffice.gov.uk/files/2013/11/C_(2013)_3559_Min_Cor_9_November_2013_Swinson-Boswell.pdf>.

4. PROCEDURAL AUTONOMY AND FUTURE INFLUENCE

With the UK scheduled to leave the EU in 2020, any restrictions placed on England's civil procedural design autonomy by its EU membership ought to cease. That the UK is to revoke the EU Regulations concerning service, the ESCP and EOP and those aspects of the CPR that implement them procedurally would seem to bear this out.[49] This would be to take a perhaps too simplistic view. There is reason to believe that the approach taken post-January 2020 is likely to be one that on the one hand maintains the pragmatic best-practice approach to procedural influence, while on the other sees the EU legislator enjoy an indirect effect on English procedural developments. The former will see EU developments treated in the same way as those from any other jurisdiction in terms of their likely influence. The latter may well see EU developments play a similar role to that taken prior to EU exit as that identified in the first part of this chapter, i.e. one of procedural autonomy with minimum discretion. Both are considered in turn.

The English common law's catholic approach to external influences whether from other common law or civilian legal systems is, as noted above, well established.[50] That willingness to examine European civil procedure in search of best practice is no exception to that. Two examples illustrate this. First, the CJC's work on collective redress reform examined both developments in common law jurisdictions and from a number of European jurisdictions, i.e. Denmark, France, Germany, the Netherlands, Norway, Spain and Sweden.[51] It drew upon the work carried out by DG Comp and DG Sanco in their respective Green and White Papers, as

49 At the time of writing prior to 29.03.2019, revocation of the various instruments and relevant Parts of the CPR was to be effected by the following: the draft Service of Documents and Taking of Evidence in Civil and Commercial Matters (Revocation and Saving Provisions) (EU Exit) Regulations 2018; European Enforcement Order, European Order for Payment and European Small Claims Procedure (Amendment etc.) (EU Exit) Regulations 2018 (SI 2018/1311); and the Civil Procedure Rules 1998 (Amendment) (EU Exit) Regulations 2019 (SI 2019/521).

50 For a discussion see, Sir John Laws, *The Common Law Constitution*, Cambridge University Press, Cambridge 2014.

51 Sorabji, Napier and Musgrove, above note 29, pp. 45 and 67ff.

well as comparative work conducted for the Commission by Stuyck et al[52] and by the European Economic and Social Committee.[53] Secondly, the Jackson Costs Review drew upon comparative examinations of civil procedure in Scotland (a distinct procedural jurisdiction from that in England), France, Germany and the Netherlands.[54] There is no reason to suppose that in the search for best practice, English procedure will look for inspiration solely from other common law jurisdictions. To do so would be to reduce the field from which it can learn and find best practice.

That it will continue to seek inspiration particularly from the EU post-January 2020 can, in fact, already by seen. At the present time the English civil justice system is undergoing a substantial modernisation programme.[55] It is digitising its processes. As part of that it is seeking to implement recommendations made by the Civil Courts Structure Review to create an online small claims procedure, which in many ways is intended to be analogous to that offered in British Columbia, Canada, by its Civil Resolution Tribunal.[56] One feature of this new online procedure is, intended, to be adjudication on the papers rather than following an oral hearing. This will be the default. English procedure does not currently adopt such an approach as a default. It would be a novel development. And it is one that is not uncontroversial given its removal of a litigant's right to appear in person to argue their case before a judge. Here EU law is being prayed in aid of the proposal. The ESCP does not have a final oral hearing as part of its process. On the contrary, its default procedure is for claims to be determined by a judge on the papers. As England looks to leave the EU and revoke the ESCP, it is also looking to rely upon the fact that the ESCP has a paper-process as a justification for its own move towards such

---

52 Ibid, pp. 25, 46 and 62. Also see J. Stuyck et al, *An analysis and evaluation of alternative means of consumer redress other than redress through ordinary judicial proceedings*, Leuven University, Leuven 2007.

53 Sorabji, Napier and Musgrove, above note 29, p. 489, in which it reprinted the Appendix to the Working Document of the Section for the Single Market, Production and Consumption on 'Defining the collective actions system and its role in the context of Community consumer law' (Own-initiative Opinion).

54 R. Jackson, *Review of Civil Litigation Costs: Preliminary Report*, TSO, London 2009, Vol. 2 Chs 54–57.

55 For a critical discussion see, J. Rozenberg, *The Online Court: Will it Work?*, Legal Education Foundation, 2019 <https://long-reads.thelegaleducationfoundation.org/hmcts-reform/>.

56 See M. Briggs, *Civil Courts Structure Review – Interim Report* (December 2015); and M. Briggs, *Civil Courts Structure Review – Final Report* (July 2016).

a process for its proposed online small claims procedure. As Lord Burnett CJ put it, these reforms may mean that

> … as already happens under the paper-based European small claims procedure … we no longer have *traditional* final hearings.[57]

As the UK leaves, it learns from the EU. There is no reason to suppose that it will do anything other than to continue to do so more generally. To do so is simply one more way in which it will manifest its general approach to looking at what works best in other jurisdictions and adopting that which it considers will work well in English procedure. Future EU procedural developments will, in all likelihood, be adopted or not depending on their perceived utility. This may lead to EU-English procedural harmonisation. To the extent that it does, it will be through the application of national procedural design choosing what works best.

There is, however, another way in which EU procedural developments may influence English procedure in the future. This second, more direct form of influence, is one that provides less procedural design autonomy for the English rule-maker. Here one can see a potential restriction on procedural design autonomy post-EU exit, or perhaps at best a strong form of indirect influence. This form of influence is likely to arise where the UK seeks to maintain regulatory alignment on areas of substantive law with the EU. An example where this is likely to be the case concerns data protection law. It is apparent, at the time of writing, that the UK government intends to incorporate the EU General Data Protection Regulation (GDPR)[58] into UK law following its departure from the EU.[59]

In order to ensure that the UK secures an adequacy decision under Article 45 of the GDPR, which will acknowledge that its data protection laws provide adequate data protection, it might be expected that the UK will ensure that it continues to mirror the GDPR in its domestic legislation, particularly the Data Protection Act 2018. In order to do so, this may require the CPR to be amended to make provision, as required by Article 80 of the GDPR for an effective collective redress mechanism. At the present time, the UK has not made provision for such a mechanism

---

57 Lord Burnett CJ, *The Cutting Edge of Digital Reform*, at [16] <https://www.judiciary.uk/wp-content/uploads/2018/12/speech-lcj-online-court.pdf>.

58 Regulation (EU) 2016/679 of the European Parliament and of the Council.

59 See the Data Protection, Privacy and Electronic Communications (Amendments etc) (EU Exit) Regulations 2019 (SI 2019/419).

to be available in its domestic legislation. Should the EU make specific provision, in its development of EU collective redress mechanisms, for collective redress to be available for data protection breaches or should the European Data Protection Supervisor make any recommendations for minimum standards for such redress mechanisms, English procedure may well have to be amended to incorporate such a mechanism.[60] In the absence of such a reform to maintain procedural alignment, the risk might arise that any adequacy decision by the EU might be placed in jeopardy.

It may be the case therefore, whether in respect of data protection law or other aspects of EU law, that where the UK seeks to or agrees to maintain regulatory alignment with the EU, that it may be required to adopt EU procedural developments as part of that regulatory alignment. In this way, following its departure from the EU, there may continue to be specific areas where English procedural design autonomy is to an extent restricted by EU procedural developments. To the extent that this arises, it might well be expected that the approach the English rule-maker will take to such an eventuality will be that outlined above, i.e. to apply it broadly when it is understood to be best practice, to minimise its influence by transposing such EU developments as particular *lex specialis*, or, to adopt a maximum discretion approach to implementation where that is possible. In each case though, EU procedural developments will continue to maintain an influence upon English procedure. The future for English national civil procedural autonomy may therefore look to a degree very much like its recent procedural history, the one difference being that to the extent that EU developments produce greater procedural harmonisation, from the English perspective they will do so through an exercise of procedural design autonomy and not through such autonomy being subject to any direct or indirect influence or legal constraints placed on it by EU law.

60 At the time of writing this issue awaits determination by the United Kingdom Supreme Court if, as is expected, the Court of Appeal's decision in *Lloyd v Google LLC* [2019] EWCA Civ 1599 is subject to appeal.

THE FINNISH WAY OF UNDERSTANDING PROCEDURAL AUTONOMY

A Practical Approach to Implementing EU Civil Procedural Law

Laura Ervo

In Finland, procedural autonomy is not a widely discussed subject. Thus, EU legislation is followed (and technically adhered to) in case law without substantial problems and without broad substantive discussions. There is not much discussion of procedural autonomy among legal scholars, either. In this chapter, an attempt will be made to map the current lay of the land as far as the limited discussion is concerned. The chapter will also try to find some answers to the question of why the Finnish discussion has been relatively so quiet. These answers can partly be found in the Finnish way of seeing legislation as a tool for organising common life in society combined with a tendency to approach especially procedural law from an instrumental point of view. Other reasons include differences in legal culture; Finns tend to readily adopt and apply legal concepts without extensive prior critical discussion thus favouring a stable national legal policy.

1. BACKGROUND

As mentioned above, in Finland, the principle of procedural autonomy is not widely debated, neither in doctrine nor in case law. Likewise, there is little evidence of Euro-scepticism among legal scholars. Especially not among experts in procedural law. One reason for this could be that Finland is a small country without many legal experts, which means that not all topics can be discussed due to a lack of human resources. Another reason could be differences in culture. Finns seem to adopt legal measures easily and tend to act operationally instead of discussing critically, in the sense that they prefer a stable national legal policy. A third reason could be the way procedural law is seen from a Finnish perspective. If seen from a practical point of view, the law has an instrumental perspective in proceedings. This means that procedural problems are principally tackled through practical solutions rather than through a system that seeks to uphold a purely procedural system.[1] All of this is important to keep in mind whenever procedural autonomy is discussed – or not discussed, and in Finland in-depth critical discussion on this topic is notably lacking. Instead, EU policy is readily accepted by the legal system which strives to follow EU law correctly and which strives to technically comply with the relevant regulation.

2. COURT PRACTICE: MODERATE BUT CONSCIENTIOUS APPLICATION

Finland has been rather moderate when asking for preliminary rulings from the European Court of Justice (ECJ). The average number of requests has been 4.8 preliminary rulings per year, which corresponds well with the average of other Nordic countries. The general average among all EU Member States is 9.1 rulings per year. But, of course, these rates need to be related to size of population as the number of court cases is naturally higher in countries with a higher population. In addition, large market areas like Germany may necessitate a greater need to turn to the ECJ for preliminary rulings.[2]

---

1 See also Section 4, below.

2 <https://www.savonsanomat.fi/kotimaa/Suomesta-maltillisesti-ennakkoratkaisupyynt%C3%B6j%C3%A4-olisi-keino-vaikuttaa-EUn-lains%C3%A4%C3%A4d%C3%A4nt%C3%B6%C3%B6n/978664>.

According to the statistics of the Finnish Supreme Court, it has asked for a preliminary ruling one to three times per year between 2013 and 2018,[3] as outlined below:

- 2018 – twice of which one concerned procedural law issues;
- 2017 – three times of which one concerned procedural law issues;
- 2016 – three times;
- 2015 – once;
- 2014 – twice of which one concerned procedural law issues;
- 2013 – once and this case concerned procedural law issues.[4]

The Finnish Supreme Court hears hundreds of cases each year that are connected with EU law in one way or another, but it has asked for preliminary rulings only in single cases.[5] Consequently, there have been occasions where there could have been much more active/interactive discourse between the Finnish instance and the ECJ.[6]

As far as Finland is concerned, about 50% of the requests for a preliminary ruling have come from the Supreme Administrative Court, followed by requests from the Supreme Court – but at a rather low frequency. The main category of cases referred seems to be taxation cases, while environmental cases constitute the second largest group. The questions raised have been important to Finland but not extremely significant as far as EU law is concerned. As a consequence, Finland has not actively affected the development of interpretation of EU law.[7] Kokko calls attention to this fact by emphasising the opportunity to affect case law by asking preliminary questions more often.[8] One reason for Finland's lack of requests to the ECJ could be that the parties in Finnish court proceedings

3 <https://korkeinoikeus.fi/fi/index/ennakkopaatokset/ennakkoratkaisupyynnoteuroopanunionintuomioistuimelle.html>.

4 <https://korkeinoikeus.fi/fi/index/ennakkopaatokset/ennakkoratkaisupyynnoteuroopanunionintuomioistuimelle.html>.

5 Tuomas Ojanen, 'Eurooppa-tuomioistuimet ja suomalaiset tuomioistuimet' (2005) 7–8 *Lakimies* 1224.

6 Taking into consideration that the Supreme Court rejects most of the appeals and only hears about 120–150 cases annually in full, this evaluation of hundreds of EU-connected cases is quite high.

7 <https://www.savonsanomat.fi/kotimaa/Suomesta-maltillisesti-ennakkoratkaisupyynt%C3%B6j%C3%A4-olisi-keino-vaikuttaa-EUn-lains%C3%A4%C3%A4d%C3%A4nt%C3%B6%C3%B6n/978664>.

8 Kai T. Kokko, 'Eurooppalainen ympäristöoikeus korkeimman hallinto-oikeuden lainkäytössä' [2011] *Lakimies* 503.

are not active in highlighting the need to ask for preliminary rulings or arguing for a change in approach. Despite the fact that requests must be made *ex officio* by the court, party activism always helps you 'see the forest for the trees',[9] but this party activism is still lacking in Finland.

The longer a Member State has been a member of the EU, the more preliminary rulings are normally asked for. In addition, the Member State's geographical location affects the rate of requests because EU law often covers cases connected to free movement. Likewise, legal culture affects Member States' relationship with the ECJ, as does the number of judges in a given Member State per inhabitant.[10]

As far as precedents at the national level are concerned, using 'EU law' or 'European Union law' as search terms in the database Finlex leads to one to three cases from the Supreme Court per year. The only exception is 2016 when six precedents were given. However, this search can be a bit misleading because often different directives and other EU norms, as well as case law, are mentioned and applied despite cases not being classified as EU law cases.[11]

The Finnish Administrative Supreme Court has been the most active in its contact with the ECJ. In Finlex, all cases that concern European law are listed separately so that those cases can be easily found. According to this classification, there were 45 cases in 2018 and 50 cases in 2017.[12] However, when 'Union law' was entered as a search term, the result was only 13 cases in total, covering the years 2011–2018.[13] Earlier, the Supreme Court collected all cases concerning EU law or the European Convention separately on their own webpage, but this system covers only

---

9 Ibid, p. 478.

10 <https://www.savonsanomat.fi/kotimaa/Suomesta-maltillisesti-ennakkoratkaisupyynt%C3%B6j%C3%A4-olisi-keino-vaikuttaa-EUn-lains%C3%A4%C3%A4d%C3%A4nt%C3%B6%C3%B6n/978664>.

11 <http://finlex.fi/fi/oikeus/kko/kko/haku/?search%5Basiasana%5D=Euroopan+unionin+oikeus&search%5Bdiaari%5D=&search%5Btaltio%5D=&search%5Botsikko%5D=&search%5Bteksti%5D=&search%5Bapvm_min%5D=&search%5Bapvm_max%5D=&search%5Bepvm_min%5D=&search%5Bepvm_max%5D=&Submit=Hae+%E2%80%BA&search%5Btype%5D=meta>.

12 <http://finlex.fi/sv/oikeus/kho/europaratts>.

13 <http://finlex.fi/fi/oikeus/kho/haku/?search%5Basiasana%5D=Unionin+oikeus&search%5Bdiaari%5D=&search%5Btaltio%5D=&search%5Botsikko%5D=&search%5Bapvm_min%5D=&search%5Bapvm_max%5D=&search%5Bkohdistuu%5D%5B%5D=vuosikirjat&search%5Bkohdistuu%5D%5B%5D=lyhyet&Submit=Hae+%E2%80%BA&search%5Btype%5D=meta>.

the years 2008–2015, when the system was abolished.[14] These statistics regrettably do not correspond with the searches in Finlex so the grounds on how to classify a case as an EU law case seem to vary.

Based on differences and errors in classifications, it is thus very difficult to obtain a general view of the real situation. The available statistics include all kinds of cases concerning EU law and not only those cases that have a procedural connection. Furthermore, the statistics also include many cases in civil and especially in criminal procedural matters, but these will not be addressed separately here because of the classificatory problems. Indeed, there are many more examples if one searches by single directives.

The above-mentioned phenomenon has been discussed by Raitio as a 'homeward trend' among Finnish courts, meaning that courts readily try to apply *lex fori* and national laws even if a link to international law, and in this case to EU law, could be established. The criticism Raitio puts forward concerns the practice of using Finnish procedural law literature in arguments whenever considering judicial problems linked with the EU law instead of using references pertaining to EU regulation. Raitio moreover highlights how the use of EU case law, when it happens, is effectuated in a very conscientious way.[15]

Elsewhere, Raitio explores the nature of EU law and its interpretation in a Finnish context, concluding that a distinctive feature of Finnish legal practice is a modification at the national level, meaning that national or local interests and traditions become key to interpreting the given applicable law.[16] This seems to prove the existence – at least to some degree – of a 'homeward' or inward-looking trend in Finnish legal practice.

Moreover, when comparing two Finnish cases, one from the Supreme Court and one from the Turku Court of Appeal, Raitio finds that the Supreme Court case indicates a more 'homeward trend' compared with the case from the Turku Court of Appeal. According to Raitio, the case from the Turku Court of Appeal is a good example of how to proceed at the

---

14 <https://korkeinoikeus.fi/fi/index/ennakkopaatokset/eu-jaihmisoikeusliitynnaisetratkaisut.html>.

15 Juha Raitio, 'Turun hovioikeuden tuomio 26.5.1998 N:o 1275 ja hovioikeuksien velvollisuus pyytää ennakkoratkaisua EY-tuomioistuimelta' [2000] 3 *Lakimies* 441, 444–445.

16 Juha Raitio, 'Kommetteja eurooppaoikeuden kansallisesta tulkinnasta' [1996] 1 *Lakimies* 318.

national level whenever the court wants to avoid asking for a preliminary ruling.[17] The question remains whether it is the correct attitude to try to find comprehensive and proper arguments 'at home' just to avoid asking for a preliminary ECJ ruling. Should the opposite not be the case? Whenever such a sentiment arises, arguably the preliminary ruling should be asked for.[18]

At the Finnish courts, then, the status of EU law has been accepted and admitted without substantial problems. The courts do their best to avoid violations and to apply EU law according to the regulation. However, the same courts normally do *not* try to reach the next level and so are usually satisfied with applying EU law at its minimum level and according to minimum standards. Arguably, there is not much 'over-harmonisation of EU law' going on in Finland.[19] The Finnish courts also seem like passive addressees concerning European courts when they could be more active in collaborative discourse that is mutual. Interactivity is one crucial component in the mechanics of EU law, and one that has not been properly understood or exploited in Finland – or at least a step that has not yet been taken.[20]

Against this background, it is rather understandable that the discussion on procedural autonomy and its limits is failing. Too much has been taken for granted as far as EU law is concerned. Consequently, there is little or no debate on procedural autonomy in Finland even if this is a hot topic in many other Member States, such as the Netherlands and Germany.[21]

---

17 In this case, the Turku Court of Appeal had researched and analysed carefully the previous case law from the ECJ and came to the conclusion that there was no need to ask a new preliminary ruling to interpret the EU law, but that the interpretation was based clearly enough on the earlier case law. Raitio, above note 15, pp. 444–445.

18 See for instance Kim Talus, 'Ennakkoratkaisumenettely Euroopan Unionin tuomioistuimessa: Velvoittavuus, vaikutukset ja sitovuus' [2013] Defensor Legis 81–84.

19 See Ojanen, above note 5, pp. 1216–1218, where he builds an argument based on the cases concerning the European Convention. However, in the author's experience, the same can be said nowadays to apply to EU law also.

20 See Ojanen, above note 5, pp. 1220 and 1222.

21 See for instance, Alain Ancery and Bart Krans, 'Consumer Protection and EU-Driven Judicial Activism in the Netherlands' in Anna Nylund and Magne Strandberg (eds), *Civil Procedure and Harmonisation of Law: The Dynamics of EU and International Treaties*, Intersentia, Cambridge 2019, pp. 115–117, and Wolfgang Hau, 'Europeanisation of Civil Procedure: Overcoming Follow-Up Fragmentation through Bottom-Up Harmonisation?' in Anna Nylund and Magne Strandberg (eds), *Civil Procedure and Harmonisation of Law: The Dynamics of EU and International Treaties*, Intersentia, Antwerp-Cambridge 2019, pp. 61–65.

It may be that Euro-passivism in general is one of the key reasons behind the lack of discussion in Finland.

3. DOCTRINE: SOME SCEPTICISM

Finnish doctrine on EU civil procedural law in general is, in keeping with the above, relatively muted. There are not many contributions on this topic in Finnish legal literature, and if views are published, the style of argumentation tends to be quite neutral, the main point being to introduce the given European instrument instead of discussing it in a critical context. There is no discussion in the doctrine on procedural autonomy as such, but this, again, is understandable because there is not that much discussion of EU civil procedural law in general, either. In addition, the tone of the discussion that does take place (which tends to concern EU civil procedural law as such) is rather neutral and descriptive instead of being critical or written on the basis of national procedural interests.

The discussion that prevails mainly concerns EU civil procedural law and cooperation in cross-border cases. There is also some more general discussion on the Europeanisation of procedural law as such. But even so, the critical debate falls shy of those situations where EU law limits national procedural autonomy. Surprisingly enough, there seem to be no comments on this aspect in the Finnish legal debate. One reason might be that the doctrine introduced below is a bit outdated, and a second reason that the otherwise vigorous European discussion on current problems has yet not reached Finland.

Some scholars *have* however expressed some critical points of view. Especially, when the European procedures (small claims and payment order) were novelties, there was also criticism in Finland but even that discussion is nowadays rather silent.[22]

Nylund wrote in 2008, for instance, that Payment Orders belong to the civil procedural periphery. With this comment, she probably meant that the harmonisation that was taking place did not involve the instruments in the procedural core but only the less fundamental instruments. Therefore,

---

22 Heidi Lindfors, 'Eurooppalainen maksamismääräysmenettely ja eurooppalainen vähäisten vaatimusten menettely – jäsenvaltioittain eroavat yhtenäistetyt menettelyt?' [2012] *Defensor Legis* 498–508, and Anna Nylund, 'Europeiskt betalningsförläggande och småmålsförfarande' [2008] *Tidskrift utgiven av Juridiska Föreningen i Finland* 241–259.

according to Nylund, the harmonisation effect of this European tool is not that profound. Conversely, she found that the harmonisation effect of the small claims procedure ran much deeper, which at the same time is riskier because of an implied lack of respect of the main procedural principles – like the right to be heard in the fair trial. The European Small Claims Procedure had been created to be quick and cheap, and, due to these aims, the principles on which this European tool is built do differ compared with the traditional hearing at the national level in most EU Member States.[23] Nylund was worried about the lacking communication in the written Small Claims Procedure and her doubts from the perspective of the fair trial were and are justified.[24]

Lindfors, next, was sceptical as far as the harmonisation of procedural law is concerned and wrote in 2012 that it is not that easy to cut loose the strong national tradition in the procedural law even in cross-border cases. Therefore, she was rather careful when estimating the future of the harmonisation of the European procedural law.[25]

In Finland, the above-named European procedures have not been adopted into the national procedural tools and so exist and find application only in European cross-border situations. Lindfors found it paradoxical that in European procedures (which are harmonised procedures for all Member States) Member States still use national, varying proceedings.[26]

In 1996, Virkkunen had already paid attention to Finnish case law and doctrine by stressing that EU law issues do not exist in a vacuum but consist of active, responsive questions affected by the surrounding society. She criticised Finnish case law and textbooks for not reflecting national problems *vis-á-vis* EU law. According to Virkkunen, the case law and textbooks contented themselves with describing the main rules of EU law without having a critical discussion on the topic, probing into questions like 'what does this mean in our Finnish case?'[27] Virkkunen however also understood the underlying problems and reasons why the situation was like that in the mid-1990s. The Finnish national judges needed to interpret the EU law in a totally different way than what they had been used to

---

23 Nylund, above note 22, p. 258.

24 Ibid, and Laura Ervo, *Oikeudenmukainen oikeudenkäynti*, WSOY, Helsinki 2005, p. 113.

25 Lindfors, above note 22, pp. 507–508.

26 Ibid, p. 500.

27 Aino Virkkunen, 'EY-tuomioistuimen eräiden keskeisten ratkaisujen heijastusvaikutuksista kansallisissa tuomioistuimissa – olisiko löydettävissä keino ennakkoratkaisupyyntöjen tason varmistamiseksi?' [1996] *Lakimies* 27.

in terms of interpreting and applying national law. The way of thinking and therefore the context was arguably very different from the tradition they had been educated in and thus were used to. Accordingly, it can be impossible to find, for instance, the core and main message in EU case law. Additionally, there are problems of understanding a language and a legal culture that is no longer national.[28] Storskrubb too has just recently paid attention to the need for creating a common European legal culture first to guarantee proper harmonisation.[29]

Niemi has discussed the Europeanisation of procedural law in general and she is of the opinion that e.g. the abolition of the *exequatur* in enforcement of judgments is a small step towards the same direction with harmonisation. She seems – more or less – to equate real harmonisation (of European procedures) with mutual recognition.[30] As Niemi has written, despite the fact that harmonisation does not have a particularly large impact on procedural law as such, there are many situations where the Europeanisation of procedural law has direct or indirect effects on national procedural law anyway.[31]

Raitio has discussed *res judicata* and the principle of efficiency in his article and quite neutrally only mentioned that Finnish supreme courts have given several precedents[32] on this topic and stressed that in case law *res judicata* at the national level remains prominent (due to the procedural autonomy) even if national judgments have been violating EU law. The requirements to obtain reversals of legally binding judgments are the same compared with cases based on national law only. Only the extraordinary appeal is possible and only within its designated time limits.[33] This approach of not wanting to change national judgments even if they violate EU law has also been criticised in the doctrine.[34] Pohjalainen especially

---

28 Ibid, p. 43.

29 Eva Storskrubb, 'Några tankar om hur EU-rättens tentakler genomtränger processrätten' (2017) 2–4 *Juridisk Tidskrift utgiven i Finland* 369.

30 Johanna Niemi, 'Prosessioikeus ja eurooppalaistumisen haaste' [2014] *Lakimies* 1061. About the history and current situation re: the harmonisation of procedural law, see also Storskrubb, above note 29, pp. 363–367.

31 Niemi, above note 30, p. 1058.

32 See KKO 2007:34, KKO 2007:35, KKO 2008:114, KKO 2016:27, KHO 2009:99, KHO 2010.44, KHO 2010:45, KHO 2011:38, KHO 2013:199, KHO 2014:183 and KHO 2017:140.

33 Raitio 2012, pp. 412–413.

34 Samuli Miettinen, 'Oikeusvoima EU-oikeudessa' [2012] *Lakimies* 430; Matti Pellonpää Pellonpää, 'Eurooppaoikeus ja ylimääräinen muutoksenhaku hallintoprosesseissa korkeimman hallinto-oikeuden viimeaikaisen oikeuskäytännön valossa' in Ida

thinks that the practice of proceeding with *res judicata* and extraordinary appeal in Finland shows the antipathy to EU law and its effects on national law because the wrong interpretation of EU law does not automatically lead to an extraordinary appeal option. Despite the fact that there is a violation, different interests (like *res judicata* and the effects of the wrong judgment) will be balanced in the discretion. She also stresses that the violation means the right to get monetary compensation, but if the wrong national judgment remains valid/is upheld, it is complicated to provide compensation through the civil proceedings due to the fact that the first judgment remains valid having a *res judicata* effect also in the ensuing trial which covers damages.[35]

In 2005, Koulu predicted that the Finnish discussion on alternative dispute resolution, which had been based mainly on national law, would become more Europeanised in the future, with European contract law especially playing a significant role due to the directive[36] against which everything should be reflected in the future.[37] This prophecy has however not totally come true despite the recent development in the EU within this area of law. Instead, the national and even the Nordic discussion remains mostly nationally or internationally oriented[38] rather than EU based.

In 2001, Välimaa wrote about the European regulation on taking evidence in other Member States.[39] He paid attention to the radical steps towards direct adjudication in the other Member States as well as the direct contacts between courts instead of contacting the central body. Clearly highlighting all relevant novelties and steps towards more efficient evidence taking, Välimaa's attitude, however, remained markedly neutral and he commented on the directive as such without any Euro-optimism or pessimism.[40]

Koivisto et al (eds), *Avoin, tehokas ja riippumaton. Olli Mäenpää 60 vuotta*, Edita, Helsinki 2010, pp. 381–393; Anna Pohjalainen, 'EU-oikeuden vastaisuus ylimääräisen muutoksenhaun perusteena – ajankohtaista oikeuskäytäntöä Suomesta' [2014] *Defensor Legis* 264, 267, and Kristiina Äimä, 'Ajankohtaista eurooppaoikeutta verotuksen alalta' [2011] *Defensor Legis* 93–103.

35 Pohjalainen, above note 34, pp. 264–267.

36 Directive 2008/52/EC of the European Parliament and of the Council of 21 May 2008 on certain aspects of mediation in civil and commercial matters.

37 Risto Koulu, 'Kommer den alternativa tvistelösningen att europeiseras?' [2005] *Juridisk Tidskrift utgiven i Finland* 552.

38 Kaijus Ervasti and Anna Nylund, *Konfliktinratkaisu ja sovittelu*, Edita, Helsinki 2014.

39 Regulation (EC) 1206/2001 of 28 May 2001 on co-operation between the courts of the Member States in the taking of evidence in civil or commercial matters.

40 Asko Välimaa, 'Todisteiden vastaanottamisesta riita-asioissa toisessa EU:n jäsenvaltiossa' [2001] *Defensor Legis* 857, 864, 866.

The most critical scholar has probably been Storskrubb, who has especially discussed the concept of mutual trust, or rather mutual distrust. Her recent article 'Mutual Trust and the Dark Horse of Civil Justice' is rather Euro-pessimistic, but it is not written particularly from a Finnish point of view but rather presents the topic at EU-law level.[41]

The discussion described above shows us how cautious the Finnish debate has actually been. There seems to be some criticism and a tendency that EU civil procedural law has not been welcomed 'free of doubt' in Finland. However, the criticism is quite moderate, with no real debate for or against other than occasional attempts by various scholars at initiating discussion. Evidently, criticism is mainly voiced behind the scenes, where attitudes seem a bit suspicious, but no one has so far been provoked enough to put up a real fight for national procedural autonomy.

4. FINNISH FOLKSY LEGAL CULTURE

The reasons for the current situation where Europeanisation and intensified cooperation in procedural matters – and particularly the debate on procedural autonomy – have not caused much discussion or explicit scepticism in Finland are historical and rooted in decision makers' personal ways of thinking/ideology. Such elements are always in play whenever legal decisions are made and these characteristics are linked with the surrounding society.[42] Adjudication is not an exact science where ideology and its significance in decision making can be totally avoided.[43] Court mentality, in other words, is a fact. Judges' individual characteristics, education, environment and world view play a role in this mentality,[44] and all of this affects the discussion of procedural law issues and the way in which those topics are debated. This fact might be one reason behind the lack of an open debate on procedural autonomy. Thus, to get the full picture of the current Finnish court mentality one needs to know the history of Finland first.

From the 1200s onwards, Finland constituted the eastern part of Sweden, a status that continued until 1809. In 1809, Finland became an

41 Eva Storskrubb, 'Mutual Trust and the Dark Horse of Civil Justice' (2018) 20 *Cambridge Yearbook of European Legal Studies* 179–201.

42 See Laura Ervo, 'Comparative Analysis Between East-Scandinavian Countries' [2015] *Scandinavian studies in law* 137–150.

43 Veli-Pekka Hautamäki, 'Teleologisk tolkningsinställning och judiciell aktivism – några teoretiska synpunkter' (2004) 2 *Juridisk Tidskrift utgiven i Finland* 133.

44 Jukka Kemppinen, *Tätä kaikki asianomaiset noudattakoot*, VAPK-kustannus, Helsinki 1992.

autonomous part of Russia but even then Swedish laws remained in force throughout the whole era of the autonomy. From 1890 onwards, a policy of 'Russification' was introduced, and this era is therefore sometimes called the period of oppression. The policy's aim was arguably to make Finland more Russian. However, whenever certain Russian exceptions were made in the field of legislation, the Finnish legal services protested widely, and the new system was never fully followed. These exceptions made in the field of legislation covered some aspects of the legal system while other aspects were still officially and formally legislated by the Finnish (formerly Swedish) laws only.[45] When the Finnish Parliament adopted the Declaration of the Independence of Finland on 6 December 1917, the new state thus already had centuries of experience in managing its own affairs. The makings of the independent nation stem partly from the times of Swedish rule (from the 13th Century until 1809) and especially from the period when Finland was an autonomous Grand Duchy of the Russian Empire (from 1809 until 1917).

Due to the political problems explained above, legislative reforms were not easy to realise during the autonomous period and thus Finnish legislation was not subject to development. The static Russian period and its challenges led to rapid developments in independent Finland and to some flexibility in applying and interpreting laws to correspond with demands in the current society. As a consequence, later legal reforms have usually been realised quickly without wide societal discussion. One of the main objectives behind this mechanism has been effectiveness.[46] The period of autonomy and ensuing legislative challenges during that period have marked Finnish legal culture and made it what it is today. Moreover, Russification caused an emphasis on legality to take root among civil servants, and this culture of legality still affects the system today.[47] Björne is nevertheless of the opinion that the passive resistance of the Finnish civil

45 See further, for instance: Osmo Jussila, *Suomen suuriruhtinaskunta 1809–1917*, WSOY, 2004, pp. 232–254; Eino Jutikkala and Kauko Pirinen, *Suomen historia*, Weilin + Göös, Helsinki 1966, p. 231; Helge Pohjolan-Pirhonen, *historia 3 1809–1855*, WSOY, 1973, pp. 157–186; and Kari O. Virtanen, *Kansakunnan historia 5 Ahdistettu kansakunta 1890–1917*, WSOY, Helsinki 1974, pp. 11–410.

46 Jukka Kekkonen, Suomen oikeuskulttuurin historiaa ja paikannusta, [1998] 6 Lakimies 7, p. 936, and Ari Saarnilehto, 'Kansallisen oikeuskulttuurin uhat' [2003] *Lakimies* 74.

47 Teemu Aalto, *Kansakunnan historia 1855–1890*, WSOY, Helsinki 1976, pp. 40–42; Jussila, above note 45, p. 254; Jukka Kekkonen, 'Suomen oikeuskulttuurin suuri linja 1898–1998' in Suomalainen Lakimiesyhdistys 100 vuotta, Helsinki 1998, pp. 162–163; and Jukka Kemppinen, 'Oikeuskulttuuri' in *Encyclopædia Iuridica Fennica Suomalainen Lakimiesyhdistys*, Suomalainen Lakimiesyhdistys, 1998; and Virtanen, above note 44, pp. 11–410.

servants and the counter measures made against the nationwide (Russian) legislation do not have that much to do with legalism as such. Instead, *Björne* posits that Finish legal culture is based on the will to interpret laws as the interpreter wants to.[48] Extra flavour to this 'cultural soup' was added by the Finnish civil war in 1918 and its consequences as well as by the Second World War and the war responsibility trials, which were of an accentuated political nature. The latter incidents may likely have resulted in accentuated demands on democracy, the rule of law, and legal protection in the Finnish legal culture.[49]

Therefore, legal culture in Finland is still today characterised by quick solutions and rapid reforms, which can be realised whenever needed through new interpretations in the case law if the legislator has not reacted to relevant new and current needs in the society. This makes flexibility, creative solutions and common sense trademarks of Finnish legal culture.[50] Discretion has in many cases been delegated from the legislator to the adjudication in the form of open norms and concepts in laws to guarantee flexible solutions in new situations of application.[51] By the same reasoning, it would be easy and non-problematic to apply EU law norms too, quickly and without extensive reflective discussions. And so, given that Finnish judges are used to working like this and given that this practice is historically rooted in legal tradition in Finland, it can be quite understandable that the critical discussion on procedural autonomy is failing. Viewed in this way, it is not a big problem for the Finnish legal practitioners to follow new EU regulations quickly and without question because they are used to acting in this manner, proceeding to apply the regulations in adjudication instead of discussing new EU legal measures

---

48 Lars Björne, 'Suomalainen legalismi – tarua vai totta?' [2012] *Lakimies* 147–149.

49 Kekkonen, above note 46, p. 936.

50 Jussi Sallila, 'Eurooppalainen oikeuskulttuuri, pohjoismainen perinne ja juristi-identiteetti. Oikeushistoria Suomen oikeustieteellisissä aikakauslehdissä n. 1945–1970' [2011] *Oikeus* 466.

51 However, this type of flexible legal culture has been found to be too restrictive in Finland. Syrjänen has paid attention to the problem and given good reasons for more creative solutions made by courts in the name of justice. See Jussi Syrjänen, *Tuomarin harkinnan rajat – irti legalismin taakasta? Oikeustiede – Jurisprudentia 2012/XLV*, Suomalainen Lakimiesyhdistys, Helsinki 2012, pp. 335–388. Hautamäki, in turn, is of the opinion that judicial activism is increasing in Finland due to more open norms which delegate more discretion to the courts. Veli-Pekka Hautamäki, 'Tuomioistuin aktivismi tutkimuskohteena' [2003] *Oikeus* 172. Tuori shares the opinion of Hautamäki and Siltala that activism is increasing and affecting more issues in the EU legislation. Kaarlo Tuori, 'Tuomarit ja tuomioistuimet suomalaisessa oikeuskulttuurissa' [2000] *Lakimies* 1051.

critically first. It is my guess that Finns implement and apply measures easily without much resistance exactly due to this tradition, whose roots can be traced back to the national history of Finland.

Finnish legal culture has also been said to be democratic, transparent, human, flexible, pragmatic and reformistic.[52] It is said that in Finland novel measures are introduced in the name of nationwide consensus. As a consequence, Finland has traditionally been a country of one truth and one type of politics.[53] This is the Finnish way of 'running things'; a culture of to *do* instead of to *discuss and reflect*. Again, this may well affect the application of EU civil procedural law, i.e. application without too much attention being paid to the limits of procedural autonomy

Siltala is of the opinion that there are two different 'trends' in Finnish adjudication; namely, the legalistic one and the more creative one. The latter is used especially whenever European legislation has to be applied to find the more corresponding interpretation between 'Finnish' and European rules.[54] However, according to Määttä, Finnish courts are passive in creating law and sometimes even respect the legislator too much. He illustrates this argument with many examples from the Supreme Courts' case law. It also seems to be disputed between legislator and courts how binding the articles, including the objectives of the act, are seen to be.[55] If Siltala is right, it might be yet another reason for the willingness to follow EU civil procedural rules without paying too much attention to formalities, like the power to invoke procedural law or not as rooted in the principle of procedural autonomy. This approach is probably not very scientific, but it is practical and practical solutions are typical in Finnish legal culture, as explained above. Still, if Määttä is right, his perspective also provides clarity. Probably, the courts also respect the European legislator and therefore want to follow EU law as best as they can. This attitude again explains the ease (or at least technical ease) with which Finnish courts follow EU law without paying attention to procedural autonomy and its limitations.

---

52 Johan Hirschfeldt, 'Domstolarna som statsmakt – några utvecklingslinjer' [2011–2012] *Juridisk Tidskrift* 5–6, and Thomas Wilhelmsson, 'Suomen kansanomaisen oikeuskulttuurin uhat' [2003] *Lakimies* 85.

53 Kekkonen, above note 46, p. 936.

54 Raimo Siltala, *Oikeustieteen tieteenteoria*, Suomalainen Lakimiesyhdistys, Helsinki 2003, p. 294.

55 Tapio Määttä, 'Lainsäätäjän kunnioittamisasenne, tavoitteellinen laintulkinta ja lakien tavoitesäännökset vallitsevassa tuomarinideologiassa' in Auri Pakarinen et al (eds), *Lainvalmistelu, tutkimus yhteiskunta Jyrki Talan juhlakirja*, Turun yliopisto, Oikeustieteellinen tiedekunta, Turku 2011, pp. 207–225.

Court mentality is one crucial factor in so-called judicial activism (or judicial law making) and in its opposite, judicial self-restraint. Judges can be like passive civil servants who just apply the law more or less technically, or they may closely resemble political actors where they actively create law and update interpretations.[56] The culture and mentality in Finland is a to *do* culture, as mentioned earlier, and therefore one cannot see the Finnish legal culture being prone to exercising self-restraint. In Finland, it is not considered that risky to make fair and rational decisions in situations where the law seems to be outdated/old-fashioned or otherwise lacking; or to include the possibility for discretion. As Mattila wrote in 1998, judges in Finland see themselves as executors of the legislator.[57] Husa shares the same opinion, and adds that activism in the courts is increasing.[58] Personally, the author of this chapter sees the Finnish courts as quite creative – at least compared with the Swedish ones[59] – but somehow this principle is not totally true when it comes to EU law. Thus, the application of EU norms remains more or less technical in nature even if consciously chosen. This is, as seen above, partially rooted in a doctrine where discussion of the remits of EU law is lacking. It might help if scholars were to pick up these questions in the legal discussion, but as long as Finnish legal culture and especially court culture continues to operate in the way that it does, this goes a long way towards explaining the current situation in Finland with its failing debate on procedural autonomy. Finns enact rules and

---

56 Hautamäki, above note 51, p. 171.

57 Heikki E.S. Mattila, 'Pohjoismainen oikeus' in *Encyclopædia Iuridica Fennica*, Suomalainen Lakimiesyhdistys, Helsinki 1998, p. 706.

58 Jaakko Husa, 'The Stories We Tell Ourselves – About Nordic Law in Specific' in Finnish Reports to the 18th Congress of the International Academy of Comparative Law (IACL), Washington D.C. 25.07.2010–01.08.2010, pp. 7–8.

59 According to Björn Bertilsson, the previously very cautious Swedish courts, which have been extremely bound to preparatory work and wording, have now become more active due to Europeanisation. He stresses, however, that this more creative way of interpreting and applying law is alien to Swedish judges, who are traditionally not used to these types of instruments in their adjudication. Björn Bertilsson, 'Förändringstendenser i svensk rättskultur, Rättskipningens funktion och domarens roll' [2010] *Svensk Juristtidning* 29–31. Elisabet Fura-Sandström shares this opinion on the diminished significance of preparatory work in Sweden. According to her, case law has grown more important and judges have become more creative and willing to solve problems within the court. Elisabet Fura-Sandström, 'Rättsbildning i en ny miljö – hur har domstolarnas roll och betydelse förändrats? Domstolarnas roll då, nu och sedan' [2004] *Svensk Juristtidning* 264–265. The above-mentioned Swedish development in response to Europeanisation has also been criticised. See Sten Heckscher, 'Finns det en europeisk rätt?' in *Festskrift till Per Ole Träskman*, Norstedts Juridik, Stockholm 2011, p. 229.

follow as well as respect the legislator, which evidently seems to include the European legislator. European legislation is therefore followed without substantial objections, and this is done, one might add, in a technical way, without recourse to creativity and/or criticism.

5. HARMONISATION AS A PRACTICAL TOOL: AN INSTRUMENTAL APPROACH TO PROCEDURAL LAW

In the age of mobile telephones, Skype and other forms of e-communication, practical cooperation in cross-border situations is easy and natural. E-communication fits into ordinary people's daily lives seamlessly. It should not therefore come as a big surprise that the same applies to courts' daily lives, too, as is the case in Finland where adjudication is widely based on paperless courts that can hear cases by phone or through video conferencing. E-mail is one of the key methods of communication and letters are no longer part of daily life at courts and law firms. Written evidence too is filed electronically. Judges are satisfied with this e-system, perhaps especially in cases involving large quantities of written evidence, because it simplifies and speeds up the practical work and helps keep files in order.[60] It has also been a recent trend to expand the use of video conferences at courts and there have been many efforts in intensifying this type of e-hearing at the Finnish courts.[61] Accordingly, the electronic trial is one of the main projects at the Finnish Ministry of Justice.[62] All of this means that Finnish courts have quite a pragmatic view of using e-communication and it is the opinion of this author that this practical perspective is quite characteristic of the Finnish courts. The attitude amongst Finnish judges is to simplify and find practical and functional tools to operate. This is one explanatory factor why EU regulation also – especially in cross-border situations – is readily followed and why there is no need to protest due to a lack of procedural autonomy. The common instruments and technical solutions as well as mutual recognition are pragmatic tools to solve cross-border cases and this practical point of view

---

60 <https://oikeus.fi/fi/index/ajankohtaista/sahkoisenoikeudenkaynninmanuaali/videoneuvottelulaitteidenkayttaminenoikeudenkaynnissa/kayttokokemukset.html>.

61 'Videoneuvottelun käytön kehittäminen' [2013] *Oikeusministeriön julkaisuja* and 'Videoneuvottelun käytön kehittäminen' [2015] *Oikeusministeriön julkaisuja*.

62 <https://oikeus.fi/fi/index/ajankohtaista/sahkoisenoikeudenkaynninmanuaali.html>.

suits Finnish courts, who are used to practical systems, extremely well. As far as digitalisation is concerned, the appropriate skills and expertise is already present at the national level and therefore extending these skills to cover cross-border situations is natural.

The benefits of digitisation in cross-border contexts are reflected in the lack of discussion of any obstacles or theoretical doubts. Instead, situations are seen from the perspective of solving cross-border adjudication in the smoothest and most practical way. The principle of procedural autonomy is simply no longer important if there is a need for practical solutions. Accordingly, European regulations on e.g. service or taking evidence are seen as practical tools to solve the cross-border situation in a simple and well-functioning way rather than a question of power exploitation. In other words, the smooth functioning of the area of freedom, security and justice by increasing the efficiency and speed of proceedings has been seen as more important than discussing procedural autonomy.

The law, especially procedural law, can be defined as an instrument. It can be applied to fix problems in our common everyday lives on the planet. The law should arguably not be seen as an isolated island, but rather as a bridge to contemporary society. And this connection should be alive and dynamic.[63] This is why European instruments have not been seen in Finland predominantly as harmonising tools, in the substantive meaning of this term, but merely as useful technical instruments to handle cross-border situations (of which there are nowadays plenty due to the free movement of persons, goods and capital in the EU). Due to the intensity of cross-border activity, adjudication too needs to become more flexible and mobile. European instruments and other international pragmatic tools are therefore needed to handle legal matters without or beyond borders. This is why this author, personally, sees cooperation in procedural matters – especially in cross-border situations – more as a practical necessity than a threat to procedural autonomy, and believes that most Finnish colleagues share this perspective given their rootedness in the very practical legal culture described above. Globalisation and Europeanisation will remain key components in people's daily lives and business and the juridical tools to handle disputes with cross-border characteristics must match this fact. This, in turn, renders the instruments a practical issue rather than a drive for further unification or harmonisation.

---

63 Laura Ervo, 'Harmonisation or Fragmentation of National Law? An East Nordic Perspective' in Anna Nylund and Magne Strandberg (eds), *Civil Procedure and Harmonisation of Law: The Dynamics of EU and International Treaties*, Intersentia, Antwerp-Cambridge 2019, p. 85.

But, embedded in EU regulation is also procedural harmonisation, which may find application not just in cross-border situations but also in national cases. The explanation provided above re: cross-border cases does *not* fit this kind of harmonisation of norms, but interestingly the same way of seeing EU law might still apply. Namely, that harmonisation as a whole is interpreted and approached from a practical perspective. Harmonisation is one of the EU's main purposes, rooted in the original idea of the Union, but also in a factual, current European society without borders. This naturally gives rise to the question of whether the EU should also harmonise procedural laws or if procedural autonomy should persist. The ways of addressing this question may vary due to national attitudes, based on local legal cultures. It could be argued that many European regulations in the field of procedural law go against state sovereignty, according to which the state has jurisdiction only over its own geographical space. However, state sovereignty is in many ways no longer a very serviceable concept if one thinks in a practical way. It is arguably more important to operate and solve international issues in procedural law than to conserve the traditional principle of state sovereignty as a pure concept in a modern Europe where there are no borders left due to both freedom of movement and technological advances.[64]

Storskrubb wrote recently that the principle of mutual trust necessarily means that state sovereignty must now be relegated to a 'deep level' and that Member States did not consider this at the early stages of developing the Union. She is sceptical as to whether the Member States are actually ready to follow this development and give up state sovereignty in such an extensive way.[65] Of course, fundamental differences in legal systems and procedural law can cause problems, like 'fishing expeditions'.[66] The other example of difficulties in harmonising procedural law could be the principle of pre-trial discovery, which is not a principle rooted in continental legal systems whereas it is a significant part in common law systems. Perhaps one can say that preserving procedural autonomy can be seen (mainly) as a practical problem *or* as a fundamental problem. For those who approach procedural law from an instrumental perspective, it is a practical issue.

64 Ervo, above note 63, p. 85.

65 Storskrubb, above note 29, p. 371.

66 According to *The Law.com Law Dictionary & Black's Law Dictionary*, 2nd ed., 'fishing expeditions' is a slang term where one party makes requests that have a very small chance of providing relevant evidence in the hope of being greatly fortunate in finding an unknown piece of relevant evidence <https://dictionary.thelaw.com/fishing-expedition/>.

As explained above, one additional reason for the lack of debate in Finland could be the predominantly practical approach that characterises Finnish legal culture, where the lack of procedural autonomy is not seen as that important and where the instrumental perspective is determinative. In that type of context, it is easier to give up state sovereignty in favour of a well-functioning procedure especially when it comes to cross-border cases. Maybe this fact can spur interest in debating the issue further. Either way, the fundamental perspectives are not seen as that important if daily life is working.

6. POSSIBILITIES OF EUROPEAN SUSTAINABILITY

Harmonisation can also be seen from the perspective of sustainability. Sustainability is associated with justice as a fair balance between mutual claims and the obligations of the community. In this context, legal proceedings can preserve all kinds of resources (human, physical, social and ecological capital).[67]

There are two main concepts of sustainability that apply in a legal context; namely, sustainability functionalism[68] and sustainability factualism. The first concept refers to those procedures whose purpose and task is to preserve existing resources. Other types of procedure can also save resources even if preserving resources is not their principal purpose. In such cases, sustainability is a by-product.[69] According to Linna, procedure as such does not produce functional sustainability because results depend on the substantive law. Thus, procedure in itself is based on sustainability-factualism, where a party can choose a type of procedural tool which allows sustainable solutions.[70] However, it is the author's opinion that there might also be *functional* sustainability whenever procedural tools are seen from practical, sustainable perspectives. Harmonisation, especially in cross-border situations, can thus be viewed as a sustainable solution. Dispute resolution processes can also be considered from a sustainability point of

67 Tuula Linna, 'Sustainability ja prosessit – kestävää siviiliprosessioikeutta?' [2018] *Lakimies* 655; Klara Helene Stumpf, Stefan Baumgärtner, Christian U. Becker and Stefanie Sievers-Glotzbach, 'The Justice Dimension of Sustainability: A Systematic and General Conceptual Framework' (2015) 7(6) *Sustainability* 7439 <https://papers.ssrn.com/sol3/papers.cfm?abstract_id=2579346>.

68 This concept refers to those procedures whose purpose and task is to keep the existing resources. Linna, above note 67, p. 658.

69 Linna, above note 67, p. 658.

70 Ibid, p. 664.

view. Process principles, such as the principle of the appropriateness of the process (re: cost, time, certainty), which will speed up dispute resolution and diminish the growth in costs, also result in sustainability. The same goes for the principle of certainty. Sustainability is not only about time and costs, but also about sustainable content, which may be deemed certain and which fulfil the requirements of fairness and quality. Technical solutions help bring about sustainability in practice, examples being witness attendance at a distance and electronic document service. These are examples of real and pragmatic sustainability at its best.

Thus harmonisation and the limits of procedural autonomy can be discussed from the perspective of sustainability, too; and it would appear that state sovereignty is usually no longer the most sustainable solution.[71] As regards cross-border situations, it is a matter of fact that European solutions to solve such situations by using common instruments is the most sustainable solution, and thus harmonisation and the limits in procedural autonomy can be defended rather than just criticised. At the same time, material harmonisation, which applies not only in cross-border situations but also in national cases (in the field of procedural law) can be a sustainable solution as well, given that such harmonisation leads to diminishing costs and better use of resources in the long run. Therefore, procedural autonomy, its future and limits should ideally be discussed from many points of view, not focusing solely on state sovereignty, mandate or the separation of power.

The ideas presented by Linna could be discussed further from a Europeanisation perspective. Maybe, by using this type of fresh opening, it could be possible to kick-start the debate on European procedural law and procedural autonomy in Finland also where 'a shot in the arm' sometimes seems necessary if the subject is to be breached.

7. EURO-OPTIMISM OR PESSIMISM?

According to Storskrubb '... to harmonize rules may in any event not succeed if procedural systems and structures remain diverse and if the vision of justice is idiosyncratic. Therefore, at present we need to deepen our understanding and be aware that the regulatory options interact.'[72] Based on this premise, it can be asked if legislators are used to cooperating

71 Ervo, above note 63, p. 85.
72 Storskrubb, above note 41, p. 23.

with each other to succeed in the harmonisation of procedural law? Are the European societies and legal systems similar enough to generate mutual trust? Indeed, mutual recognition and technical cross-border solutions (like taking evidence or serving documents) could be a proper compromise in the field of harmonisation, because national procedural law would still have autonomy even if cross-border issues were solved mainly through mutual recognition. In that case, the principle of state sovereignty is seen as old-fashioned, while procedural law would be seen from the instrumental perspective that is prevalent in Finland. The lack of mutual trust and demands to preserve procedural autonomy have not been problems in Finland or at least these are not issues that have been voiced openly in discussion amongst legal practitioners. The author of this chapter sees mutual trust and mutual recognition not from a perspective of mistrust, but as tools to retain procedural autonomy at the national level[73] – retaining each Member State's original procedural laws and at the same time solving at least the cross-border situations in a sustainable way.

The other point of view is that the obligation to apply and interpret EU law at the national level has led to more independent national courts as far as the relation between the national courts and the national legislator is concerned. This might be a problem, too. Often, this topic has been discussed under the heading of 'judicial activism'. Is it correct to increase the power of judges at the expense of the legislator? This question can of course also be addressed from the fundamental or practical perspective and there has been a fundamental discussion of this in Finland, too.[74] Still, in Finnish court practice, judicial activism is seen predominantly as a practical tool to solve new problems quickly. This is achieved by finding the best possible solution in the case, corresponding with legal principles and international instruments instead of waiting for the reaction of the national legislator who would adjust the details of the national law according to the changing demands of interpretation. This does also happen rather often, but the first step can be taken in case law which directs the legislator's attention to the given current problem and perhaps leads to changes in the legislation.[75]

---

73 Ervo, above note 63, pp. 69–71.

74 Ojanen, above note 5, pp. 1214–1215.

75 This was the case, for instance, when Finnish national law on mediation in criminal cases was developed. In the beginning, prosecutors applied an open list of reasons not to accuse – seeing successful mediation as one reason not to start criminal proceedings at the court. Later on, the legislator adjusted the law and wrote mediation into the law text as one particular reason not to accuse.

At its best, judicial activism can offer quick and flexible solutions to new types of legal problems. In common law countries, laws are improved through case law and this practice seems to be working. One could thus argue that there is no need to be that 'unwelcoming' as concerns creative court practice. As far as Finland is concerned, and based on the discussion of doctrine above, courts could be even more creative than they are today. Accordingly, the obligation to apply and interpret EU law at the national level even more than it is done today could be welcomed in Finland. At least the risks associated with judicial activism and independent national courts in relation to the legislator are not seen by scholars as too significant. In conclusion, procedural autonomy is not a concept to be defended at all costs if relinquishing the principle in fact leads to pragmatic and sustainable solutions, which work well.

What will happen in the future, then? Aalto argued that the EU seems to exist from one crisis to the next. He already suggested in 2000 that judicial cooperation in civil matters will not be easy. He was right. Still, he also emphasised that this is normal given the history of the EU, the main achievements of which have been fostered by crises. He guessed in 2000 that judicial cooperation in civil matters would happen in waves and based on single projects. He also wrote that the main challenges for those who defend national sovereign integrity as well as those who promote cooperation are still ahead of us.[76] He was right about this, too. Further crises lie in wait for us along the horizon and the quarrelling between collaboratively minded and more nationally oriented colleagues continues. Let us hope that Aalto is right: the main achievements have been realised due to crises. If this is true, there is still a lot of hope.

One concrete way to reach consensus in the discussion on procedural autonomy and the need to harmonise could be the practical and instrumental approach to court proceedings seen in Finland. As long as our national procedural law is not enough and cannot solve all new problems caused by free movement, Europeanisation and globalisation, something must be done. From a practical perspective, there is no longer a need to maintain or defend procedural autonomy. At least at the cross-border level, new instruments are necessary. Why make this too problematic when there is the possibility of addressing it in a pragmatic way? It is clearly possible to regard procedural law from an instrumental point of view also at the EU level.

---

[76] Pekka Aalto, 'Yksityisoikeuden alan yhteistyö EU:ssa' (2000) 3 *Lakimies* 335.

All in all, the Finnish way of seeing the question of procedural autonomy tends to be a bit different compared with other legal cultures. Based on what has been described above, the characteristics, perspectives and the way of thinking that prevails in Finnish national legal culture can be good explanations of why there has not yet been a very active debate on procedural autonomy in Finland. There might, of course, also be other, more practical, reasons for the lack of debate – like a lack of human resources, for example; as explained in the beginning of this chapter. Still, from a Euro-optimistic perspective, there is no reason to create problems that do not exist. The highly practical and instrumental perspective on procedural law, including European procedural law, is clearly one solution to the overall debate on procedural autonomy – which might indeed partially be the reason why the very same discussion has so far been absent in Finland.

A GERMAN PERSPECTIVE ON THE WANING PROCEDURAL AUTONOMY IN CIVIL MATTERS

Who is Afraid of European Civil Procedure?

Wolfgang Hau

1. STARTING POINT: PROCEDURAL AUTONOMY AS A MATTER OF HIERARCHY OF RULES

According to Article 81 TFEU,[1] the EU is competent to harmonise procedural rules for judicial cooperation in civil matters with cross-border

[1] Consolidated version of the Treaty on the Functioning of the European Union [2012] OJ C 326/47.

implications. This explicitly includes the elimination of obstacles to the proper functioning of civil proceedings, if necessary, by promoting the compatibility of the rules on civil procedure applicable in the Member States (Article 81(2)(f)). In contrast, the legislative competence of the EU to harmonise or at least approximate civil procedure is much more limited as regards mere domestic disputes, because, in this respect, the TFEU contains no general legal base equivalent to Article 81. On the other side of that coin is what is often referred to as 'procedural autonomy of the Member States' (in German, usually referred to as 'Verfahrensautonomie der Mitgliedstaaten'[2]): in principle, it is for each national legal system to designate which court has jurisdiction and to determine the procedural conditions governing actions at law to ensure the protection of rights of individuals.[3]

Below the line, however, procedural autonomy is limited and increasingly waning, if not eroding. Firstly, national procedural rules are only applicable in so far as they are consistent with higher-ranking principles:

> In accordance with the principle of sincere cooperation enshrined in Article 4(3) TEU, the detailed procedural rules governing actions for safeguarding an individual's rights under EU law must be no less favourable than those governing similar domestic actions (principle of equivalence) and must not render impossible in practice or excessively difficult the exercise of rights conferred by EU law (principle of effectiveness).[4]

---

2 For recent accounts from a German perspective see Malte Kramme, 'Verfahrensautonomie der Mitgliedstaaten im Zivilverfahrensrecht – Grundsatz des Unionsrechts oder Phantom?' in Caspar Behme and Matthias Fervers (eds), *Perspektiven einer europäischen Privatrechtswissenschaft*, Nomos, Baden-Baden 2016, p. 407; Markus Ludwigs, 'Die Verfahrensautonomie der Mitgliedstaaten – Euphemismus oder Identitätsfaktor?' [2018] *Neue Zeitschrift für Verwaltungsrecht* 1417; Jan Lüttringhaus, *Vertragsfreiheit und ihre Materialisierung im Europäischen Binnenmarkt – Die Verbürgung und Materialisierung unionaler Vertragsfreiheit im Zusammenspiel von EU-Privatrecht, BGB und ZPO*, Mohr Siebeck, Tübingen 2018, pp. 459ff.

3 Judgment of 16.12.1976, Case 33/76, *Rewe-Zentralfinanz eG and Rewe-Zentral AG v. Landwirtschaftskammer für das Saarland*, ECLI:EU:C:1976:188, is usually cited as a starting point for this well-established position. For a recent confirmation see the Grand Chamber's Judgment of 24.10.2018 in Case C-234/17, *XC and Others v. Generalprokuratur*, ECLI:EU:C:2018:853 at [21].

4 This formula was used, for example, in the Grand Chamber's Judgment of 24.10.2018 in Case C-234/17, *XC and Others v. Generalprokuratur*, ECLI:EU:C:2018:853 at [22], citing older landmark decisions to that point.

Secondly, several provisions of the TFEU (such as Articles 114, 115 and 169) allow for the adoption of measures for the approximation of the laws of the Member States.[5] While such rules primarily aim at the harmonisation of substantive law in a number of areas of private law (for example, consumer protection, anti-discrimination, insurance law, labour law, company law and competition law), it is generally recognised that they can also serve as a legal basis for uniform procedural rules or standards even in purely domestic civil cases. In this context, it should be noted that such EU requirements can go far beyond the simple effectiveness test normally applied in the context of procedural autonomy.[6]

In other words: where EU procedural rules apply, they simply prevail over national procedural rules in accordance with the principle of supremacy. In so far as no EU procedural rules exist, it is settled case law of the Court of Justice of the European Union (ECJ) that EU law can still interfere into national procedural law through the principle of effectiveness where the enforcement of EU law is in question. As a result of the foregoing, one must emphasise from the outset that, while the concept of the Member States' procedural autonomy is, in principle, still recognised in jurisprudence and literature, it is today of a mere subsidiary nature.[7] Against this backdrop, this chapter provides some personal views and selected examples from a German perspective.[8]

---

5 For a more detailed discussion see, for example, Gerald Mäsch, 'Zivilprozessrecht' in Katja Langenbucher (ed.), *Europäisches Privat- und Wirtschaftsrecht*, 4th ed., Nomos, Baden-Baden 2017, pp. 526, 531–532 and 540–543.

6 This was correctly highlighted by Advocate General Maciej Szpunar in his Opinion of 06.06.2018 in Case C-149/17, *Bastei Lübbe GmbH & Co. KG v. Michael Strotzer*, ECLI:EU:C:2018:400, dealing with the procedural requirements set out in Directive 2001/29/EC of 22 May 2001 on the harmonisation of certain aspects of copyright and related rights in the information society ([2001] OJ L 167/10) and Directive 2004/48/EC of 29 April 2004 on the enforcement of intellectual property rights ([2004] OJ L 157/45).

7 Maciej Szpunar, 'Procedural Autonomy and Private Law' [2018] *Zeitschrift für Europäisches Privatrecht* 1, 4.

8 It goes without saying that the author does not claim to present the (one and only) German perspective on such a controversial topic, and it seems even hardly possible to identify at least the prevailing German opinion on most of the questions discussed.

2. EUROPEAN AND GERMAN CIVIL PROCEDURE

2.1. NO CLASH OF CULTURES

Maybe surprisingly, notwithstanding the long tradition of procedural doctrine and legislation in Germany,[9] there are occasionally some, but not too many voices warning against a decline of procedural autonomy in civil matters. That might be due to the fact that there is no clash of cultures: the procedural concepts behind European instruments are in many respects in line with the ones known and applied in Germany. In particular, at least in principle, both systems pay heed to the idea that procedural law does not only deal with technical issues such as case management, expediting proceedings and cost-efficiency, but that the design of procedural rules as such must serve the ends of justice: not only the decision on the merits but also the procedure leading to it has to be fair and in line with the rule of law.[10] It is, thus, common ground both in Germany and on the European level that the quality of a procedural system depends on its willingness to give more weight to procedural justice than to mere efficiency. Of course, it does not follow from this that procedural justice is already sufficiently paid heed to in every single respect by every single German or European procedural instrument and that in case of doubt it is always preferred over cost considerations. But it is the thought that counts and, here too, the better is always the enemy of good.

2.2. COMMON MINIMUM STANDARDS OF CIVIL PROCEDURE

In Germany, it is regarded as a matter of course to comply with the procedural minimum standards as set out in Article 47 ChFR,[11]

---

9 For introductions to German civil procedure in English see Stephan Rützel, Gerhard Wegen and Stephan Wilske, *Commercial Dispute Resolution in Germany*, 2nd ed., Beck, Munich 2016; Peter L. Murray and Rolf Stürner, *German Civil Justice*, Carolina Academic Press, Durham 2004; for a shorter account see Wolfgang Hau, 'The Law of Civil Procedure' in Gerhard Wagner and Joachim Zekoll (eds), *Introduction to German Law*, 3rd ed., Wolters Kluwer, Alphen aan den Rijn 2018, p. 479.

10 On this fundamental understanding see, for example, Rolf Stürner, 'Verfahrensrecht und materielle Gerechtigkeit' in Joachim Münch (ed.), *Prozessrecht und materielles Recht – Liber Amicorum für Wolfram Henckel*, Mohr Siebeck, Tübingen 2015, p. 359.

11 Charter of Fundamental Rights of the European Union [2012] OJ C 326/391.

Article 19(1) TEU[12] and the jurisprudence of the ECJ thereto. Fortunately, at least for the time being, it seems most unlikely that developments similar to the ones that have recently given rise to proceedings before the ECJ[13] could occur in Germany. It is to be hoped that the constitutional safeguards which have been implemented in the Grundgesetz of 1949 (such as, in particular, the embedding of the rule of law as leitmotif of all public action, its affirmation by the so-called eternity clause in Article 79 and the establishment of the Bundesverfassungsgericht as guardian) will deter Germany from relapsing into sin.

Another remarkable development in the context of defining European procedural standards is the European Parliament Resolution of 4 July 2017 with recommendations to the Commission on common minimum standards of civil procedure in the European Union.[14] From a German perspective, there is little concern as to the content of the proposed standards. Nevertheless, the project is facing criticism with regard to the apparently rather random choice of aspects dealt with.[15] More importantly, it is questioned whether Article 81 TFEU provides a sufficient legal competence: it seems doubtful whether the Parliament's very broad interpretation of 'civil matters having cross-border implications' stays in

---

12 Consolidated version of the Treaty on European Union [2012] OJ C 326/13.

13 Some very remarkable recent cases raise issues related to the national organisation of the judiciary: The Judgment of the Grand Chamber of 27.02.2018, Case C-64/16, *Associação Sindical dos Juízes Portugueses v. Tribunal de Contas*, ECLI:EU:C:2018:117, deals with the question whether the European principle of judicial independence could preclude general salary reduction measures for judges. Furthermore, on 23.09.2018 the European Commission decided to refer Poland to the ECJ alleging violations of the principle of judicial independence created by the new Polish Law on the Supreme Court (Case C-619/18, *European Commission v. Republic of Poland*, ECLI:EU:C:2019:325). For an overview of the proceedings so far see the Order of the President of the Court of 15.11.2018, ECLI:EU:C:2018:910.

14 European Parliament Resolution of 4 July 2017 with recommendations to the Commission on common minimum standards of civil procedure in the European Union, 2015/2084, [2018] OJ C 334/39.

15 Cf. Astrid Stadler, 'Harmonisierung des Europäischen Zivilprozessrechts - Mindeststandards oder Modellregeln?' [2017] *Juristenzeitung* 693. For further German discussions on the common minimum standards project see the contributions in Christoph Althammer and Matthias Weller (eds), *Mindeststandards im europäischen Zivilprozessrecht – Grundvoraussetzung für gegenseitiges Vertrauen*, Mohr Siebeck, Tübingen 2015, and Christoph Althammer and Matthias Weller (eds), *Europäische Mindeststandards für Spruchkörper – Unabhängigkeit, Effizienz und Spezialisierung als Kernanforderungen*, Mohr Siebeck, Tübingen 2017.

line with the intention of the TFEU and is likely to convince the Member States, or eventually the ECJ.[16]

2.3. PROCEDURAL PRINCIPLES

Since procedural law in Germany is mainly determined by statutory law, not by case law, for German lawyers the handling of EU regulations is not very different from working with the *Zivilprozessordnung* (German Code of Civil Procedure). As regards content, some of the most controversially discussed peculiarities of EU procedural law that are felt hard to accept from the perspective of some national systems readily comply with the German legal tradition and are not understood as particularly problematic.[17]

This holds true, for instance, for the required *ex officio* application of consumer protection law.[18] As the ECJ has pointed out on several occasions, the 1993 Unfair Terms in Consumer Contracts Directive[19] must be interpreted as to mean that it is for the national court to identify of its own motion, in the place of the consumer in his capacity as an applicant, any unfairness of a contractual term, provided that it has available to it the legal and factual elements necessary for that task.[20] In principle, this

---

16 Cf. Wolfgang Hau, 'Europeanisation of Civil Procedure: Overcoming Follow-Up Fragmentation through Bottom-Up Harmonisation?' in Anna Nylund and Magne Strandberg (eds), *Civil Procedure and Harmonisation of Law: The Dynamics of EU and International Treaties*, Intersentia, Antwerp-Cambridge 2019, pp. 61, 62–54.

17 For a discussion of such coherence with regard to German and European principles of international civil procedure see Wolfgang Hau, 'The European Union and Civil Procedure from a German Perspective' in Anna Nylund and Bart Krans (eds), *The European Union and National Civil Procedure*, Intersentia, Antwerp-Cambridge 2016, pp. 59, 64–65.

18 For detailed accounts see Ivo Bach, 'The Role of Judges in Consumer Cases – A German Perspective' in Anna Nylund and Magne Strandberg (eds), *Civil Procedure and Harmonisation of Law: The Dynamics of EU and International Treaties*, Intersentia, Antwerp-Cambridge 2019, pp. 141 and 142ff; Jan Lüttringhaus, above note 2, pp. 467ff. For a comparative analysis see Anna Nylund and Magne Strandberg, 'Conclusions on Civil Procedure and Harmonisation of Law' in Anna Nylund and Magne Strandberg (eds), *Civil Procedure and Harmonisation of Law: The Dynamics of EU and International Treaties*, Intersentia, Antwerp-Cambridge 2019, pp. 231 and 234–238.

19 Directive 93/13/EEC of 5 April 1993 on unfair terms in consumer contracts [1993] L 95/29.

20 For recent confirmations of this position see the Judgments of the ECJ of 20.09.2018 in Case C-51/17, *OTP Bank Nyrt., OTP Faktoring Követeléskezelő Zrt. V. Teréz Ilyés, Emil Kiss*, ECLI:EU:C:2018:750 at [84 et seq] and in Case C-448/17, *EOS KSI Slovensko s.r.o. v. Ján Danko and Margita Danková*, ECLI:EU:C:2018:745 at [45 et seq]. See also Anthi Beka, *The Active Role of Courts in Consumer Litigation – Applying EU Law of the National Courts' Own Motion*, Intersentia, Antwerp-Cambridge 2018.

is completely in line with the German position, and this was the case even long before the 1993 Directive entered into force. There are, however, ongoing discussions whether the German summary procedure for an order to pay debts ('Mahnverfahren', §§ 688ff of the Code of Civil Procedure) is in every respect sufficiently fitted for the required *ex officio* application of EU consumer protection provisions.[21] Further questions are raised when the ECJ concludes that a national court must investigate on its own motion whether a contract falls within the scope of a Consumer Protection Directive[22] and must even decide on a remedy that the consumer plaintiff has not applied for.[23] At first glance, this hardly seems reconcilable with the German principles of party presentation ('Verhandlungsmaxime') and of party disposition ('Dispositionsmaxime').[24] In most cases, however,

---

21 Cf. Bach, above note 18, pp. 143–145. For more detailed discussions in German see Anatol Dutta, 'Nationales Mahnverfahren und die Effektivität des europäischen Verbraucherschutzes' (2013) 126 *Zeitschrift für Zivilprozess* 153; Björn Laukemann, 'Unionsrechtsschutz und res judicata im Zivilprozess' (2017) 130 *Zeitschrift für Zivilprozess* 439; Lüttringhaus, above note 2, pp. 503–515; Andreas Piekenbrock, 'Mahnverfahren, Rechtskraft und Unionsverbraucherrecht' [2018] *Juristenzeitung* 855; Michael Stürner, 'Amtsprüfung im Mahnverfahren und Unzulässigkeit der Vertragsanpassung bei missbräuchlicher Verzugszinsklausel' [2013] *Zeitschrift für Europäisches Privatrecht* 666.

22 Judgment of 04.06.2015, Case C-497/13, *Froukje Faber v. Autobedrijf Hazet Ochten BV*, ECLI:EU:C:2015:357: 'Directive 1999/44/EC of the European Parliament and of the Council of 25 May 1999 on certain aspects of the sale of consumer goods and associated guarantees must be interpreted as meaning that a national court before which an action relating to a contract which may be covered by that directive has been brought, is required to determine whether the purchaser may be classified as a consumer within the meaning of that directive, even if the purchaser has not relied on that status, as soon as that court has at its disposal the matters of law and of fact that are necessary for that purpose or may have them at its disposal simply by making a request for clarification.'

23 Judgment of 03.10.2013, Case C-32/12, *Soledad Duarte Hueros v. Autociba SA and Automóviles Citroën España SA*, ECLI:EU:C:2013:637: 'Directive 1999/44/EC of the European Parliament and of the Council of 25 May 1999 on certain aspects of the sale of consumer goods and associated guarantees must be interpreted as precluding legislation of a Member State, such as that at issue in the main proceedings, which does not allow the national court hearing the dispute to grant of its own motion an appropriate reduction in the price of goods which are the subject of a contract of sale in the case where a consumer who is entitled to such a reduction brings proceedings which are limited to seeking only rescission of that contract and such rescission cannot be granted because the lack of conformity in those goods is minor, even though that consumer is not entitled to refine his initial application or to bring a fresh action to that end.'

24 On these principles see Murray and Stürner, above note 9, pp. 156–160; Hau, above note 9, p. 481.

the ECJ's requirements can be met via recourse to the rather active role of German courts ('materielle Prozessleitung')[25] and the far-reaching rights of the parties to complement the facts relied upon and to modify the complaint in the course of the proceedings.

2.4. INTERLOCKING OF EUROPEAN AND NATIONAL PROCEDURAL LAW

A context of great practical importance in which European and national procedural rules encounter each other very often is international litigation. An interesting instrument that serves to coordinate both sets of rules in cross-border cases are residual application clauses, such as Article 6(1) and Article 41(1) of the Brussels *Ibis* Regulation[26] or Article 19 of the Small Claims Regulation.[27] In practice, however, it sometimes turns out to be very difficult to define the scopes of application of both sets of rules and to ensure a smooth interplay: if drafted too vaguely or applied without sufficient regard to the relevant principles of differentiation, such clauses can turn out to be sources of confusion or even bones of contention.

---

25 §139(1) of the Code of Civil Procedure: 'To the extent required, the court is to discuss with the parties the circumstances and facts as well as the relationship of the parties to the dispute, both in terms of the factual aspects of the matter and of its legal ramifications, and it is to ask questions. The court is to work towards ensuring that the parties to the dispute make declarations in due time and completely, regarding all significant facts, and in particular is to ensure that the parties amend by further information those facts that they have asserted only incompletely, that they designate the evidence, and that they file the relevant petitions.' For a comparative analysis see Oscar Chase and Helen Hershkoff, *Civil Litigation in Comparative Context*, 2nd ed., West Academic, St Paul 2017, pp. 258–260.

26 Regulation No 1215/2012 of 12 December 2012 on jurisdiction and the recognition and enforcement of judgments in civil and commercial matters [2012] OJ L 351/1. Article 6(1): 'If the defendant is not domiciled in a Member State, the jurisdiction of the courts of each Member State shall, subject to Article 18(1), Article 21(2) and Articles 24 and 25, be determined by the law of that Member State.' Article 41(1): 'Subject to the provisions of this Section, the procedure for the enforcement of judgments given in another Member State shall be governed by the law of the Member State addressed. [...]'

27 Regulation No 861/2007 of 11 July 2007 establishing a European Small Claims Procedure ([2007] OJ L 199/1), amended by Regulation No 2015/2421 of 16 December 2015 ([2015] OJ L 341/1). Article 19: 'Subject to the provisions of this Regulation, the European Small Claims Procedure shall be governed by the procedural law of the Member State in which the procedure is conducted.'

A recent illustration of this is the ECJ's assumption that German courts are free to apply a German provision limiting the enforcement period of a preventive attachment order to only one month[28] also to an enforceable Italian order, although Italian law knows no equivalent expiration date for court orders.[29] The ECJ apparently means well and tries to preserve procedural autonomy for the national (here: German) *lex loci executionis*. But there is a catch: the application of such rules of the state of enforcement is not in line with the well-established principle that under the Brussels I regime of recognising foreign decisions it is up to the law of the state of origin, not the state of enforcement, to define the effects and limits of the decision in question.[30] At the end of the day, the ECJ restricts the free movement of decisions in the European area of justice.

3. PROCEDURAL AUTONOMY AS AN END IN ITSELF?

Such observations lead to the question whether the Member States' procedural autonomy should anyway be regarded as an end in itself. As already mentioned, due to the still increasing relevance of EU law, the scope for procedural autonomy is waning. This may explain the doomsday mood of some traditional proceduralists: they face the much-discussed phenomenon of the vanishing trial, since for many years the numbers of new civil cases brought to the courts have been drastically declining in Germany as well as in many other countries.[31] Even worse, they also have to accept the vanishing relevance of their cherished national procedural law.

---

28 §929(2) of the Code of Civil Procedure: 'The enforcement of the writ of seizure is no longer an available remedy if one month has lapsed since the date on which the writ of seizure was issued or on which it was served on the party at the request of which it was issued.'

29 ECJ Judgment of 04.10.2018, Case C-379/17, *Proceedings brought by Società Immobiliare Al Bosco Srl*, ECLI:EU:C:2018:806, thereby departing from the much more convincing Opinion of Advocate General Maciej Szpunar of 20.06.2018, ECLI:EU:C:2018:472.

30 For a discussion of this principle of extension of effects ('Wirkungserstreckung', as opposed to 'Gleichstellung') and its conceivable limits see Partick Wautelet, Article 36 paras 6–9, in Peter Mankowski and Ulrich Magnus, *Brussels Ibis Regulation – Commentary*, Dr. Otto Schmidt, Cologne 2016.

31 For accounts of the situation in Germany see Gerhard Wagner, *Rechtsstandort Deutschland im Wettbewerb: Impulse für Justiz und Schiedsgerichtsbarkeit*, Beck, Munich 2017; Monika Nöhre, 'Wie viel Streitschlichtung verträgt der deutsche Zivilprozess? Der Rückgang der Eingangszahlen im Zivilprozess und mögliche Auslöser' [2019] *Anwaltsblatt* 91.

Of course, this attitude does not only reflect nostalgia: at least ideally, legal diversity makes sense since it can stimulate a competition of ideas and thereby boost conceptual progress. Indeed, in the wake of Brexit there has been a remarkable increase in competition between Member States that aims at attracting work for national providers of legal services.[32] It would seem, however, over-optimistic to consider this as a process of cross-border learning between the Member States. Rather, it is appropriate to emphasise the importance of Europeanisation as a means of improving the quality of procedural law – as long as it is not achieved as a result of a race to the bottom by way of settling for mere minimum standards but by identifying and promoting best standards.[33] A very strong argument for more, not less, European rules can be made in particular with regard to the enforcement of consumers' rights,[34] but the same holds true for other types of disputes, for example for cross-border cases.

4. WAIVER OF PROCEDURAL AUTONOMY: BOTTOM-UP HARMONISATION

The existing European procedural provisions are only meant to enhance the practical application of rights as guaranteed by particular European instruments (for example regarding consumer or cross-border cases), but do not require the Member States to modify their national procedural regimes in general. This leads to the unwanted phenomenon of follow-up fragmentation on the Member State level with a dividing line running between ordinary disputes on the one hand, and disputes with a relevant EU impact on the other hand. This, in turn, can either be shrugged off as an unpleasant side effect of procedural autonomy or, at least in suitable contexts, be overcome through bottom-up (or: spontaneous)

---

32 Just think of the continental race to establishing commercial courts with English as working language. In Germany, there is a remarkable official initiative named 'Law – Made in Germany' (see <www.lawmadeingermany.de>).

33 Cf. Eva Storskrubb, 'EU Civil Justice at the Harmonisation Crossroads?' in Anna Nylund and Magne Strandberg (eds), *Civil Procedure and Harmonisation of Law: The Dynamics of EU and International Treaties*, Intersentia, Antwerp-Cambridge 2019, pp. 11 and 33: 'if the purpose of the European Parliament's proposal is to start a debate on civil procedural standards in Europe, it is concerning that its starting point is common minimum practices, rather than best practices'.

34 See the powerful plea by Anne-Marie Van den Bossche, 'Private Enforcement, Procedural Autonomy and Article 19(1) TEU: Two's Company, Three's a Crowd' (2014) 33 *Yearbook of European Law* 41.

harmonisation, understood as autonomous reception of European solutions into areas of national law that are per se not affected by EU law.[35]

The voluntary transplant of European rules for international cases to merely domestic disputes is feasible and has happened on many occasions. Accordingly, the concept of broadening the scope of European procedural solutions – and thus waiver of procedural autonomy – can gain momentum in other contexts, too: it seems advisable to take a closer look at European procedural rules that were designed either for particular disputes (for example, over intellectual property rights, anti-trust or unlawful discrimination) or for the protection of particular groups of litigants (e.g. consumers or small and medium-sized enterprises) and consider their transferability into the Member States' general law of civil procedure. Instead of going into detail, two remarks should be made.[36]

Firstly, such a 'trickle-down effect' from the European to the Member States' level is obviously far less effective than a top-down harmonisation of procedural law. Indeed, it is clear that this approach does not lead to Europe-wide harmonisation but depends on every single Member State's actions. In consequence, the direct harmonising effect of voluntary over-implementation is limited to the very Member State(s) adapting to the European standards, not horizontally between all Member States. However, given the limited legislative competence of the EU in the field of civil procedure, trickle-down harmonisation accomplished is better than top-down harmonisation awaited.

Secondly, it has to be borne in mind that bottom-up harmonisation is not about safeguarding minimum standards but about promoting best practice. In other words, quality is of the essence: although it seems reasonable to expect that the ongoing competition between civil justice systems (in particular in the wake of Brexit) will increase Member States' readiness for reception, the concept of over-implementation stands or falls by the quality of each and every European procedural solution in question.

5. TESTING THE WATERS: STANDARD OF PROOF

The tiptoeing – but arguably quite reasonable – rise of EU procedural law even in areas traditionally considered as a matter for the *lex fori*

35 For a more detailed discussion and examples see Hau, above note 16, pp. 67–73.
36 Hau, above note 16, pp. 73–75.

and therefore falling within the procedural autonomy of the Member States may be illustrated by discussing in more detail the presumably increasing number of EU provisions that determine or at least influence the applicable standard of proof in private law cases. Whereas the burden of proof determines which party has to prove disputed facts relevant for the outcome of the dispute, the standard of proof addresses the question which degree of certainty is required for the court to accept a fact as established and therefore to base its decision upon. One would think that such a central procedural problem has long been settled and that at most some details are still under discussion. But way off the mark: although the German Code of Civil Procedure provides a general rule which, in principle, requires a remarkably high standard of proof ('full judicial conviction', § 286(1) of the Code of Civil Procedure[37]), many facets of the problem are as intensely debated as ever.[38] It has already been thoroughly discussed from interdisciplinary and comparative perspectives[39] and with regard to its conflict of laws implications. Of particular interest for this chapter, however, are the more or less hidden European provisions for the determination of the standard of proof, an aspect which has not been given a lot of attention so far.

37 This provision reads: 'The court is to decide, at its discretion and conviction, and taking account of the entire content of the hearings and the results obtained by evidence being taken, if any, whether an allegation as to fact is to be deemed true or untrue. The judgment shall state the reasons that have guided the judicial conviction.' The leading case is the Federal Court of Justice's Judgment of 17.02.1970 – III ZR 139/67 [1970] *Neue Juristische Wochenschrift* 946, 948: 'What is required is a degree of conviction that for all practical purposes silences doubts without necessarily eliminating them completely.' It seems safe to say that this 'full conviction test' comes at least very close to the 'beyond reasonable doubt' test which was developed in common law jurisdictions for criminal law cases. A lesser standard of proof which under German law only applies under exceptional circumstances is met when the relevant fact is more likely than not and therefore can be demonstrated to the satisfaction of the court ('Glaubhaftmachung'; cf. §294 of the Code of Civil Procedure).

38 For contributions in English see Moritz Brinkmann, 'The Synthesis of Common and Civil Law Standard of Proof Formulae in the ALI/UNIDROIT Principles of Transnational Civil Procedure' (2004) 9 *Uniform Law Review* 875; Julia Caroline Scherpe, 'Alleviations of Proof in German and English Civil Evidence' (2016) 80 *Rabels Zeitschrift* 888; Mark Schweizer, 'The civil standard of proof – what is it, actually?' (2016) 20 *Int. J. Evidence & Proof* 217. For a recent monographic account in German see Mark Schweizer, *Beweiswürdigung und Beweismaß – Rationalität und Intuition*, Mohr Siebeck, Tübingen 2015.

39 For a new collection of essays see Luboš Tichý (ed.), *Standard of Proof in Europe*, Mohr Siebeck, Tübingen 2019.

Since the EU does not have general legislative power in the area of civil procedure, there is no 'European law of evidence' but merely piecemeal legislation.[40] For example, EU law is of practical importance for the judicial cooperation in cross-border taking of evidence, but the Evidence Regulation of 2001[41] is limited to international legal assistance and extraterritorial taking of evidence and does not govern the question of interest here. Nor is the standard of proof in civil proceedings laid down in any other European instrument of general application. Surprisingly, even the comprehensive procedural regime created for the so-called Unitary Patent[42] does not contain an explicit general rule on the standard of proof.[43] It would, however, be premature to conclude that the standard of proof falls within the scope of procedural autonomy of the Member States. Rather, there are several provisions in different areas of law where it stands to reason that the European legislator wants to regulate or at least influence the standard of proof.[44]

5.1. EXAMPLES

5.1.1. Competition Law

Regulation No 1/2003[45] governs the implementation of the primary law rules on competition which today are laid down in Articles 101 and 102 TFEU. Whereas Article 2 of the Regulation allocates the burden of proof, its Recital No 5 clarifies that it does not affect the national rules on the

---

40 Cf. the various contributions in Thilo Marauhn, *Bausteine eines europäischen Beweisrechts*, Mohr Siebeck, Tübingen 2007.

41 Regulation No 1206/2001 of 28 May 2001 on cooperation between the courts of the Member States in the taking of evidence in civil or commercial matters [2001] OJ L 174/1.

42 Laid down in the Agreement on a Unified Patent Court [2013] OJ C 175/1.

43 Hans-Jürgen Ahrens, 'Besonderheiten der Beweiserhebung im EPG-Verfahren' [2017] *Gewerblicher Rechtsschutz und Urheberrecht* 323, 326, suggests a high regular standard of proof, based on a conclusion drawn from Article 55(2) of the Agreement.

44 For a more detailed analysis see Wolfgang Hau, 'Europarechtliche Vorgaben zum Beweismaß im Zivilprozess' in Moritz Brinkmann et al (eds), *Dogmatik im Dienst von Gerechtigkeit, Rechtssicherheit und Rechtsentwicklung – Festschrift für Hans Prütting*, Carl Heymanns, Cologne 2018, p. 325 (also examining further examples taken from EU anti-discrimination directives).

45 Regulation No 1/2003 of 16 December 2002 on the implementation of the rules on competition laid down in Articles 81 and 82 of the Treaty [2003] OJ L 1/1.

standard of proof. The ECJ, however, has overcome this tribute to the principle of procedural autonomy of the Member States by emphasising the principle of effectiveness according to which national procedural law may not render excessively difficult or practically impossible the effective application of EU competition law. From this the ECJ concludes, for example, that an infringement can be demonstrated by means of mere circumstantial evidence.[46]

In order to improve the practical implementation of competition law, in 2014 the EU adopted a Directive dealing with certain rules governing actions for damages.[47] The Directive contains a number of provisions dealing with aspects of evidence, in particular with regard to disclosure (Articles 5 et seq.), obstruction of the taking of evidence (Article 8), *prima facie* evidence (Article 9) and burden of proof (Articles 13–15 and 17). More interestingly for our topic, some of these provisions are evidently based on an autonomous standard of proof: Article 5 speaks of 'a claimant who has presented a reasoned justification containing reasonably available facts and evidence sufficient to support the plausibility of its claim'. Article 4 expressly confirms the principle of effectiveness as developed by the ECJ, requiring all national rules and procedures relating to the exercise of claims for damages to be designed and applied in such a way that they do not render practically impossible or excessively difficult the exercise of the Union right to full compensation for harm caused by an infringement of competition law. And Article 17(1) further clarifies that this also applies to the national law of evidence: 'Member States shall ensure that neither the burden nor the standard of proof required for the quantification of harm renders the exercise of the right to damages practically impossible or excessively difficult.' Referring to these autonomous EU provisions, the Bundesgerichtshof (German Federal Supreme Court) held that the question whether and to what extent an infringement of competition law has caused damages is not governed by the general standard of proof (full judicial conviction), but that it is sufficient to establish a mere preponderance of probability.

---

46 Judgment of 21.01.2016, Case C-74/14, *Eturas UAB and Others v. Lietuvos Respublikos konkurencijos taryba*, ECLI:EU:C:2016:42.

47 Directive 2014/104/EU of 26 November 2014 on certain rules governing actions for damages under national law for infringements of the competition law provisions of the Member States and of the European Union [2014] OJ L 349/1.

5.1.2. *Cross-Border Civil Procedure*

EU regulations on procedural issues are of particular importance in the field of international litigation. They concern issues such as international jurisdiction, enforcement of foreign decisions and cross-border legal assistance, but do not, at least not explicitly, address the standard of proof. So, for example, Article 7 No 2 of the Brussels I*bis* Regulation provides that the occurrence of a harmful event constitutes a basis for jurisdiction in a tort case. The question under which conditions the judge may assume that such an event has indeed occurred within the forum is not governed by harmonised European law, but the *lex fori*. Accordingly, when a German court decides whether or not the claimant has produced sufficient facts to establish jurisdiction, it will refer to the traditional full conviction test of § 286(1) of the Code of Civil Procedure. This is the position of the prevailing opinion,[48] but nevertheless not a matter of course: is such a high threshold really acceptable while in other EU Member States a mere preponderance of probability would be sufficient?

One is more likely to find autonomous European specifications on standard of proof issues in instruments creating genuine European procedures. Under which conditions, for example, can an application for a European Payment Order be rejected on the basis that 'the claim is clearly unfounded' as stated in Article 11(1) of the European Payment Order Regulation[49] or, quite similar, when is it possible to issue a European Certificate of Succession because the relevant elements are 'established' as required by Article 67 of the Succession Regulation?[50]

Another and maybe even more striking example that strongly suggests an autonomous standard is the Regulation establishing a European

48 On the applicability of the national law as regards the required standard of proof see ECJ Judgment of 07.03.1995, Case C-68/93, *Fiona Shevill, Ixora Trading Inc., Chequepoint SARL and Chequepoint International Ltd v. Presse Alliance SA*, ECLI:EU:C:1995:61 at [37]; Peter Mankowski, Article 7 para. 228, in Peter Mankowski and Ulrich Magnus, *Brussels Ibis Regulation – Commentary*, Dr. Otto Schmidt, Cologne 2016.

49 Regulation No 1896/2006 of 12 December 2006 creating a European order for payment procedure [2006] OJ L 399/1.

50 Regulation No 650/2012 of 4 July 2012 on jurisdiction, applicable law, recognition and enforcement of decisions and acceptance and enforcement of authentic instruments in matters of succession and on the creation of a European Certificate of Succession [2012] OJ L 201/107.

Account Preservation Order Procedure.[51] According to its Article 7(1), the court shall issue the Preservation Order 'when the creditor has submitted sufficient evidence to satisfy the court' on certain points. In Germany, several scholars have argued that this wording can only mean that the Account Preservation Order Regulation does not refer to the *lex fori* but rather creates an autonomous standard of proof.[52] And this position promptly achieved support by the German legislator: the government draft of the German implementing act states that the Regulation does not require the creditor to provide full proof as it normally would be necessary under German law, but that a lesser degree of probability is sufficient.[53] In consequence, Berlin felt bound by this alleged autonomous test provided in the Regulation and expressly refrained from defining the applicable standard of proof.[54] The main argument for this self-restraint of the German legislator was the idea that the German language version of the Regulation in other contexts (namely in Article 14(3) and Recital No 15) uses the term 'Überzeugung' (which can be translated as 'conviction') and that in consequence the softer wording of Article 7 ('berechtigte Annahme') must mean something different. This, however, is by no means a matter of course. This becomes obvious when taking a look, for example, at the English version of the Regulation which in all relevant contexts requires that the court must be 'satisfied' or at the French version which consistently uses the verb 'convaincre'. This is why it is suggested that the German legislator was simply deceived by the Regulation's inconsistent

[51] Regulation No 655/2014 of 15 May 2014 establishing a European Account Preservation Order procedure to facilitate cross-border debt recovery in civil and commercial matters [2014] OJ L 189/59.

[52] Cf. Jan Lüttringhaus, 'Die Europäisierung des Zwangsvollstreckungsrechts im Bereich der vorläufigen Kontenpfändung – Der Europäische Beschluss zur vorläufigen Kontenpfändung und seine Wechselwirkungen mit der deutschen Zivilprozessordnung' (2016) 129 *Zeitschrift für Zivilprozess* 187, 199; Burkhard Hess, Artikel 7 EuKtPVO para. 4 and Artikel 9 EuKtPVO para. 3, in Peter Schlosser and Burkhard Hess, *EU-Zivilprozessrecht*, 4th ed. Beck Munich, 2015. For Austria see Barbara Köllensberger, Artikel 7 para. 18, in Hubertus Schumacher, Barbara Köllensberger and Martin Trenker, *Kommentar zur EU-Kontenpfändungsverordnung*, Manz, Vienna 2017. See also Gilles Cuniberti and Sara Migliorini, *The European Account Preservation Order Regulation – A Commentary*, Cambridge University Press, Cambridge 2018, Article 7 para. 16: 'it is submitted that, although an autonomous interpretation should arguably be developed, the courts of the Member States will simply continue to follow their judicial practice in this respect'.

[53] Bundestags-Drucksache (German Parliament Document) 18/7560, p. 42.

[54] The relevant provision, §947(1) of the Code of Civil Procedure, carefully only addresses the admissible means of proof, but not the applicable standard of proof.

German language version. This, however, only leads to the conclusion that there are not necessarily different standards of proof applicable within the Regulation. Nevertheless, there is still room for discussion on what exactly the relevant standard is and whether this is a matter of autonomous interpretation or rather left to the *lex fori*.

5.2. CONCLUSIONS

The few examples taken from different EU instruments provide neither a complete nor a representative selection, but might nevertheless elucidate the problem and permit some cautious conclusions. First of all, procedural autonomy, understood as a reference to the *lex fori*, is not a general rule, but merely one possible solution among others for a choice of law problem. As far as the applicable law for the determination of the standard of proof in an EU law context is concerned, there seem to be three conceivable solutions. The required degree of probability may firstly be exclusively governed in accordance with the *lex fori*, secondly be governed by the *lex fori* but with an autonomous hint as to whether the standard shall be rather high or rather low, or thirdly be exclusively governed by autonomous EU rules. Whereas the first and, to a lesser degree, also the second approach preserve some procedural autonomy, the third one does not.

As there are only a few genuine procedural legal instruments in EU law, it cannot be ruled out that European specifications on the measure of proof – either express or implied – could be found in instruments that mainly deal with substantive law. Notwithstanding this, one should subscribe to the prevailing opinion that the standard of proof – unlike the burden of proof – is a matter of procedural law (and therefore outside the scope of, e.g. Article 18 of the Rome I-Regulation[55] or Article 22 of the Rome II-Regulation[56]). In particular, even when the standard is specified in a substantive law context, it does not follow from this that it is to be governed by the *lex causae*.

When there are EU specifications regarding the standard of proof, this does not seem problematic as far as legislative competence is

55 Regulation No 593/2008 of 17 June 2008 on the law applicable to contractual obligations [2008] OJ L 177/6.

56 Regulation No 864/2007 of 11 July 2007 on the law applicable to non-contractual obligations [2007] OJ L 199/40.

concerned: there is no general mandate of the EU in the field of civil procedural law, but the principle of effectiveness as developed by the ECJ proves to be a sufficient justification when procedural provisions supplementing the substantive law are required in order to ensure the effective application of EU law by national courts. Another, more technical, problem of law-making occurs when the EU opts for an autonomous regime for a particular piece of legislation, because this makes it considerably more difficult to ensure consistency than in a purely national context. This already follows from the need to create several equally valid and consistent language versions. Moreover, legislation is further complicated by the fact that European law lacks a default rule (such as the German full conviction test anchored in § 286(1) of the Code of Civil Procedure). In the future, it would be useful to pay greater attention to the issue. Ideally it should be emphasised at least in the recitals of an instrument that on certain matters either an autonomous legal standard – to be described in further detail – applies or, while remaining within the respective *lex fori*, the court should apply a rather high or rather low standard within this national spectrum.

Against this backdrop, it would be a considerable step forward if a European default rule regarding the standard of proof in private law instruments could be established. In this context, the European Law Institute's plan to draft 'European Rules of Civil Procedure' deserves special attention.[57] This project builds upon the 'Principles of Transnational Civil Procedure' published by the American Law Institute and UNIDROIT in 2004. The European Rules will focus more specifically on European affairs and cover both cross-border and domestic matters. An important topic in this context is 'access to information and evidence', which is dealt with by a special ELI working group. A draft of the working group expressly points out that it seems 'necessary to assume that there is certain flexibility and a need to adapt to the circumstances in order to decide when a court is 'reasonably convinced'. As mentioned, this would not be in line with the stricter German standard rule. From a German perspective, it is therefore important to pay very close attention to which

[57] For an introduction see John Sorabji, 'The ELI-UNIDROIT Principles: An Introduction and an English Perspective' in Anna Nylund and Magne Strandberg (eds), *Civil Procedure and Harmonisation of Law: The Dynamics of EU and International Treaties*, Intersentia, Antwerp-Cambridge 2019, p. 35.

formulation on the regular standard of proof will be adopted in the final version of the European Rules – and thus possibly at some point in a future European Code of Civil Procedure.

6. FINAL REMARKS

It might have become clear that this chapter, although maybe suggested by its title, does not end with warnings against the big bad wolf. Nor is it appropriate to think of the Europeanisation of civil procedure as a Cinderella story:[58] there is no guaranteed happy ending and the process of Europeanisation is rather like marching a rocky road than dreaming of having a ball. Nevertheless, one should not be discouraged by that but think of other tales where in the end the one that is rewarded is the one who plucks up the courage to experience adventures and to meet tricky challenges.

---

[58] See Helen E. Hartnell, 'A Cinderella Story: Judicial Cooperation in Civil Matters Meets the Prince' (2010) 29 *Yearbook of European Law* 483: 'Once upon a time, procedural law in all its peculiarity stayed home in the scullery, while public and even private law went off to attend the European integration ball.' But who has to act as wicked stepmother oppressing poor Cinderella and who is entrusted the much more gratifying role of the good fairy (or, in the German version, white doves) coming to her help?

PROCEDURAL AUTONOMY IN THE NETHERLANDS

A Fading Relic?

Bart Krans

1. A FIRM STARTING POINT IN EU LAW

The relationship between EU law and national civil procedure law is developing quite rapidly. That might be considered as surprising because the starting point is clear and simple: EU law is law of the EU and the rules and regulations concerning civil procedure are up to the Member States. Member States have the authority over their own procedural system. This outset from the start also means that proceedings concerning EU law before national courts are conducted along the lines set out by the national civil procedure system. There is no EU law that provides a general system for all types of civil cases that must be applied by Member States. EU Member States are free to set up their own system concerning civil procedural law.

That has been settled case law for many years. In the classic case *Rewe* from 1976, the ECJ placed emphasis on the concept of procedural autonomy.[1] In many cases since then the ECJ has referred to this starting point.[2] In the *EOS/Danko* case from September 2018 the question at the table was whether Directive 93/13 on unfair terms precludes certain national legislation which prevents a consumer protection organisation from intervening in proceedings seeking an order for payment. On its way to the answer the ECJ ruled that in the absence of EU legislation concerning the possibility for consumer protection associations to intervene in individual disputes involving consumers, it is for the national legal order of each Member State to establish such rules, in accordance with the principle of procedural autonomy.[3] By doing so, the ECJ once again reconfirmed the principle of procedural autonomy.[4] There are many more cases in which the ECJ has referred to this starting point.[5]

By the term 'procedural autonomy', only the freedom of the Member States to organise their procedural law for civil proceedings is referred to. Nevertheless, it is worth mentioning that procedural autonomy is not the

1 The ECJ states that in the absence of Community rules (…) it is for the domestic legal system of each Member State to designate the courts having jurisdiction and to determine the procedural conditions governing actions at law intended to ensure the protection of the rights which citizens have from the direct effect of Community law (16.12.1976, C-33/76, *Rewe-Zentralfinanz eG and Rewe-Zentral AG v. Landwirtschaftskammer für das Saarland*, ECLI:EU:C:1976:188, sub 5).

2 See on the dual requirement of equivalence and effectiveness and at the notion of 'procedural autonomy' of the Member States in the area of procedures and remedies for the enforcement of EU law based rights before the Member States' courts, M. Bobek, 'Why is there no principle of "Procedural Autonomy" of the Member States, the European Court of Justice and autonomy of the Member States' in B. de Witte and H. Micklitz (eds), *The European Court of Justice and Autonomy of the Member States*, Intersentia, Antwerp-Cambridge 2011, pp. 305–322, and M. Hoskins, 'Tilting the balance: supremacy and national procedural rules' [1996] *European Law Review* 365–377.

3 ECJ 20.09.2018, C-448/17, *EOS KSI Slovensko s.r.o. v. Ján Danko and Margita Danková*, EU:C:2018:745, sub 36.

4 See on procedural autonomy in the context of administrative law, R. Ortlep and M. Verhoeven, 'The principle of primacy versus the principle of national procedural autonomy' [2012] April–June *NALL*.

5 Just to mention a few examples: ECJ 25.07.2018, C-338/17, *Guigo/Fond Garantirani*, ECLI:EU:C:2018:605; ECJ 31.05.2018, C-306/17, *Nothartová/Boldizsár* ECLI:EU:C:2018:360; ECJ 03.09.2009; C-2/08, *Fallimento Olimpiclub*, ECLI:EU:C:2009:506; ECJ 23.04.2009, C-378/07–C-380/07, ECLI:EU:C:2009:250; ECJ 27.02.2014, C-470/12, *Pohotovost*, ECLI:EU:C:2014:101; ECJ 21.02.2013, C-471/11, *Cido Grupa SIA v. Valsts ieņēmumu dienests*, ECLI:EU:C:2012:555 and ECJ 14.06.2012, C-618/10, *Banco Espanol de Crédito*, ECLI:EU:C:2012:349.

only type of autonomy that plays a role in the ECJ case law.[6] For example, in several combined cases on possible state aid and tax measures adopted by a regional or local authority the ECJ also refers to the concept of institutional autonomy, economic autonomy and regional autonomy.[7] This chapter deals with procedural autonomy of the Netherlands.[8]

2. EXCEPTIONS TO THE STARTING POINT: SEVERAL SECTORS

In spite of the above-mentioned deeply rooted starting point of procedural autonomy in the case law of the ECJ, the relationship between EU law and national procedural law is far from dull.[9] This relationship is, as stated, changing rapidly. The EU legislator has not held its breath the last decades, on the contrary. There is EU law on many sectors. Parts of that EU law are also relevant for Dutch national civil procedure law.

A well-known sector where a serious amount of EU law can be found is consumer law. Consumer sale, consumer credit, unfair terms and unfair commercial practices are examples of sectors where EU law plays a

---

6 It may vary per Member State whether a topic is considered procedural or more substantive of nature (see A.S. Prechal and K. Cath, 'The European Acquis of Civil Procedure: constitutional aspects' (2014) 19 *Unif L Rev* 180). See on EU internal market law and autonomy in general (so, not specific to procedural autonomy), A. Nordhausen Scholes, 'Autonomy' in N. Reich, A. Nordhausen Scholes and J. Scholes (eds), *Understanding EU Internal Market Law*, Intersentia, Antwerp-Cambridge 2015, Ch. V, pp. 491–602.

7 ECJ 11.11.2008, C-428/06–C-434/06, *Comunidad Autónoma de la Rioja*, ECLI:EU:C:2008:488.

8 There is also a vast amount of case law concerning cross-border cases. This chapter on the Netherlands will not deal with cross-border cases but focusses on purely national cases.

9 The relationship between EU law on the one hand and procedural autonomy of a Member State on the other hand was already pointed at by, *inter alia*, E.M. Szyszczak and J. Delicostopoulos, 'Intrusions into national procedural autonomy: the French paradigm' (1997) 22-2 *European Law Review* 140–141, and A. Biondi, 'The European Court of Justice and Certain National Procedural Limitations: Not such a tough Relationship' (1999) 36 *Common Market Law Review*. One example, of many, of more recent attention on the topic is offered by C. Krönke, *Die Verfahrensautonomie der Mitgliedstaten der Europaïschen Union, Jus Internatioanle et Europeum*, Mohr Siebeck, Tübingen 2013, and M. Kramme, 'Verfahrensautonomie der Mitgliedstaaten im Zivilverfahrensrecht – Grundsatz des Unionsrechts oder Phantom?' in C. Behme et al. (eds), *Perspektiven einer europäischen Privatrechtswissenschaft, Jahrbuch Junger Zivilrechtswissenschaftler*, Nomos, Munich 2017, p. 407.

pivotal role. In all Member States, the EU regulatory framework regarding consumer protection needs to be taken into account. The presumption on lack of conformity in the Directive on consumer sales and guarantees is just one example: if a product is sold to a consumer and any lack of conformity which becomes apparent within six months of delivery of the goods is, as a starting point, presumed to have existed at the time of delivery.[10] *Ex officio* application of EU Consumer law forms another example.

Intellectual Property law is another field of law where EU law plays an important role. The Directive on enforcement of IP rights was introduced because 'the protection of intellectual property is an essential element for the success of the internal market'.[11] The objective of this Enforcement Directive is to 'approximate legislative systems so as to ensure a high, equivalent and homogeneous level of protection in the internal market'.[12] Therefore this directive regulates matters of, *inter alia*, evidence, measure for preserving evidence, on right of information, on provisional and precautionary measures, injunctions and legal costs. As a result of this directive a new section in the Dutch Code of Civil Procedure (CCP) was introduced concerning litigation in IP cases.[13]

Another sector where EU law has become more and more important for the law of civil procedure is competition law. The Treaty on the Functioning of the European Union (TFEU) prohibits agreements between companies which prevent, restrict or distort competition in the EU and which may affect trade between Member States (anti-competitive agreements).[14] The TFEU also prohibits abusive conduct by companies that have a dominant position on a particular market.[15] When it comes to proceedings before national courts concerning the enforcement of these well-known and important regulations, it is obvious that rules of national civil procedure must be taken into account. For those competition law cases, there are some special aspects concerning civil procedure.

---

10 Article 5, para 3, Directive 1999/44/EC of the European Parliament and of the council of 25 May 1999 on certain aspects of the sale of consumer goods and associated guarantees. This EU rule is implemented in Article 7:18, section 2 CC. There is a lot of case law in the Netherlands on this rule.

11 Directive 2004/48/EC of the European Parliament and of the Council of 29 April 2004 on the enforcement of intellectual property rights, recital sub 1.

12 Enforcement Directive, recital sub 10.

13 Section 7.15 of the Dutch of Civil Procedure (CCP): Articles 1019–1019i.

14 Article 101 of the TFEU.

15 Article 102 of the TFEU.

The fields of labour law and equal treatment law also contain many EU law base regulations. Several pieces of it can be relevant for Dutch national civil procedure law. This 'list of sectors' where the EU plays a role or even an important role is longer.[16]

A first glance at these sectors makes clear the way national civil procedure systems may have to be applied or adjusted to meet EU rules and requirements on enforcement in these sectors. The EU influence on national civil procedure law per sector is relatively obvious and demonstrates a clear impact of EU law on national civil procedure law. This first glance is underlined by the notion that there is also another type of EU relevance for national civil procedure law. The famous *Rewe/Comet* doctrine may also result in European requirements for parts of Dutch national civil procedure law.[17] The applicable national rules to adjudicate claims that are based on EU law cannot be less favourable than claims with just a national dimension, so follows from the principle of equivalence. The effectiveness principle requires that national rules relevant for claims based on EU law may also not render it virtually impossible of excessively difficult to exercise EU rights.[18]

3. LIMITATIONS TO PROCEDURAL AUTONOMY: GENERAL REMARKS

Several general aspects concerning limitations to procedural autonomy can be identified for the Netherlands.[19] First of all, a vast part of the limitations to Dutch national procedural law concern procedural topics which target certain groups of people or certain interests. Even for

16 For example, procurement law and corporate law are other sectors where EU law is quite visible. The relation between EU corporate law and national civil procedure law will not be dealt with in this chapter. The same counts for the possible interference between EU procurement law and Dutch civil procedure law. See on state aid and procedural autonomy, A. Metselaar, 'Drie rechters en één norm: handhaving van de Europese staatssteunregels voor de Nederlandse rechter en de grenzen van de procedure autonomie', diss. Wolters Kluwer, Leiden 2016 (696 pages).

17 See B. Krans, 'EU Law and National Civil Procedure Law: An Invisible Pillar' (2015) 4 *ERPL* §4, 571–573.

18 Ibid, §4, 571–573.

19 One could also use the wording 'infringements on procedural autonomy', but 'limitations to procedural autonomy' seems to fit the relationship between EU law and national law better.

pure national cases, so without any cross-border aspect, more and more parts of civil procedural law have been constructed at EU level.[20]

The EU legislation is based on a different kind of legislative process. The way the EU legislation is put on the map is not the same as the legislative process of all, or at least most, Member States. EU legislation is the result of a process that seems to have more of an ad hoc basis. The absence of a generally binding EU Code on civil procedure law on the one hand, and the sector approach on the other hand result in more or less fragmented limitations in the civil procedure law systems of the Member States.[21]

The sector approach seems to be part of a more general development. Instead of working with traditional fields (or distinctions) like contract law, liability law and property law, EU legislation seems to be developing more towards different categories of law. Perhaps one can say that the EU level has demonstrated some shifting of the paradigm towards lawmaking from a more sector-based approach. In the author's view it is this development that has resulted in a lot of the changes of Dutch national civil procedure law.

Do EU rules have consequences for Dutch national civil procedure law? For certain EU rules, the answer is doubtless positive. Several levels of limitations to the procedural autonomy can be identified: limitations that are clear at first sight and limitations that are less visible at first glance.[22]

4. LIMITATIONS TO PROCEDURAL AUTONOMY: THE FIRST LEVEL

A first level of limitations to the procedural autonomy of the Netherlands has come in through the front door. Some parts of the Dutch procedural landscape have been adjusted or changed as a result of EU law. EU law,

---

20 Attention for the autonomy of Member States is not limited to civil cases. See, for example, for administrative law E. Hofmann, 'Der Abschied von der (ohnehin meist falsch verstandenen) Verfahrensautonomie der Mitgliedstaaten? Anmerkung zu EuGH v. 15. 10. 2015, Rs. C-137/14' (2016) 15 *Europarecht* Heft 2, 188, and J.H. Jans, 'Naar een Europese Awb ?, Enkele opmerkingen over het slaan van piketpaaltjes, rechterlijke dialoog en harmonisatie via de achterdeur' in T. Barkhuysen, W. Den Ouden and J.E.M. Polak (eds), *Bestuursrecht Harmoniseren*, Boom Juridische uitgevers, The Hague 2010, pp. 609–626.

21 See on internal fragmentation, Krans, above note 17, §10, pp. 582–584.

22 The typology of the limitations and their levels is mapped and analysed by the author for the purpose of this chapter and does not necessarily reflect the opinion of all Dutch scholars.

in particular directives, has directly led to several direct changes in Dutch civil procedure law. This type of limitations to the autonomy of the Dutch legislator in civil procedure matters can be referred to as first level limitations.[23] Dutch procedural law offers several examples.

4.1. EU-DRIVEN MECHANISMS AND INSTRUMENTS: SOME EXAMPLES

The protection of intellectual property rights was considered an essential element for the success of the internal market.[24] Therefore the above-mentioned Enforcement Directive was introduced. As a result, the Dutch Code on Civil Procedure was extended with a special section on IP rights.[25] This section in the Dutch Code of Civil Procedure regulates, for example, seizure of evidence, cases concerning urgent matters, witness hearings and costs in civil proceedings concerning the enforcement of intellectual property rights. This section of the Dutch Code of Civil Procedure entered into force on 1 January 2007.[26]

Without going into details on the regulations in this section, it can be stated that several regulations in that section on proceedings in IP cases did not pre-exist in Dutch procedural law.[27] The above-mentioned new section in the Dutch Code of Civil Procedure on proceedings in IP cases has brought several changes for this type of proceedings.[28] It concerns special rules on, *inter alia*, access to documents (Article 1019a of the CCP), seizure of evidence (Article 1019c of the CCP) and costs awards (Article 1019h of the CCP). These rules are, as a starting point, only

23 The terminology first, second and third does not refer to a chronological order of limitations. It also does not intend to define the level of importance of the several level of limitations.

24 See above note 11.

25 Section 15, Book 3 CCP: article 1019–1019i CCP. The Enforcement directive has also led to changes in several Dutch Acts on IP rights.

26 See Act of 08.03.2007, Stb. 2007/108. The enforcement directive (2004/48/EG) should have been implemented by 29.04.2006. There is case law (by lower courts) on the interpretation in conformity with the directive from the end of the implementation period (see for example Court of Appeal, The Hague 08.12.2009, BIE 2010/62).

27 See B. Krans, 'The Impact of EU Law on Dutch Civil Procedure Law' in A. Nylund and B. Krans (eds), *The European Union and National Civil Procedure*, Intersentia, Antwerp-Cambridge 2016, pp. 93–94.

28 See on this section on IP rights Krans, above note 27.

applicable in IP cases and deviate from the (pre-existing) general rules on civil cases.[29] For those aspects where the Enforcement Directive has brought changes, the diminishing procedural autonomy is obvious.

Costs related to legal proceedings in civil cases seems to be a topic with a pure national dimension.[30] One can perceive this topic as firmly related to the national procedural system, and perhaps even to national legal culture. An example of this level of limitations as far as legal cost is concerned results from this Enforcement Directive. According to Article 14 of that directive Member States shall ensure that reasonable and proportionate legal costs and other expenses incurred by the successful party shall, as a general rule, be borne by the unsuccessful party, unless equity does not allow this. The implementation of this prescription has introduced a regime in the Dutch Code of Civil Procedure for the awarding of legal costs which deviates from the general regime on costs (in the sense that it is more favourable for the winning party than for the winning party in other civil cases). There is a lot of case law on this EU-based regime for IP cases, both from lower courts as well as from the Dutch Supreme Court. Special guidelines for judges were introduced concerning the assessment of the amount of the award on legal costs in IP cases.[31] This EU rule has diminished the procedural autonomy in the Netherlands on legal cost awards in IP cases.[32]

4.2. EU-DRIVEN MECHANISMS AND INSTRUMENTS: OTHER EXAMPLES

This first level of diminishing procedural autonomy also offers a slightly different type of limitation to procedural autonomy. The Directive on

29 See for an extension of a part of this section to other certain other cases the decision of the Dutch Supreme 28 September 2018, ECLI:NL:HR:2018:1775.

30 See on costs and EU law, Krans, above note 17, pp. 567–587, in particular para. 6.

31 These are the so-called *indicatietarieven in IE-zaken*. They are developed for courts of first instance, courts of appeal and the Supreme Court. These various *indicatietarieven* are public and can be found on the website of the judiciary <www.rechtspraak.nl>.

32 C. Vrendenbargh wrote a dissertation on this regime, also addressing the question on the compatibility of Dutch costs systems with EU law (*Proceskostenveroordeling in IE-zaken en toegang tot de rechter*, Wolters Kluwer, Alphen aan den Rijn 2018, 421 pages).

product liability offers an example.[33] In cases concerning product liability the injured person shall be required to prove the damage, the defect of the product and the causal relationship between defect and damage.[34] At the time the Dutch legislator started drafting the act to implement this directive there was no intention of enacting a special rule or provision to implement this regulation from the Directive.[35] Implementation was deemed not necessary because this rule in the Directive was considered to be already in line with Dutch law. If the general rule in Dutch law on burden of proof is applied, the same result will be achieved as is aimed for by the Directive, so was the idea at the beginning of the legislative process of the implementation of the product liability Directive.[36] Nevertheless, later on in this legislative process, the special rule was proposed and introduced, probably to be on the safe side.[37] Dutch civil procedure law has some techniques, which can only be applied in certain circumstances, to give some relief to a burden of proof for certain civil cases in general. Among Dutch scholars, there is some attention to the question whether this special rule in the Dutch Civil Code that is enacted to implement the rule on burden of proof in the Directive leaves room for the use of these techniques.[38]

There are more directives with a specific rule on burden of proof.[39] Several EU rules on burden of proof have led to direct changes in Dutch legislation.[40]

---

33 Council Directive of 25 July 1985 on the approximation of the laws, regulations and administrative provisions of the Member States concerning liability for defective products, OJ EC, L 210/29.

34 Article 4 of this Directive.

35 See on the Directive product liability, in a paragraph with the heading Procedural Autonomy revisited, F. Wilman, *Private Enforcement of EU law before national courts*, Edward Elgar, Cheltenham 2015, para. 10.1.3.

36 Parliamentary Documents II, 1985/1986, 19 636, no. 3, p. 4 and 1987/1988, 19 636, nr. 6, pp. 5–6.

37 This has led to Article 6:188 of the Dutch Civil Code (CC).

38 See *inter alia* Asser/Hartkamp and Sieburgh 6-IV 2015/269 and C.J.M. van Doorn and S.B. Pape, 'Productaansprakelijkheid en productveiligheid' in E.H. Hondius and G.J. Rijken (eds), *Handboek consumentenrecht. Een overzicht van de rechtspositie van de consument*, Uitgeverij Paris, Zutphen 2015, pp. 333–334, also containing references to case law.

39 For example, Directive (93/13) on unfair terms (Article 3), Directive (2005/29) on unfair commercial practices (Article 12), Directive (99/44) on consumer sale (Article 5). See Krans, above note 27. Directive (2002/73/EG) on equal treatment of men and women also covers burden of proof.

40 All of the national rules on civil procedure which are within the scope of the Directive do now have an EU background.

5. LIMITATIONS TO PROCEDURAL AUTONOMY: THE SECOND LEVEL

Limitations to the Dutch procedural autonomy can be less visible than the ones referred to in the first level because they do not result directly from a directive as such. EU-driven exceptions to the procedural autonomy can be necessary as a result of the application of the *Rewe/Comet* rule: the requirements being effectiveness and equivalence.

5.1. A MORE ACTIVE ROLE OF COURTS IN CONSUMER CASES

It is not an exaggeration to state that the role of Dutch courts in certain consumer cases has become more active as a result of ECJ case law on *ex officio* application of EU consumer law. In the Netherlands *ex officio* application of consumer law, at least of certain areas of consumer law, is a topic that is far from unnoticed. What started with two European rulings on several specific types of general terms on the list to the Directive on unfair contract terms,[41] has led not only to a serious amount of cases of the ECJ, but also of cases in Dutch courts. This chapter will not go into the specifics of the vast amount of case law and literature on that topic in the Netherlands, but will be limited to refer to earlier publications on that topic.[42] To put it in short: it is clear that the Dutch courts have to take an active approach.

5.2. *RES JUDICATA*

The well-known topic of *res judicata* is acknowledged in most, probably all, Member States. Its application seems to be a topic that is really a matter of national law. At first glance, one might wonder if there is an EU

41 Council Directive 93/13/EEC of 5 April 1993 on unfair terms in consumer contracts.

42 See, *inter alia*, A. Ancery and B. Krans, 'Consumer Protection and EU-Driven Judicial Activism in the Netherlands' in A. Nylund and M. Strandberg (eds), *Civil Procedure and Harmonisation of Law*, Intersentia, Antwerp-Cambridge 2019, pp. 125–139, with further references. There are many publications on the topic in Dutch, for example A.G.F. Ancery, 'Ambtshalve toepassing van EU-recht', dissertation, Kluwer, University of Groningen, Deventer 2012.

dimension to this important topic. If one takes a closer look it appears that EU law can be relevant even for *res judicata*.

The *Eco Swiss/Benetton* case from June 1999 concerned the relation between EU law and an arbitral interim award. The case was referred to the ECJ by the Dutch Supreme Court. One of the questions was whether an agreement that is declared valid in an arbitral interim award still can be void because it violates Article 101 of the TFEU (at that time Article 81 EC). The answer of the ECJ is negative. The ECJ ruled that EU law (at that time Community law) does not require a national court to refrain from applying domestic rules of procedure according to which an interim arbitration award which is in the nature of a final award and in respect of which no application for annulment has been made within the prescribed time limit acquires the force of *res judicata* and may no longer be called into question by a subsequent arbitration award. This is even so, still according to the ECJ, if this is necessary in order to examine, in proceedings for annulment of a subsequent arbitration award, whether an agreement which the interim award held to be valid in law is nevertheless void under Article 81 EC (now Article 101 of the TFEU).[43] In this decision the ECJ respects the national rules on *res judicata* in arbitral interim-decisions.

In the *Kapferer* case the ECJ also acknowledges the importance of the principle of *res judicata*.[44] This case, referred to the ECJ by an Austrian court, concerned prize notification and misleading advertising. The ECJ reminds the importance of the principle of *res judicata*. In order to ensure both stability of the law and legal relations and the sound administration of justice, the ECJ considers it important that judicial decisions which have become definitive after all rights of appeal have been exhausted or after expiry of the time limits provided for in that connection can no longer be called into question.[45] Therefore EU law does not require a national court to disapply domestic rules of procedure conferring finality on a decision, even if to do so would enable it to remedy an infringement of the EU by the decision at issue, so rules the ECJ.[46]

The *Lucchini* case from 2007 concerned an application for state aid. Strongly summarised, the facts come down to the following. Lucchini

43 ECJ 01.06.1999, C-126/97, *Eco Swiss/Benetton*, ECLI:EU:C:1999:269, in particular at [48].

44 ECJ 16.03.2006, C-234/04, *Kapferer/Schlank&Schick*, ECLI:EU:C:2006:178.

45 The ECJ refers to its decision in C-224/01, *Köbler*, ECLI:EU:C:2003:513 at [38].

46 C-234/04, *Kapferer/Schlank&Schick*, ECLI:EU:C:2006:178 at [21] (the ECJ uses the terminology Community law (at the time of the ruling the right terminology)).

applied to the competent authorities for state aid. These authorities granted Lucchini state aid on a provisional basis. This was on the condition of approval by the European Commission. Lucchini started proceedings against the competent authorities before an Italian court to establish his right to payment. Afterwards the European Commission stated that all of the aid intended for Lucchini was incompatible with the common market. Lucchini did not file an appeal against that decision of the EC within the prescribed period. Nevertheless, the Italian courts, ruling on Lucchini's request for payment, decided that Lucchini was entitled to payment. The EC called on the authorities to recover the state aid. Lucchini started proceedings before the Consiglio di Stato. This Consiglio asked questions to the ECJ. According to the ECJ the national court asked essentially whether Community law precludes the application of a provision of national law which seeks to lay down the principle of *res judicata* in so far as the application of that provision prevents the recovery of State aid granted in breach of Community law which has been found to be incompatible with the common market in a Commission decision which has become final.[47] The main question was therefore whether a judgment of a national court has the authority of *res judicata*. The ECJ ruled that it follows from settled case law that a national court which is called upon, within the exercise of its jurisdiction, to apply provisions of Community law is under a duty to give full effect to those provisions, if necessary refusing of its own motion to apply any conflicting provision of national legislation.[48] The ECJ concluded by ruling that Community law precludes the application of a provision of national law which seeks to lay down the principle of *res judicata* in so far as the application of that provision prevents the recovery of State aid granted in breach of Community law which has been found to be incompatible with the common market in a decision of the Commission which has become final.[49] The conclusion is that EU law prohibits in this case a national regulation on *res judicata* in so far as its application prevents recovery of state aid.

This ruling in *Lucchini* does not mean that the principle of *res judicata* is now entirely an EU matter.[50] On the contrary: it seems that the more or

[47] ECJ 18.07.2007, C-119/05, *Lucchini*, ECLI:EU:C:2007:434 at [48].

[48] ECJ 18.07.2007, C-119/05, *Lucchini*, ECLI:EU:C:2007:434 at [61].

[49] ECJ 18.07.2007, C-119/05, *Lucchini*, ECLI:EU:C:2007:434 at [63].

[50] See on *res judicata* in relation to EU law also, S. Wagner, 'Unionsrechtliche Rechtskraftdurchbrechung? Zu den Grenzen der mitgliedstaatlichen Verfahrensautonomie auf dem Gebiet der Rechtskraft nach der Rechtsprechungdes EuGH' (2014) 2 *ZeuS* 211–234.

less special circumstances in the *Lucchini* case are crucial for the decision in this case.[51] This view is underlined by the decision in *Olimpiclub* from 2008. The ECJ ruled in *Olimpiclub* that in the absence of Community legislation in this area, the rules implementing the principle of *res judicata* are a matter for the national legal order, in accordance with the principle of the procedural autonomy of the Member States.[52] The decision in *Lucchini* learned that an exception is possible, but it is still a firm starting point that EU law respects national rules on *res judicata*, just as demonstrated in *Eco Swiss/Benetton* and *Kapferer*.

6. LIMITATIONS TO PROCEDURAL AUTONOMY: THE THIRD LEVEL

A third level of limitations can be identified. The first two categories concerned limitations to procedural autonomy that are directly visible, either in EU-driven new or adjusted national legislation either in Dutch case law that results from or is based on EU law. The EU dimension of a procedural topic can also be relevant in spite of the fact that it has not yet resulted in action of the Dutch legislator or Dutch case law.[53]

An example is offered by the Directive on late payment.[54] This directive aims at combating late payment in commercial transactions in the internal market. In the Dutch Civil Code a special provision was introduced to implement the requirements on legal interest of this directive.[55] According to the Directive on late payments in commercial transactions the creditor is entitled to obtain reasonable compensation for any recovery costs.[56]

---

51 See also Advocate-General Mazak in his conclusion for *Olimpiclub*, sub 61–64.

52 ECJ 03.09.2009, C-2/08, Olimpiclub, ECLI:EU:C:2009:506 at [24].

53 Compare Krans, above note 27, para. 3.4.

54 Directive 2011/7/EU of the European Parliament and of the Council of 16 February 2011 on combating late payment in commercial transactions. This directive repealed the earlier Directive 2000/35/EC of the European Parliament and the Council of 29 June 2000 on combatting late payment in commercial transactions.

55 This provision, Article 6:119a CC, was originally introduced with a view to implement Directive 2000/35/EC of the European Parliament and of the Council of 29 June 2000 on combating late payment in commercial transactions (*PbEG* L 200/35). Article 6:119a CC was amended in 2012 (enacted in 2013) as a result of Directive 2011/7/EU of the European Parliament and of the Council of 16 February 2011 on combating late payment in commercial transactions.

56 Article 6 Directive 2011/7/EU. In the directive of 2000, it concerned Article 3.

The Dutch legislator decided not to implement this rule on recovery for costs.[57] The rationale for this non-action was that there was already a procedural system that leads to fair compensation.[58] Some Dutch scholars criticised this choice, arguing that the Dutch system does not meet this requirement of the Directive. The core of their argument was the existing Dutch rules on a part of the costs (the so-called *buitengerechtelijke incassokosten* (which can be translated more or less as extrajudicial collective costs)) is insufficiently transparent.[59] Without going into the details and discussing whether the choice of the legislator was right or not, it is clear that the final say whether there is a system that meets this requirement is up to the ECJ, if necessary. So, the system of compensation for costs has a European dimension.

7. LIMITATIONS TO PROCEDURAL AUTONOMY: THE FOURTH LEVEL?

A national legislator can make adjustments or changes in its national procedural system which are not required by EU law, but which are nevertheless some kind of follow up of the enactment of EU law. A national legislator can for example, decide to broaden the scope of an EU rule. If the Directive on combatting on late payments in commercial transactions requires Member States to set rules for awarding costs, a Member State can as a starting point decide to apply these rules also for other types of transactions.[60] If the directive on IP rights prescribes Member States several procedural mechanisms for IP cases, a national legislator has the option, at least in principle, to enact those rules for IP cases and other cases. This decision can also be taken by courts. If it is decided at the national level that the rules and regulations for IP cases will also apply to other cases, this is referred to as spontaneous harmonisation. For the Netherlands an example is provided by seizure of evidence. As stated before, a special rule

---

57 This was decided at the time of the implementation of the directive from 2000. After the enactment of Directive 2011/7/EU no special rule on this point was introduced.

58 Parliamentary Documents 28 239 (2001–2002), no. 3, para. 3.

59 See, *inter alia*, G.J. Knijp and S.D. Lindenbergh, 'Buitengerechtelijke kosten in Europees perspectief' (2002) 7/8 NbBW 100–103, and M. Freudenthal, J.M. Milo and H.N. Schelhaas, 'Europese wanbetalers: geen krediet na aanvaarding richtlijn' (2000) 7 NTBR 293.

60 This has not happened in the Netherlands.

for IP cases was enacted in Dutch law to implement the Directive on IP rights. The EU bases rule played a role in the acceptance by the Dutch Supreme Court of a general power of seizure of evidence in civil cases.[61]

This spontaneous harmonisation comes down to harmonisation at the national level between rules with an EU background and other rules. In that sense it is primarily a form of harmonisation of national law of a Member State. If, and only if, other several Member States will adopt this technique an indirect result may very well be that it also leads to harmonisation in procedural regime of different Member States on topics without a direct EU background. One could argue that this spontaneous harmonisation cannot be perceived as a real fourth level of limitations on procedural autonomy. The changes for national law are more or less 'voluntary limitations'. The concept of voluntary limitations seems to be a *contradictio in terminis*. Real limitations are not voluntarily, in the sense that that are a direct result from EU law.[62] Nevertheless, this kind of spill over effect of the EU is triggered by EU law and has brought changes to national civil procedure law. These changes can be considered individually on their merits and can on that basis deserve a positive mark. At least, the national legislator, or the national court that harmonised its national law spontaneously, must have considered it a step forward in some way. In that sense one can argue this is not really a kind of limitation to procedural autonomy of the Member State, and therefore not a fourth level. That is a sound point. That might be underlined by the following. It is clear that the final word on the interpretation of rules on civil procedure which have an EU background, if necessary, is not up to the Dutch Supreme Court, but up to the ECJ. This does not count for rules resulting from the spontaneous harmonisation of Dutch law. National rules which do not fall within the scope of the EU regulations belong to the domain of the Dutch Supreme Court and are not up to the ECJ.

On the other hand, the scope of the EU rules might be widened with the sole purpose of maintaining or achieving coherence of procedural law at the national level, If the adjustments to national law outside the scope of, for example, a directive, are made by national legislators or courts, just to maintain coherence at the national level which was broken as a result of that specific directive, those additional changes are not

61 See for more details of this example, Krans, note 29, para. 4, with further references.

62 This a factual statement. Whether one considers an individual limitation an improvement or a deterioration of the national system is another question. That question can be answered by looking at the merits of that individual change.

really voluntary. To that extent, this type of 'voluntary' changes can be considered as limitation to the national procedural autonomy.

8. FINAL REMARKS

Several conclusions can be drawn for the Netherlands. First, there are more EU-based limitations to procedural autonomy than one might expect. More procedural topics are related to or can be related to EU law than one might see at first sight.[63] It concerns topics in various stages of civil proceedings.

Several types of limitations to procedural autonomy can be identified. Four levels of limitations were distinguished. The main difference between the various levels concerns the relationship between the relevant element of EU law and the infringement on the procedural autonomy. A clear distinction between the various levels cannot always be made. The boundaries can be vague. Case law (level 2), for example, may easily result from new rules and prescriptions in Codes (level 1). A clear-cut distinction is not necessary. The various levels demonstrate that the procedural autonomy of the Member States is diminishing via several channels. In various ways EU law can be relevant for or make limitations to Dutch national procedural law. Limitations do not only follow from directives which have to be implemented, but also from case law,[64] and from the TFEU itself.

Is procedural autonomy a firm starting point or a fading relic? Procedural autonomy is still a firm starting point. The majority of the civil procedure law in the Netherlands is pure Dutch. Procedural autonomy is fading, but it is not a relic, at least from a Dutch point of view. Procedural autonomy may be diminishing, but the 'body of procedural autonomy' is still intact.

Are the EU-driven limitations to be considered positive or negative? That was not the topic of this chapter, but from a national judicial point

63 Krans, note 29, p. 90, following up on the wording used in the report 'Europeanisation of civil procedure' of the European Parliamentary Research Service (author R. Manko), 2015 <www.europarl.europa.eu>, para. 4.1.

64 The *ex officio* application can serve as an example. See on *ex officio* application also A. Adinolfi, 'The "procedural autonomy" of member states and the constraints stemming from the ECJ's case law: is judicial activism still necessary?' in H.-W. Micklitz and B. De Witte (eds), *The European Court of Justice and the Autonomy of the Member States*, Intersentia, Antwerp-Cambridge 2011, Pt V.

of view, as far as this author is concerned, one simply has to deal with the EU-driven limitations. All the Member States are, in some way, EU legislators. Even if one sets aside the role of Member States in the EU legislative process, one does not have to be negative by definition about all the limitations. The EU dimensions on rules and regulations can be considered individually on their merits. Some limitations can be considered positive in themselves, because they are an improvement of the Dutch system. Some limitations have led to spontaneous harmonisation in a positive way.[65] Other limitations, this author does not necessarily consider positive.

65 The acceptance (by the Dutch Supreme Court) of the seizure of evidence for civil cases in general is a form of spontaneous harmonisation that this author considers positive.

PROCEDURAL AUTONOMY, THE EEA AGREEMENT AND NORWEGIAN LAW

The Art of Bridging a Gap and Maintaining it Too

Anna Nylund

1. THE EEA AGREEMENT, EU AND PROCEDURAL LAW

Until the early 1990s Western Europe consisted of two trade blocks: the European Free Trade Association (EFTA) and the European Economic Community (EEC), which subsequently became the European Union (EU). As dual blocks were considered suboptimal, steps were taken to extend the single market and the four freedoms to EFTA states and to ease the transition to full EU membership. The result was the Agreement on the European Economic Area (EEA),[1] which entered into force in 1994. Today, the EEA has three Member States: Iceland, Liechtenstein and Norway.[2]

Article 1 of the EEA Agreement reiterates the fundamental principle of homogeneity, which requires EEA/EFTA states to ensure uniform interpretation and application of EEA law, (i.e. EU law that has been adopted and general principles of EEA law). Within the scope of the EEA law, EU and EEA/EFTA states have, by far, the same obligations. Nevertheless, dissimilarities in institutional design engender certain differences.[3] EEA law does not encompass home and justice affairs, which has resulted in a palpable – and growing – gap between EEA and EU law in the area of civil procedure.[4] Although the density of EU civil procedure law constantly increases, the EEA Agreement reflects the situation where EU civil procedure law was virtually non-existent, except for the then Brussels Convention,[5] which later became the Brussels I (*bis*) Regulation.[6] The Norwegian government and Norwegian courts, as well as the EFTA Court, attempt to bridge this gap by dynamic interpretation that recognises the interlinkages between substantive and procedural law and the need for effective and equal enforcement of rights. Since Norway – and the other EEA/EFTA states – have explicitly rejected full EU membership, retaining the gap between EEA and EU law is essential for political reasons.

1 Agreement of the European Economic Area [1994] OJ L1/572.

2 Switzerland decided not to enter into the EEA Agreement. Instead, they decided to remain in the EFTA only and to adopt a system where EU Directives and regulations are incorporated on a case-by-case basis.

3 See e.g. C.N.K. Franklin, 'Synthesis: Drawing Some Lines on the Application of the Principle of Consistent Interpretation in National Courts' in C.N.K. Franklin (ed.), *The Effectiveness and Application of EU and EEA Law in National Courts*, Intersentia, Antwerp-Cambridge 2018, pp. 7–10, and G. Baur, 'Decision-Making Procedure and Implementation of New Law' in C. Baudenbacher (ed.), *The Handbook of EEA Law*, Springer, Cham 2016, pp. 45–67.

4 H.H. Fredriksen, 'Bridging the Widening Gap between the EU Treaties and the Agreement on the European Economic Area' (2012) 18 *European Law Journal* 868.

5 Brussels Convention on the Jurisdiction and the Enforcement of Civil and Commercial Matters [1972] OJ L 299/32.

6 Council Regulation (EC) No 44/2001 of 22 December 2000 on jurisdiction and the recognition and enforcement of judgments in civil and commercial matters [2001] OJ L 12/1 (Brussels I Regulation), which was repealed by the European Parliament and Council Regulation (EU) 1215/2012 of 12 December 2012 on jurisdiction and the recognition and enforcement of judgments in civil and commercial matters [2012] OJ L 351/1 (Brussels I *bis* Regulation).

Thus, being an EEA/EFTA state is a constant exercise in simultaneously bridging and maintaining this gap.

Since justice affairs are not part of EEA law, one could draw the conclusion that EEA/EFTA states have full procedural autonomy and that the growing body of EU civil procedure law is mostly irrelevant. However, the conclusion is clearly erroneous: both the intimate connection between civil procedure law and substantive law (rights are of little value if they are not enforceable in practice) and the importance of general principles of law require some level of European inference with national civil procedure law. Thus, a study of procedural autonomy in an EEA/EFTA state also yields an indication of how multi-speed integration effects procedural autonomy, in particular how institutional and legal differences may or may not result in various levels of procedural autonomy.

This chapter investigates how the procedural autonomy of Norway, as an EEA/EFTA state, is limited in practice. Section 2 discusses procedural autonomy under EEA law in general to establish the conception of it under EEA and Norwegian law. Section 3 explores how the legal and institutional setup of the EEA influences procedural autonomy, while section 4 explores new developments in EU and EEA law limits procedural autonomy in novel ways. In section 5, selected problems in bridging and maintaining the gap between EEA and EU law are disseminated in more detail. Finally, some concluding remarks will be offered.

2. PROCEDURAL AUTONOMY, EEA LAW AND NORWEGIAN LAW

Procedural autonomy is not discussed in Norway – it is simply assumed to be a basic principle or doctrine of EEA law, so is the fact that EEA law limits procedural autonomy when national procedural rules hinder effective and equal protection of rights derived from EEA law. The acceptance of the influence of EU law follows partly from the nature of EC/EU law in the early 1990s, prior to the EEA Agreement. Since civil justice matters do not fall under the scope of the EEA Agreement, the perception is that EEA/EFTA states have ample procedural autonomy.[7] The impact of EEA law on Norwegian civil procedure has been discussed

[7] A. Robberstad, *Sivilprosess*, 4th ed., Fagbokforlaget, Bergen 2018, pp. 68–69; J.E.A. Skoghøy, *Tvisteløsning*, 3rd ed., Universitetsforlaget, Oslo 2017, pp. 591–593; I.L. Backer, *Norsk Sivilprosess*, Universitetsforlaget, Oslo 2015, p. 49.

by legal scholars both on the general level and on specific topics.[8] Norwegian authorities appear, however, to believe that the influence is less pronounced than it actually is.[9] In recent years, the topic of the duty to apply EU/EEA consumer law *ex officio* has spurred debate among scholars.[10] However, courts and practitioners have so far not joined the discussion. One reason for their disinterest in the topic could be that scholars assume that the obligations arising from EU/EEA law are aligned with the general duty for substantive case management, in particular the duty to clarify the legal and factual aspects of the case. Another reason might be that the concept of procedural autonomy, and some of its limitations, are built in by design into EEA law.

First, the doctrine of procedural autonomy, and the requirements of effective and equivalent protection forming bounds on autonomy, were well established in the early 1990s when the EEA Agreement was drafted and thus would also be part of the general principles of EEA law.[11] Moreover, Article 3 of the EEA Agreement includes a duty of loyalty, which indirectly requires equal and efficient application of EEA law.

8 E.g. H.H. Fredriksen and M. Strandberg, '*Ex Officio* Application of EU Consumer Protection Law in Norwegian Courts' in A. Nylund and M. Strandberg (eds), *Civil Procedure and Harmonisation of Law*, Intersentia, Antwerp-Cambridge 2019, p. 171; M.A. Hjort, 'The EU's Influence on Norwegian Civil Procedure through National Substantive Law' in A. Nylund and M. Strandberg (eds), *Civil Procedure and Harmonisation of Law*, Intersentia, Antwerp-Cambridge 2019, pp. 111–124; H.H. Fredriksen and M. Strandberg, 'Norwegian Civil Procedure Under the Influence of EU Law' in A. Uzelac and C.H. van Rhee (eds), *Transformation of Civil Justice. Unity and Diversity*, Springer, Heidelberg 2018, p. 41; Skoghøy, above note 7, pp. 600–604; E. Eldjarn, *Materiell prosessledelse*, Cappelen akademisk, Oslo 2016, pp. 237ff; A. Nylund, 'Norway: An Insider Outside – or an Outsider Inside – European Civil Justice' in A. Nylund and B. Krans (eds), *The European Union and National Civil Procedure*, Intersentia, Antwerp-Cambridge 2016, p. 101; H.H. Fredriksen, 'Tvisteloven og EØS-avtalen' [2008] *Tidskrift for Rettsvitenskap* 289.

9 The Expert Committee Report on which the current Norwegian civil procedure act – the Dispute Act (Act of 17.06.2005 No. 90 relating to mediation and procedure in civil disputes *Lov om mekling og rettergang i sivile tvister (tvisteloven)* – is based, only contains a few references to EU/EEA law, see NOU 2001: 32, *Rett på sak*, pp. 154–155. The same applies to the Government Bill on the Dispute Act Ot. prp. No. 51, *Om lov om mekling og rettergang i sivile tvister (tvisteloven)* (2004–2005), p. 32.

10 See Fredriksen and Strandberg, above note 8, for further references.

11 This limitation of procedural autonomy can be traced to the *Rewe/Comet* case. Case 33-76, *Rewe-Zentralfinanz eG et Rewe-Zentral AG v. Landwirtschaftskammer für das Saarland*, ECLI:EU:C:1976:188. For an account of the impact ensuing from non-discrimination, effectiveness and equivalence, see Fredriksen and Strandberg, above note 8, p. 5057.

Second, the Brussels Convention was intimately connected with the EEC from the start, and even more so after the Luxembourg Protocol[12] of 1971 gave the European Court of Justice (ECJ) a pivotal role in ensuring equal interpretation of the Convention. The 1988 Lugano Convention[13] extended the Brussels Convention to EFTA states. The free movement of judgments, 'the fifth freedom', is a natural extension of the internal market. The 2007 Lugano Convention[14] is, with some exceptions, parallel to the Brussels I *bis* Regulation and has to be interpreted uniformly with the Regulation. To increase coherence of the rules on venue, the Dispute Act, the Norwegian civil procedure act, was modelled after the Lugano Convention.[15]

Nevertheless, one would expect more discussion on the topic for at least three reasons. First, the concept of procedural autonomy is unclear in itself; it could be conceptualised as a principle, a shorthand for the CJEU case law on the issue, a doctrine or perhaps something else. Procedural autonomy in EU law is the starting point for procedural autonomy in EEA law. Second, there are clear differences between the institutions and procedures in EEA law and in EU law. These differences may result in differences in the extent and nature of procedural autonomy. These differences will be discussed in further detail in section 3 below.

Third, since the turn of the millennium, rules directly or indirectly relevant for civil procedure law have proliferated in EU hard law, case law and soft law. The interface between procedural law, falling outside the scope of the EEA Agreement, and substantive law, falling under its scope, is blurred because procedural rules are embedded in substantive law. The question is to which extent procedural content falls under the EEA Agreement, and hence restricts procedural autonomy, and whether content that is not EEA-relevant *de facto* restricts procedural autonomy, even if Norway is not obliged to implement it under the EEA law. These questions will be discussed in section 4 below.

---

12 Protocol on the interpretation by the Court of Justice of the Convention of 27 September 1968 on jurisdiction and the enforcement of judgments in civil and commercial matters [1975] OJ L 204/28.

13 Convention on jurisdiction and the enforcement of judgments in civil and commercial matters – Done at Lugano on 16 September 1988 [1988] OJ L 319/9.

14 Convention on jurisdiction and the enforcement of judgments in civil and commercial matters [2007] OJ L 339/3.

15 Nylund, above note 8, pp. 103–106.

3. INSTITUTIONAL DIFFERENCES BETWEEN EEA AND EU LAW AND THEIR IMPACT ON PROCEDURAL AUTONOMY

3.1. DIFFERENCES BETWEEN PRELIMINARY RULINGS AND ADVISORY OPINIONS

The EFTA Court is the equivalent of the Court of Justice of the European Union (CJEU); its main task is to ensure uniform implementation and application of EEA law. The principle of homogeneity requires the EFTA Court to follow the CJEU, but in the absence of rulings from the CJEU, the EFTA Court must interpret EEA law independently. Differences in EEA and EU law sometimes result in disparate interpretation, argumentation and outcomes.[16]

According to Article 34 of the Surveillance and Court Agreement (SCA),[17] courts and tribunals in EEA/ EFTA states have a right to request an advisory opinion on questions of interpretation of EEA law. It is important to notice the differences between Article 34 of the SCA and Article 267 of the Treaty on the Functioning of the European Union (TFEU).[18] First, under Article 34 of the SCA even the highest courts do not have a duty to request an advisory opinion, only a right to do so. As this author has previously written elsewhere,[19] there was a dry spell in Norwegian requests for advisory opinions, particularly from the Supreme Court, but the *Holship* case[20] in 2015 marked a shift in the relations between the EFTA Court and the Norwegian Supreme Court.

---

16 Article 6 of the EEA Agreement which mandates the EFTA Court to interpret EEA law in conformity with the relevant rulings of the Court of Justice of the European Union rendered prior to the EEA Agreement. Under Article 3.2 of the Agreement between the EFTA States on the Establishment of a Surveillance Authority and a Court of Justice, the EFTA Court is obliged to take 'due account' to CJEU rulings. C.N.K. Franklin, 'The EEA Principle of Consistent Interpretation (Or Something that Looks Like It) and Norwegian Courts' in C.N.K. Franklin (ed.), *The Effectiveness and Application of EU and EEA Law in National Courts*, Intersentia, Antwerp-Cambridge 2018, pp. 318–332. H.H. Fredriksen, 'One Market, Two Courts: Legal Pluralism vs. Homogeneity in the European Economic Area' (2010) 79 *Nordic Journal of International Law* 481.

17 Agreement between the EFTA States on the Establishment of a Surveillance Authority and a Court of Justice.

18 Consolidated version of the Treaty on the Functioning of the European Union [2012] OJ C 326/47.

19 Nylund, above note 8, pp. 109–112.

20 Case E-14/15, *Holship* [2016] EFTA Ct. Rep. 240 at [123].

Nevertheless, due to the narrower scope of the EEA Agreement compared to EU law and the relative lower status of the EFTA Court, the number of annual requests is expected to remain considerably lower than in EU Member States.

Second, the opinions are advisory, and therefore not formally binding. This creates some room for manoeuvre for Norwegian courts, which the Supreme Court particularly has utilised.

The Norwegian Supreme Court exploits the leeway by emphasising the non-binding nature of advisory opinions. However, it immediately adds that national courts must give particular weight to EFTA Court judgments because the EFTA Court provides for uniform interpretation and application of EEA law. Therefore, national courts must follow the opinions of the EFTA Court unless 'special circumstances' (i.e. weighty grounds) so require.[21] The Supreme Court expresses a loyalty towards the EFTA Court but also claims a certain space for independent decision-making and, therefore, more procedural autonomy than in EU Member States.

This approach follows directly from the wording of Article 34 of the SCA combined with the duty to loyalty in Article 3 of the EEA Agreement. The gap between EEA and EU law is intentional and EEA courts have a duty to maintain it while remaining loyal to the aim of creating uniform rules.

---

21 E.g. HR-2016-2554-P (*Holship*) at [76]–[77]. An unofficial translation of the judgment is available at <https://www.domstol.no/globalassets/upload/hret/decisions-in-english-translation/case-2014-2089.pdf>. In *Fosen-Linjen* (LF-2015-187242) the Frostating Court of Appeal chose not to follow the reasoning in the advisory opinion it had requested from the EFTA Court (E-16/16, *Fosen-Linjen* [2017] EFTA Ct. Rep. 617). The case was appealed to the Supreme Court, which decided to request a new advisory opinion on substantially the same issue to clarify the content of the first advisory opinion which appear to deviate from CJEU case law (Supreme Court case number 18-077187SIC-HR). According to draft new Rules of Procedure of the EFTA Court Article 97 it is for the national courts 'to assess whether they consider that sufficient guidance is given by an advisory opinion, or whether it appear so them that a further reference to the Court is required' (<https://eftacourt.int/wp-content/uploads/2019/01/EFTA_Court_Draft_RoP_04072018.pdf >). Although the rules of procedure have not entered into force, the Norwegian Supreme Court answered the invitation to further dialogue by asking for 'clarification and amplification, and possibly reconsideration' of the first ruling (E-07/18, *Fosen-Linjen AS II* [2019] EFTA Ct. Rep. xx, at [38]). Fosen-Linjen AS II should therefore not be interpreted (primarily) as the Supreme Court defying the EFTA Court. The EFTA Court did modify the interpretation, although it did not formally revoke it. Other cases where the Supreme Court, having analysed CJEU case law pointing at an alternative conclusion, has distanced itself – tacitly or openly – from the advisory opinion are HR-2009-1319-A (*Pedicel*) and HR-2013-496-A (*STX*).

Furthermore, the Norwegian Supreme Court exploits this autonomy by referring directly to CJEU case law and as long as the analysis results in a fairly clear outcome, it will not request an advisory opinion.[22] The Supreme Court relies on case law from the more prominent court, the CJEU, rather than the 'little brother', the EFTA Court. Moreover, the Norwegian Supreme Court frequently expresses that courts in EEA/EFTA states have an obligation to interpret EEA law independently.

The differences between preliminary references and advisory opinions result in EEA law affording more procedural autonomy to national courts and legislators. However, the degree of the difference should not be exaggerated because the threshold to put aside advisory opinions is high and Norwegian courts actively use CJEU case law and assign it strong persuasive authority.

3.2. DIFFERENCES IN THE CONTENT OF EU AND EEA LAW

The EEA consists of two pillars: the EU pillar and the EEA/EFTA pillar. When the EU adopts EEA-relevant legislation, the EU Commission labels the legislation so. Then, the EEA Joint Committee decides to incorporate it into EEA law by amending one of the annexes to the EEA Agreement. The Joint Committee consists of the Ambassadors of the EEA/EFTA states and representatives of the EU, through the European External Action Service. In theory, EEA/EFTA states are entitled to reject the incorporation of an act but because a rejection undermines the EEA Agreement and

22 The Norwegian Supreme Court has long had a troubled relationship with the EFTA Court, in particular the perceived lack of requests for advisory opinions has been vividly discussed. See e.g. C. Baudenbacher 'The EFTA Court: Structure and Tasks' in C. Baudenbacher (ed.), *The Handbook of EEA Law*, Springer, Cham 2016, p. 157; T.C. Poulsen, 'Norwegian Courts' in C. Baudenbacher (ed.), *The Handbook of EEA Law*, Springer, Cham 2016, p. 271; Nylund, above note 8, pp. 109–112; H.H. Fredriksen and C.N.K. Franklin, 'Of Pragmatism and Principles: The EEA Agreement 20 Years on' (2015) 52 *Common Market Law Review* 629, 672–673; H.H. Fredriksen and G. Mathisen, *EØS-rett*, 2nd ed., Fagbokforlaget, Bergen 2014, pp. 196–203; H.H. Fredriksen, 'The troubled relationship between the Supreme Court of Norway and the EFTA Court: recent developments' in P.C. Müller-Graff and O. Mestad (eds), *The Rising Complexity of European Law*, Berliner Wissenschafts-Verlag, Berlin 2014, pp. 11–37; H.H. Fredriksen, *EU/EØS-rett i norske domstoler, Europautredningen* – Rapport no. 3. Oslo 2011.

the mechanisms of it, EEA/EFTA states refrain from using their right of reservation.[23]

Because the scope of the EEA Agreement is limited, not all EU law is EEA relevant. Factors influencing relevance are *inter alia* whether the piece of legislation falls thematically under the EEA Agreement; the extent to which it enhances the four freedoms and the functioning of the internal market; the nature and extent of the obligations arising out of it; and the extent to which it establishes cooperation beyond the internal market. Additionally, the Norwegian government requires that the contents of the Directive or Regulation must be acceptable.[24]

Based on these criteria, the Norwegian government usually denies the EEA relevance of EU law with primarily procedural content. The more the substantive content dominates, the more likely the legislation will be EEA relevant. The Norwegian government has a consistent policy of rejecting the EEA relevance of civil procedure content. Consequently, sometimes a Directive, Regulation or parts of it, are not incorporated into the EEA Agreement. These policies follow directly from the ambit of EEA law: accepting instruments with significant procedural law content amount to a tangible extension of the EEA Agreement. Despite the inclination to reject civil procedural content, the Norwegian government recognises the need for some procedural approximation and is thus willing to make exceptions.[25] Moreover, Norway has voluntarily implemented some of the procedural EU law. Voluntary harmonisation will be discussed in more detail below in section 4.

The scope of the EEA Agreement combined with the criterion of acceptability increases procedural autonomy of EEA/EFTA states, because they can – at least to some extent – pick and choose which acts they consider binding upon themselves.

---

23 Norway originally rejected the third Postal Directive (European Parliament and Council Directive 2008/6/EC of 20 February 2008 amending Directive 97/67/EC with regard to the full accomplishment of the internal market of Community postal services [2008] OJ L 52/3) in 2013. However, after the 2013 Parliamentary elections, the Directive was implemented in Norway. See also K. Almestad, 'The Notion of "Opting Out"' in C. Baudenbacher (ed.), *The Handbook of EEA Law*, Springer, Cham 2016, pp. 85–94.

24 See e.g. Nærings- og fiskeridepartementet, *Høringsnotat. Forslag til endringer i konkurranseloven – gjennomføring i norsk rett av direktiv 2014/104/EU om privat håndheving av EU/EØS-konkurransereglene*, pp. 10–14.

25 See e.g. Nærings- og fiskeridepartementet, above note 24, pp. 10–14.

3.3. THE JURISDICTION OF THE EFTA COURT

Another institutional difference between EEA and EU law impacting procedural autonomy is that the jurisdiction of the EFTA Court is limited to EEA law. Thus, it does not have the power to rule on the Lugano Convention, which, although it is not formally a part of EEA law, is essentially an extension of EEA law. Courts in EEA/EFTA states must consequently interpret the Convention without having the option of requesting an advisory opinion. Under Protocol 2 on the uniform interpretation of the Convention and on the Standing Committee Lugano states have an obligation to interpret the Convention uniformly.[26]

The Norwegian Supreme Court has been loyal to CJEU case law except for cases where the question of whether the Convention is applicable.[27] In these cases, the Norwegian Supreme Court has departed from the method of interpretation the CJEU uses and thus it has wrongly rejected Norwegian jurisdiction in cases where the connection to Norway is weak. However, these cases reflect, in the author's opinion, insufficient knowledge of the Convention rather than the Supreme Court being deliberately defiant.[28] The lack of access to preliminary rulings impedes uniform interpretation and application of European law although uniformity is the express aim of the Lugano Convention. Thus, slightly more leeway for national courts could have, and in this case has, detrimental effects on legal certainty and equal interpretation. Due to the obligation to ensure uniform interpretation and the paramount role of the CJEU in interpreting and developing the Brussels I bis Regulation, and thus the parallel provisions in the Lugano Convention, the room for manoeuvre for Norwegian courts should be the same as for courts in EU Member States.

Voluntary implementation of EU civil procedure law results in lack of access to advisory opinions. Because implementation is voluntary and

---

26 A. Borrás, I. Neophytou and F. Pocar, *13th Report on National Case Law Relating to the Lugano Conventions* (May 2012) <https://www.bj.admin.ch/dam/data/bj/wirtschaft/privatrecht/lugjurispr-13-e.pdf>.

27 A. Nylund, 'Luganokonvensjonen i Høyestererett – et kritisk blikk' in T. Haugli, G. Eriksen and I.U. Jakobsen (eds), *Rettsvitenskap under nordlys og midnattssol*, Fagbokforlaget, Bergen 2018, footnote 19 which lists 10 cases in the period 2010–2015. In 2016–2018, the Supreme Court ruled on the Lugano Convention in HR-2018-936-U, HR-2018-869-A, HR-2017-2472-U, HR-2017-1297-A. Considering that in only two of these cases the Supreme Court interpreted the Lugano Convention in a manner that is not consistent with CJEU case law, the Court can be characterised as predominantly loyal. See Nylund, above note 8, pp. 105–106.

28 Nylund, above note 27, p. 227.

does not follow from an obligation to do so, the EFTA Court does not have jurisdiction in these cases. CJEU case law related to this legislation is not binding for Norwegian courts, even if Norwegian courts will assign it persuasive authority. When in doubt of how to interpret voluntarily implemented EU law, Norwegian courts must manage on their own.

Both these situations illustrate how procedural autonomy comes with caveats. The rationale of common rules is harmonisation and thus Norwegian courts should as far as possible be bound by CJEU case law. When encountered with hard cases, Norwegian courts must solve difficult cases to their best abilities, and they are barred from contributing to the development of European law.

4. THE CHANGING LANDSCAPE OF EEA LAW AND PROCEDURAL AUTONOMY

At least four developments influencing procedural autonomy have arisen or have been strengthened since Norway entered into the EEA Agreement 25 years ago.

4.1. FUNDAMENTAL RIGHTS IN EU AND EEA LAW

In contrast to the 1990s, fundamental rights, which include the right to a fair trial, are explicitly recognised as a part of EU and EEA law. The EU Fundamental Rights Charter[29] as such is not part of EEA law and therefore not binding for Norway. It is, however, indirectly included in EEA law and thus limits procedural autonomy.

The EFTA Court has established in a range of judgments that 'provisions of the EEA Agreement [...] are to be interpreted in the light of fundamental rights',[30] in particular the European Convention on Human Rights and European Court of Human Rights (ECtHR) judgments.[31]

29 Charter of Fundamental Rights of the European Union [2000] OJ C 364/1.

30 Case E-2/03, *Ásgeirsson* [2003] EFTA Ct. Rep. 185 at [23].

31 See also Joined Cases E-3/13 and E-20/13, *Fred. Olsen* [2014] EFTA Ct. Rep. 400 at [224]; Case E-14/11, *DB Schenker v. ESA (Schenker I)* [2012] EFTA Ct. Rep. 1178 at [166]; Case E-18/11, *Irish Bank* [2012] EFTA Ct. Rep. 592 at [63]; Case E-15/10, *Posten Norge* [2012] EFTA Ct. Rep. 246 at [85]; Case E-4/11, *Arnulf Clauder* [2011] EFTA Ct. Rep. 216 at [49]; Case E-12/10, *ESA v. Iceland* [2011] EFTA Ct. Rep. 117 at [60]; Case E-2/02, *Bellona* [2003] EFTA Ct. Rep. 52 at [37]; Case E-8/97, *TV 1000 Sverige v. Norway* [1998] EFTA Ct. Rep. 68 at [26].

The EFTA Court has also found that the 'principle of effective judicial protection including the right to a fair trial … is a general principle of EEA law'[32] and that '[f]undamental rights form part of the unwritten principles of EEA law.'[33] By using creative interpretation, the EFTA Court has been able to fill the lacuna that the absence of an EEA equivalent of the EU Charter has created, and therefore bridged the gap between EU and EEA law.[34]

In the *Holship* plenary judgment,[35] the Norwegian Supreme Court had to strike a balance between the freedom of association and the freedom of establishment. It interpreted both rights in the light of domestic and supranational law. The majority of justices held that '[f]undamental rights under EU and EEA law include, inter alia, the European Convention on Human Rights and other fundamental international human rights'.[36] In discussing the human rights enshrined in EEA law, the Supreme Court consistently referred to EU law, in particular CJEU case law.[37]

Although the Supreme Court acknowledged the status of fundamental rights in EEA law, and thus, indirectly, that these rights limit national procedural autonomy, it still tried to distance itself from being bound by fundamental rights in EEA and EU law. Most provision on human rights in the Norwegian Constitution entered into force in 2014. They are modelled after the ECHR, the EU Charter and other international documents, and therefore case law on these instruments is of paramount importance when

---

32 Case E-15/10, *Posten Norge*, above note 27, at [86].

33 Case E-14/15, *Holship* [2016] EFTA Ct. Rep. 240 at [123].

34 R. Spano, 'The EFTA Court and Fundamental Rights' (2017) 13 *European Constitutional Law Review* 475; D.T. Björgvinsson, 'Fundamental Rights in EEA Law' in EFTA Court (ed.), *The EEA and the EFTA Court – Decentered Integration*, Hart Publishing, Oxford 2014, p. 278.

35 *Holship*, above note 21.

36 *Holship*, above note 21, at [111]. The majority of ten justices of the Norwegian Supreme Court referred to Case C-260/89, *ERT (Elliniki Radiophonia AE and Panellinia Omospondia Syllogon Prossopikou v. Dimotiki Etairia Plifoforissis and Sotirios Kouvelas and Nicolaos Avdellas and others)*, ECLI:EU:C:1991:254 at [41]; Case C-112/00, *Eugen Schmidberger, Internationale Transporte v. Republik Österreich*, ECLI:EU:C:2003:333 at [71ff]; Case C-341/05, *Laval un Partneri Ltd v. Svenska Byggnadsarbetareförbundet, Svenska Byggnadsarbetareförbundets avdelning 1, Byggettan and Svenska Elektrikerförbundet*, ECLI:EU:C:2007:809 at [90]; Case C-438/05, *International Transport Workers' Federation and Finnish Seamen's Union v. Viking Line ABP and OÜ Viking Line Eesti*, ECLI:EU:C:2007:772 at [43ff]; Case C-271/08, *The European Commission v. The Federal Republic of Germany*, ECLI:EU:C:2010:426 at [37ff]. The Supreme Court explicitly mentioned the EU Charter and its relevance for EU law. The minority of seven justices did not discuss whether fundamental rights are part of EEA and EU law.

37 *Holship*, above note 21, at [111]–[113].

interpreting the Constitution. In *Holship*, the Supreme Court stated *obiter dictum* that although section 101 of the Constitution enshrining freedom of association is interpreted in the same manner as the corresponding provisions in the ECHR and the EU Charter, it retains the right to interpret section 101 in a different manner than the European courts do.[38] This comment is a disclaimer creating leeway for autonomy in the future. Although the *Holship* case concerned labour rights, the argumentation is applicable to rights enshrined in Article 6 of the ECHR and Article 47 of the EU Charter.[39]

The *Holship* case illustrates how the gap between EU and EEA law can be bridged by pragmatism and the tacit cooperation between the CJEU, the ECtHR, the EFTA Court and the Norwegian Supreme Court. Therefore, differences in procedural autonomy between EEA and EU law are perhaps not very considerable, after all.

4.2. PROCEDURAL RULES IN EU/EEA SUBSTANTIVE LAW

Procedural rules deriving from EU substantive law influence Norwegian procedural law. Substantive law of the internal market is binding for Norway as EEA law. Norway consequently has an obligation to implement hard law and case law with procedural implications.[40] The presumption that a non-conformity of goods that appear within six months of purchase have existed at the time of delivery of the goods serves as an example.[41] It has been implemented in Norwegian law in the Consumer Sales Act section 18 subsection 2.[42] There are numerous other examples.[43]

Norwegian courts are obliged to apply selected aspects of consumer and competition law *ex officio*, in the same manner as courts in EU Member States. These obligations have not been problematised in Norwegian law: they are accepted as an inevitable consequence of EEA law.[44]

---

38 *Holship*, above note 21, at [86].

39 For examples of potential situations where the Charter could impact Norwegian Law, see Fredriksen and Strandberg, above note 8, pp. 45–49.

40 For an overview, see Hjort, above note 8; Fredriksen and Strandberg, above note 8.

41 Article 5.3 of European Parliament and Council Directive 1999/44/EC of 25 May 1999 on certain aspects of the sale of consumer goods and associated guarantees [1999] OJ L 171/12.

42 Lov 21. juni 2002 nr. 34 om forbrukerkjøp.

43 For a more detailed analysis of the impact of EU hard law and case law, see Fredriksen and Strandberg, above note 8.

44 See text and references accompanying note 8 above.

4.3. THE WIDENING SCOPE OF THE EEA AGREEMENT

As mentioned above, cooperation in justice matters are not included in the EEA Agreement. Thus, neither Norway nor the EU consider EU hard law enacted under the competencies foreseen in TFEU Article 81 on judicial cooperation in civil matters EEA-relevant. When TFEU Article 114 on approximation of laws to ensure the functioning of the internal market constitutes the legal basis for EU law with procedural content, the outcome is less clear. These rules, which are oftentimes sectoral, appear to pass the barrier more often than procedural rules intended for general cases. Again, consumer law serves as an example.

Norway has implemented the Consumer Alternative Dispute Resolution (ADR) Directive[45] and the Consumer Online Dispute Resolution (ODR) Regulation[46] and accepted them as EEA relevant, because otherwise Norwegian consumer would have had a disadvantage in cross-border cases vis-à-vis consumers in EU Member States. Although consumer dispute resolution boards have been omnipresent in Norwegian consumer law for decades, implementing the Consumer ADR Directive allowed for consolidation of the boards and their regulations and the Consumer ODR Regulation introduced electronic platforms facilitating cross-border disputes. EU law was an impetus for national reforms and served as a benchmark.[47] Their primarily procedural content raised the threshold of accepting them as EEA relevant, yet the fact that consumer ADR and ODR are situated at the interface of procedural and substantive law, and thus that they defy being placed primarily in either domain, is likely to have paved the way.

The rules on consumer ADR and ODR indicate that maintaining the gap between EEA law and EU law is increasingly difficult as the density

---

45 European Parliament and Council Directive 2013/11/EU of 21 May 2013 on alternative dispute resolution for consumer disputes and amending Regulation (EC) No 2006/2004 and Directive 2009/22/EC (Directive on consumer ADR) [2013] OJ L 165/63.

46 European Parliament and of the Council Regulation (EU) No 524/2013 of 21 May 2013 on online dispute resolution for consumer disputes and amending Regulation (EC) No 2006/2004 and Directive 2009/22/EC (Regulation on consumer ODR) [2013] OJ L 165/1.

47 Prop.145 L (2015-2016) Lov om Forbrukerklageutvalget (forbrukerklageloven), pp. 7–8; Prop.32 L (2015-2016) Lov om klageorganser for forbrukersaker (gjennomføring av direktiv 2013/11/EU af forordning nr. 524/2013) og endringer i enkelte andre lover, p. 12; NOU 2010:11 Nemndsbehandling av forbrukertvister. Barne-, likestillings- og inkluderingsdepartementet, pp. 56–59.

of EU civil procedure law increases. Hence, differences in procedural autonomy decreases accordingly.

4.4. 'VOLUNTARY' IMPLEMENTATION

Harmonisation through 'voluntary' implementation poses a *de facto* limit to procedural autonomy of EEA/EFTA states. Although Norway does not have a duty under the EEA Agreement to implement EU civil procedure law it may be sensible or even necessary to do so to create a level playing field in the internal market. Harmonisation, or at least approximation, of procedural rules is essential to maintain a single market where all players play by the same rules, at least for a small country such as Norway. While Norway has no formal obligation to implement EU procedural law, due to the possibly considerable adverse consequences of non-implementation, the procedural autonomy of Norway is *de facto* limited. Intellectual property rights are one example.

Norway has implemented the IP Rights Enforcement Directive[48] on a 'voluntary' basis in Chapter 28A of the Dispute Act.[49] Affording intellectual property rights less protection in Norway than in EU Member States would have been highly problematic considering Norway is part of the internal market.[50]

However, Norway is unable to participate in the unitary patent protection through European patents[51] and the Unified Patent Court,[52] even though it would desire to do so, because cooperation is limited to EU Member States.[53] As a result, obtaining a patent is more costly for Norwegian companies, because they must apply for both a Norwegian and a European unified patent to obtain protection across the internal market

---

48 European Parliament and Council Directive 2004/48/EC of 29 April 2004 on the enforcement of intellectual property rights [2004] OJ L 157/45.

49 For a more detailed discussion of the implementation of the Directive, see Hjort, above note 8, pp. 121–123.

50 Prop.81 L (2012-2013) Endringer i lovgivningen om industrielt rettsvern m.m. (styrking av håndhevingsreglene), p. 13.

51 European Parliament and Council Regulation (EU) No 1257/2012 of 17 December 2012 implementing enhanced cooperation in the area of the creation of unitary patent protection [2012] OJ L 361/1.

52 Agreement on a Unified Patent Court 2013/C/175/01 [2013] OJ C 175/1.

53 In Opinion 1/09 of the Full Court, ECLI:EU:C:2011:123, the CJEU opined that a court system including non-Member States is not compatible with EU law.

and they risk patent litigation concerning both the European and the Norwegian patent.

A challenge associated with voluntary implementation is, as explained above in section 3.3, that the EFTA Court lacks jurisdiction to give advisory opinions in these cases. Since implementation is voluntary, so is ensuring uniform application. As a result, Norwegian courts could use their room for manoeuvre by interpreting and applying the rules differently than in EU Member States. It should be noted, however, that exploiting procedural autonomy comes with a cost: the less uniform the application of the 'voluntarily' implemented rules, the less the rationale of voluntary implementation – ensuring equal enforcement of rights – is fulfilled. 'Voluntary' implementation requires in effect equal application, where the room for manoeuvre is confined in practice although not formally. Indeed, one could question whether using the word 'voluntary' is appropriate at all.

5. ROAD BUMPS IN THE IMPLEMENTATION OF PROCEDURAL EEA LAW

Certain features of the EEA Agreement impede voluntary implementation by creating bumps in the road to equal and effective protection of rights. The Directive on private enforcement of competition law (Antitrust Damages Directive)[54] serves as an example. The Directive obliges Member States to implement specific mechanisms facilitating private enforcement of competition law, *inter alia* rules on disclosure of evidence and consensual dispute resolution processes.

Private enforcement of competition law is tied to public enforcement of the same rules. Articles 53 and 54 of the EEA Agreement correspond to the provisions on enforcement of competition law in Articles 101 and 102 of the TFEU. The Regulation 1/2003[55] is transposed in EEA law. The Regulation creates a decentralised system, where national competition authorities cooperate directly and have the primary responsibility for

[54] European Parliament and Council Directive 2014/104/EU of 26 November 2014 on certain rules governing actions for damages under national law for infringements of the competition law provisions of the Member States and of the European Union [2014] OJ L 349/1.

[55] Council Regulation (EC) No 1/2003 of 16 December 2002 on the implementation of the rules on competition laid down in Articles 81 and 82 of the Treaty [2003] OJ L 1/1.

enforcing EU competition law.[56] The decentralised system does not apply across the EU and EEA pillars, only within them. Thus, authorities and courts in EU Member States can request information from authorities in other EU Member States, but not from authorities in EEA/EFTA states, and vice versa, at least according to the official Norwegian view.[57] The Norwegian government maintains that the EEA Agreement as such does not allow decentralised enforcement, and that decentralised enforcement ensues from national law,[58] in Norway section 9 of the Competition Act.[59] Articles 4–6 of Protocol 4 of the SCA could also be considered as the legal basis for decentralised enforcement within the EEA pillar.

The Norwegian government accepted immediately that articles regulating substantive issues in the Antitrust Damages Directive are EEA relevant. After careful consideration, it found that the same is true for the civil procedural rules in the Directive.[60] The reason is that the adverse effects of non-incorporation would be tangible: Residents of EEA/EFTA states would not be able to enforce their rights on an equal footing with residents of EU Member States. Nevertheless, the Norwegian government also underlined that accepting procedural rules as EEA relevant was an exception. The strategy of insisting on this being an exception is a logical consequence of differences in EEA law and EU law, ensuing from the wish to remain outside the EU.

Accepting the entire Directive as EEA relevant did not suffice: A significant obstacle remains. The Antitrust Damages Directive requires, in practice, decentralised enforcement of competition law, i.e. direct cooperation between national authorities across the two pillars of EEA law. As mentioned above, there is currently no cross-pillar decentralised enforcement in place. The Norwegian government has commenced negotiations with the EU Commission on decentralising enforcement of competition law across the two EEA pillars. Additionally, a new chapter

56 E.g. F. Müller, 'The New Council Regulation (EC) No. 1/2003 on the Implementation of the Rules on Competition' (2004) 5 *German Law Review* 721.

57 Cooperation between the Nordic countries is an exception to this rule due to the existence of an agreement from 2001 on cooperation between the competition authorities of the Nordic countries. See S. Teigum, 'Competition Law: A National Perspective' in C. Baudenbacher (ed.), *The Handbook of EEA Law*, Springer, Cham 2016, p. 557.

58 Nærings- og fiskeridepartementet, above note 24, p. 8.

59 Lov 5. mars 2004 nr. 12 om konkurranse mellom foretak og kontroll med foretakssammenslutninger (konkurranseloven).

60 Nærings- og fiskeridepartementet, above note 24, pp. 10–14.

to the Competition Act[61] that would implement the Directive has been drafted. The drafted legislation would add many procedural rules which would deviate from the general rules in the Dispute Act, *inter alia* rules on disclosure of evidence, and rules mandating courts to suspend proceedings when the parties are engaged in consensual dispute resolution.

The negotiations between Norway (and other EEA/EFTA states) and the Commission have stranded since the Government Consultation Paper was sent in December 2015. The Brexit election in June 2016 has hindered the negotiations because resources have been devoted to the Brexit process, so has the reluctance of the EU to accept symmetrical decentralised enforcement.[62] The timeline of incorporation of the Antitrust Damages Directive is still unknown.

The Antitrust Damages Directive illustrates how the pragmatic attitude of the Norwegian government helps solve many of the problems arising from multi-speed integration, but it cannot smooth all bumps in the road.

6. CONCLUDING REMARKS ON PROCEDURAL AUTONOMY AND MULTI-SPEED INTEGRATION

Norway has, in theory, a considerably wider procedural autonomy than EU Member States, since far from all EU civil procedure hard law is EEA relevant and thus transformed to EEA law. In practice, differences in procedural autonomy are much smaller. The increasing density of procedural rules in EU law, as well as its constitutionalisation, bring procedural rules into EEA law in multiple ways: through general principles of EEA law, hard law, international treaties serving as an informal extension of EEA law,[63] case law and voluntary harmonisation. Due to institutional and legal

---

61 Lov om konkurranse mellom foretak og kontroll med foretakssammenslutninger, lov av 5. mars 2004 nr. 12.

62 Fredriksen and Strandberg, above note 8, p. 60.

63 The Lugano Convention is the main example, but the Convention of 23 November 2007 on the International Recovery of Child Support and Other Forms of Family Maintenance is entangled with EU maintenance law and partly also interconnected with EEA law. See V. Lipp, 'Maintenance and Multi-Level Harmonisation: A European Union Perspective' in A. Nylund and M. Strandberg (eds), *Civil Procedure and Harmonisation of Laws*, Intersentia, Antwerp-Cambridge 2019, pp. 193–208; A. Nylund, 'Family Maintenance and Multi-Speed Integration: A Norwegian Perspective' in A. Nylund and M. Strandberg (eds), *Civil Procedure and Harmonisation of Laws*, Intersentia, Antwerp-Cambridge 2019, pp. 209–230.

differences between EU and EEA law as well as the need to keep the gap between these manageable, establishing the exact nature and extent of the procedural autonomy in EEA law is onerous.

On the one hand, the Norwegian government and Norwegian courts must insist on the differences between EU law and EEA law and consequently maintain a perception of more room to manoeuvre within the realm of EEA law. On the other hand, a level playing field necessitates identical, or at least very similar, procedural rules across the single market to the extent that harmonisation has taken place at the EU level. Hence, the Norwegian government and Norwegian courts must simultaneously maintain the gap and bridge the gap.

Voluntary implementation illustrates that insisting on maximum procedural autonomy is not advisable; rather exploiting the additional autonomy that EEA law bestows may be an impediment, at least for small states such as Norway. The cost of autonomy is a cumbersome enforcement of rights, thus Norway and other EEA/EFTA states increasingly exchange procedural autonomy for efficient and equal enforcement of EU/EEA law. Procedural autonomy is not an end in itself and it is in many aspects void of intrinsic value.

The future of multi-speed integration and EEA law depends *inter alia* on whether Brexit will have a detrimental effect on the possibilities to adopt European treaties on judicial cooperation such as taking of evidence,[64] and on labelling EU hard law with a significant procedural component as EEA relevant. For the latter, the question is also whether the Norwegian stance on accepting the EEA relevance turns to be a slippery slope, where the threshold to incorporate procedural content diminishes for each act that is incorporated into EEA law.

64 See Fredriksen and Strandberg, above note 8, p. 58 for further details on ongoing and proposed negotiations on the topics.

A POLISH PERSPECTIVE ON COLLECTIVE CIVIL PROCEEDINGS

Reluctance to Follow EU Recommendations?

Anna Piszcz*

1. INTRODUCTION

In Poland, there exist a few systems and hierarchies of state courts (as well as the State Tribunal and the Constitutional Tribunal) with hugely varied procedures and differentiated structures. The Polish judicial system consists of the Supreme Court, administrative courts (including the Supreme Administrative Court), military courts and ordinary courts (civil cases, among others, are dealt with by them). Ordinary courts include 321 district courts (*sądy rejonowe*), 45 regional courts (*sądy okręgowe*) and 11 courts of appeal (*sądy apelacyjne*). They are organised into divisions,

* This chapter is related to the author's single scientific activity Miniatura 2 financed by the National Science Centre, Poland (reg. no. 2018/02/X/HS5/03367). ORCID: 0000-0001-7163-3292.

first and foremost criminal divisions and civil divisions; judges are usually specialised in certain fields of law. Decisions of district courts can be appealed to a competent regional court and decisions adopted by regional courts as courts of first instance to a competent court of appeal (two-instance proceedings).

There is one thing on which both Polish EU-sceptics and Polish EU-enthusiasts must agree: for over a dozen years Polish civil law, including civil procedural law, has been undergoing intensive EU-Europeanisation.[1] The main focus of this chapter is on the relationship between EU law and Polish civil procedural law in the area of collective civil proceedings; the impact of other European fora on Polish law, including the impact of the European Court of Human Rights, are not going to be analysed therein.

The normative (formal) Europeanisation is the process whereby domestic civil law is adapted to conform to EU rules and may be related to substantive laws, the institutional design of administration of justice, as well as procedural laws. The first and second are beyond the scope of this chapter and the latter may be associated with the phenomenon traditionally branded as national procedural autonomy. According to *Rewe/Comet* doctrine,[2] in the absence of EU rules on the subject, it is for the domestic legal system of each Member State to determine the procedural framework (procedural autonomy) governing actions at law intended to ensure the protection of the rights which citizens derive from the direct effect of EU law,[3] but this national design must fully respect the EU principles of equivalence and effectiveness. This analysis will be

---

1 Rafał Mańko, 'The Unification of Private Law in Europe from the Perspective of the Polish Legal Culture' (2007–2008) 11 *Yearbook of Polish European Studies* 123; Anna Piszcz, 'Polish Civil Proceedings: How Much Europeanised?' in Anna Nylund and Bart H. Krans (eds), *The European Union and National Civil Procedure. A smooth process or a rocky road for Member States?*, Intersentia, Antwerp-Cambridge 2016, p. 115. Also, Robert Grzeszczak, 'Europeanisation of Polish Law Following Poland's Accession to the European Union' (2017) 71 *Studia Iuridica* 61. On the 'EU-Europeanisation' or 'Unionisation', Andrea Lenschow, 'Europeanisation of public policy' in Jeremy John Richardson (ed.), *European Union: Power and Policy-making*, Routledge, Abingdon 2006, p. 59.

2 Case 33/76, *Rewe-Zentralfinanz eG et Rewe-Zentral AG v. Landwirtschaftskammer für das Saarland*, ECLI:EU:C:1976:188; Case 45/76, *Comet BV v. Produktschap voor Siergewassen*, ECLI:EU:C:1976:191. For more see, Marcus Klamert, *The Principle of Loyalty in EU Law*, Oxford University Press, Oxford 2014, p. 125.

3 It is also for them to designate the courts having jurisdiction internally (institutional autonomy).

accommodated within this conceptual framework, even though some commentators emphasise that the concept of national procedural and institutional autonomy of the Member States no longer explains the very complicated relationship between the EU law and national rules.[4]

The purpose of this chapter is to assess the phenomenon of the procedural autonomy of Poland in the area of collective civil proceedings against the background of the current legislation and jurisprudence. The second section attempts to answer a conceptual question: is the procedural autonomy principle conceptualised in Poland at all, and if so, how is it conceptualised? The second question is purely descriptive: is there any impact of EU soft law regarding collective civil proceedings on Polish procedural law and what are the differences between the former and the latter? These questions are ancillary to the third question and provide the frameworks on the basis of which a concrete assessment will be done. The third question, finally, is a contextualised question: how can the discussed phenomena be assessed taking into account, among others, recent developments and future prospects in EU legislation?

2. RECOGNITION OF THE CONCEPT

How is procedural autonomy understood and conceptualised in Poland? It is well worth researching how it is recognised not only by the judiciary (state courts and tribunals) but also by the two other 'arms' of the state (legislature and executive), as well as by academics.

The views on procedural autonomy taken by legislature, executive and the judiciary (see below) may be derived from academia and vice versa,

---

4 Michal Bobek, 'Why There Is No Principle of "Procedural Autonomy" of the Member States?' in Bruno de Witte and Hans Micklitz (eds), *The European Court of Justice and the Autonomy of the Member States*, Intersentia, Antwerp-Cambridge 2012, p. 305; Fabrizio Cafaggi, 'Towards Collaborative Governance of European Remedial and Procedural Law?' (2018) 19 *Theoretical Inquiries in Law* 254; Andrzej Wróbel, 'Autonomia proceduralna państw członkowskich. Zasada efektywności i zasada efektywnej ochrony sądowej w prawie Unii Europejskiej' ['Procedural Autonomy of EU Member States: Principle of Effectiveness and Effective Judicial Protection'] (2005) 67(1) *Ruch Prawniczy, Ekonomiczny i Socjologiczny* 35. See also, Katri Havu, 'EU law in Member State courts: "Adequate judicial protection" and effective application – ambiguities and nonsequiturs in guidance by the Court of Justice?' (2016) 8(1) *Contemporary Readings in Law and Social Justice* 159; Anna Wallerman, 'Towards an EU law doctrine on the exercise of discretion in national courts? The Member States' self-imposed limits on national procedural autonomy' (2016) 53(2) *Common Market Law Review* 339–340.

since many experts of the Bureau of Research at the Chancellery of the *Sejm* (the lower house of the Polish Parliament), governmental experts and judges are at the same time researchers. There are plenty of publications by Polish authors recognising the procedural autonomy as well as their limits, both classics and newer ones recognising developments of the concept.[5]

As for legislature and executive, their views on the concept discussed here may be found mainly: (1) in the case of legislature – in opinions of the Bureau of Research at the Chancellery of the *Sejm* and in

---

5 E.g. Andrzej Wróbel, 'Autonomia proceduralna państw członkowskich. Zasada efektywności i zasada efektywnej ochrony sądowej w prawie Unii Europejskiej' ['Procedural autonomy of member states. Principle of effectiveness and principle of effective judicial protection in EU law'] (2005) 67(1) *Ruch Prawniczy, Ekonomiczny i Socjologiczny* 35 (the author is a judge of the Supreme Court); Andrzej Wróbel, 'Europeizacja polskiego prawa o postępowaniu administracyjnym a autonomia proceduralna państw członkowskich Unii Europejskiej' ['Europeanisation of Polish law on administrative proceedings and the procedural autonomy of member states of European Union'] in Ireneusz Nowikowski and Iwona Rzucidło (eds), *Europeizacja prawa administracyjnego* [*Europeanisation of administrative law*], UMCS, Lublin 2011, p. 24; Zbigniew Kmieciak, 'Zasada autonomii proceduralnej państw członkowskich UE i jej konsekwencje dla procesu orzekania przez sądy administracyjne i organy administracji publicznej' ['The principle of procedural autonomy of EU member states and its consequences for the process of adjudication by administrative courts and public administration bodies'] (2009) 2 *Zeszyty Naukowe Sądownictwa Administracyjnego* 9 (the author is a judge of the Supreme Administrative Court); Monika Domańska, 'Miejsce zasady autonomii proceduralnej państw członkowskich wśród zasad ogólnych prawa wspólnotowego' ['The place of the principle of the procedural autonomy of member states among the general principles of Community law'] in Cezary Mik (ed.), *Zasady ogólne prawa wspólnotowego* [*General principles of Community law*], TNOiK, Toruń 2007, p. 111 (the author is an assistant to a judge of the Supreme Court); Tomasz T. Koncewicz, 'Autonomia proceduralna państw członkowskich' ['Procedural autonomy of member states'] (2003) 11–12 *Palestra* 207; Tomasz T. Koncewicz, 'Autonomia proceduralna państw członkowskich. Pragmatyczne przewartościowanie czy pryncypialne utrzymywanie status quo? Cz. 1 i 2' ['Procedural autonomy of member states. Pragmatic reevaluation or principled maintenance of the status quo? Part 1 and 2'] (2011) 5–6 *Palestra* 187 and (2011) 7–8 *Palestra* 167. Tomasz T. Koncewicz, 'Autonomia proceduralna państw członkowskich. Zmierzch czy nowe otwarcie? Uwagi na marginesie wyroku Trybunału Sprawiedliwości w sprawie Unibet' ['Procedural autonomy of member states. Twilight or new opening? Observations on the sidelines of the judgment of the Court of Justice in the Unibet case'] (2012) 11–12 *Palestra* 194; Katarzyna Gajda-Roszczynialska, 'Test sześciu warunków unijnego standardu pojęcia „sądu" a polski wymiar sprawiedliwości – rozważania na kanwie wyroku TSUE z 27.2.2018 r. w sprawie C-64/16 Associação Sindical dos Juízes Portugueses' ['Test of six conditions of the EU standard for the concept of "court" and the Polish administration of justice system – considerations based on the CJEU judgment of 27.2.2018 in case C-64/16 Associação Sindical dos Juízes Portugueses'] (2018) 2 *Iustitia* 61 (the author is a judge of a district court, civil division).

facts of the Constitutional Tribunal judgments, where standpoints of the *Sejm* as one of the participants to proceedings are presented; and (2) in the case of executive – in explanatory notes accompanying draft statutes from the government. It can be found that the Constitutional Tribunal presented standpoints of the *Sejm* recognising the procedural autonomy and the requirement of effectiveness regarding national solutions.[6] The Bureau of Research used to recognise the procedural autonomy together with the limiting role of the principles of equivalence and effectiveness.[7] Also, the government referred to the procedural autonomy (even though not to its limits) and the *International Fruit* case[8] when amending provisions of the Law on Ordinary Courts Organisation with regard to the competence of courts issuing writs of execution.[9]

Have legislature and executive changed the way they understand the procedural autonomy in recent years? It is not, as a rule, explicitly manifested in official documents. Explanatory notes accompanying draft statutes that re-organise the Polish judiciary[10] show no traces of references to the procedural (or institutional) autonomy of Poland. Explanatory notes accompanying the draft 2017 Act on the Supreme Court prepared by the President of the Republic of Poland only mention that the draft Act intends to avoid bringing Poland to a situation where, in the face of previous judgments of the EU Court of Justice (CJEU), which specify the conditions of lawful interference in the judiciary personnel, retired Supreme Court judges would have to be reinstated or paid high compensations. The President assessed his proposed draft Act as balanced, but at the same time radical as far as it is possible respecting the Constitution of the Republic of Poland. At the same time, he stated that the subject matter of the draft Act is not covered

---

6 Judgment of 11.03.2015, No. P 4/14; judgment of 16.10.2012, No. K 4/10. The cases were not related to private law provisions.

7 E.g. opinions of 10.09.2012, No. BAS-WAPEiM-2194/12, 12.08.2010, No. BAS-WAPEiM-1471/10, 12.08.2010, No. BAS-WAPEiM-1472/10.

8 Joined cases 51/71 to 54/71, *International Fruit Company NV and others v. Produktschap voor groenten en fruit*, ECLI:EU:C:1971:128.

9 Explanatory notes accompanying the 2011 draft Amendment Act to the Law on Ordinary Courts Organisation. In Polish, available at: <http://orka.sejm.gov.pl/Druki6ka.nsf/wgdruku/3833>.

10 Explanatory notes accompanying draft 2017 Act on the Supreme Court (Journal of Laws of 2018, item 5, as amended) and statutes amending the 2011 Act on the National Council of the Judiciary (consolidated text Journal of Laws of 2018, item 389, as amended), the 2001 Law on Ordinary Courts Organisation (consolidated text Journal of Laws of 2018, item 23, as amended).

by EU law. Explanatory notes accompanying draft statutes amending statutes that organise the Polish judiciary either mention briefly that the draft statute is compliant/is not incompliant with EU law or that it is not covered by EU law.

However, on 23 August 2018 the Minister of Justice, acting at the same time as the Prosecutor General, submitted a request to the Constitutional Tribunal to examine the compliance of Article 267 TFEU with the Polish Constitution, so far as it allows the reference for preliminary ruling regarding: (1) questions bearing no relevance to the subject matter of the main case, and (2) the organisation of the national judiciary.[11] The Prosecutor General demands that the Constitutional Tribunal declare the unconstitutionality of Article 267 TFEU, so far as it permits the national court to make preliminary references in matters relating to the system, form and organisation of the judiciary as well as proceedings before judicial authorities of the EU Member State. He explicitly refers to institutional and procedural autonomy in his pleading of 4 October 2018.[12] The case is pending. Moreover, at the end of September 2018 the Minister of Justice said in a radio interview that the EU Court of Justice was not competent to interfere in the internal organisation of the national judiciary.[13]

There are, however, commentators who have recognised the recent events in Poland regarding judiciary as infringement of the autonomy.[14]

---

[11] Case K 7/18. In Polish, available at: <https://ipo.trybunal.gov.pl/ipo/view/sprawa.xhtml?&pokaz=dokumenty&sygnatura=K%207/18>. The second question has been added with a pleading of 4 October 2018.

[12] Retrieved from: <https://ipo.trybunal.gov.pl/ipo/view/sprawa.xhtml?&pokaz=dokumenty&sygnatura=K%207/18>, pp. 25–26.

[13] In Polish, available at: <https://www.polskieradio.pl/13/53/Artykul/2194796,Sygnaly-Dnia-27-wrzesnia-2018-roku-rozmowa-ze-Zbigniewem-Ziobro>.

[14] Cf. Gajda-Roszczynialska, above note 5, pp. 61ff; Stanisław Biernat and Monika Kawczyńska, 'Though this be Madness, yet there's Method in't: Pitting the Polish Constitutional Tribunal against the Luxembourg Court' [2018] *Verfassungsblog on matters constitutional*, 26.10.2018, <https://verfassungsblog.de/though-this-be-madness-yet-theres-method-int-the-application-of-the-prosecutor-general-to-the-polish-constitutional-tribunal-to-declare-the-preliminary-ruling-procedure-unconstitut/>. As for the rule of law concerns see, Wojciech Sadurski, 'Bad Response to a Tragic Choice: the Case of Polish Council of the Judiciary' [2018] *Verfassungsblog on matters constitutional*, 16.04.2018 <https://verfassungsblog.de/bad-response-to-a-tragic-choice-the-case-of-polish-council-of-the-judiciary/>; Laurent Pech and Patryk Wachowiec, 'Rule of Law in Poland (or lack thereof): 7 Questions for the Article 7 Hearing' [2018] <https://www.euronews.com/2018/09/17/rule-of-law-in-poland-or-lack-thereof-7-questions-for-the-article-7-hearing-view>.

So far there has been no evidence that the Constitutional Tribunal or the Supreme Court have changed their approach to the concept of national procedural autonomy following the newest legislative changes relating to these bodies, since there are no published decisions thereof that refer to the concept discussed in this chapter.

When it comes to the Constitutional Tribunal, which is responsible for judging whether statutory legislation complies with the Constitution, references to the discussed concept have rarely been made. Only two of its judgments delivered before 2016 can be found that mention the procedural or institutional autonomy. The Constitutional Tribunal confirmed that there was no autonomy of the Member States with regard to competences that result from directly applicable provisions of EU law.[15] It also recognised the limiting role of the EU principles of equivalence and effectiveness for national decision makers.[16]

The procedural autonomy has been invoked with a much higher frequency by the Supreme Court which hears cassation complaints and adopts resolutions to clarify legal issues, among others in civil cases. The practice of the Supreme Court was that it used to refer to EU law provisions as limiting procedural autonomy.[17] In two of the decisions the explicit references to *Rewe/Comet* doctrine took place.[18] In another three decisions the Supreme Court recognised the links between the national procedural autonomy and the principles of equivalence and effectiveness referring to the CJEU's settled case law.[19]

Regarding specifically collective civil proceedings, the Supreme Court only expressed its view on Poland's autonomy in one decision,[20] even though it did not refer explicitly to the concept of procedural autonomy. In the facts of the case, the claimant claimed, among others, that the Court of Appeal's interpretation of national provisions had been contrary

---

15 Judgment of 10.02.2015, No. SK 50/13. The case was not related to private law provisions. The database of Legalis C.H. Beck has been used to look for judgments of Polish courts referred to in this chapter.

16 Judgment of 12.12.2011, No. P 1/11. The case was not related to private law provisions.

17 Ruling of 28.01.2015, No. III SK 37/14 and judgments of 15.07.2009, No. III SK 2/09; 08.10.2014, No. III SK 85/13; 05.12.2016, No. III SK 18/14 and 18.01.2017, No. III SK 20/14.

18 Ruling of 18.02.2015, No. III SK 18/14 and resolution of 19.10.2017, No. III CZP 42/17.

19 Ruling of 20.02.2008, No. III SK 23/07 and judgments of 21.09.2011, No. II PK 36/11 and 04.10.2011, I PK 56/11.

20 Ruling of 28.01.2015, No. I CSK 533/14. Translation into English by the author of this chapter.

to the EU Commission's Recommendation[21] on common principles for injunctive and compensatory collective redress mechanisms in the Member States concerning violations of rights granted under Union Law (hereafter, Commission's Recommendation). This allegation was dismissed since, in the Supreme Court's view, EU law does not oblige Member States to regulate in any certain way collective civil proceedings, but only provides recommendations on this topic. The Commission's Recommendation does not reveal anything specific or unknown to Polish law that would be useful for interpreting Polish provisions on collective civil proceedings. It results from EU law only that it recommends introducing collective redress mechanisms to the national legal systems, including collective actions for damages, because they can facilitate access to justice. This led the Supreme Court to the conclusion that:

> if provisions on collective civil proceedings already exist in the system of national law, their interpretation should foster their effective operation. Such a line of interpretation under Polish law is, however, obvious and independent of EU recommendations, as it corresponds to typical mechanisms of teleological interpretation applied also in the case examined by the Supreme Court, without the need for recourse to EU law.

3. IS THERE ANY IMPACT OF THE EU RECOMMENDATION ON POLISH PROCEDURAL LAW?

In cases of soft law (as well as merely coordinative policy of the EU) the explicit hierarchical pressure on domestic institutions is weak; instead of complying with rules, national actors are expected to widen their ideational horizon due to the exposure to European or neighbour country discourses and to reconsider previously held beliefs, expectations and preferences.[22] EU soft law may cause national laws to be Europeanised

---

21 2013/396/EU, OJ L 201, 26.07.2013, p. 60.

22 Cf. Lenschow, above note 1, p. 66. The author mentions the European Employment Strategy as an example. It may be added that discourses concerning unfair trading practices in the food supply chain influenced domestic strategies employed to protect food producers even before the EU's initiative to ban such practices (proposal for a directive).

in 'spontaneous' ('soft') ways. However, it is believed that Member States' legislatures have little incentive to undertake reforms in national civil procedural rules in accordance with the mandates incorporated in non-legally binding recommendations.[23] Rules on civil procedure are strongly rooted in the national procedural autonomy. If the implementation of soft law instruments by Member States occurs, it is often explained by the principle of sincere and loyal cooperation. The principle of sincere and loyal cooperation together with the principle of effectiveness and the application of Article 47 of the European Charter of Fundamental Rights are believed to be a means of the evolution of procedural autonomy (and more precisely its erosion).[24]

It is important to recognise that Member States – even though they cannot see their discretion limited by a soft-law instrument which is exterior to them[25] – can voluntarily implement EU soft law related to procedural issues (spontaneous Europeanisation). Even in the absence of such specific legislation, Europeanisation may occur through the CJEU's decisions, though these changes are incremental as well as less systematic than legislative reforms and their impact on the various Member States remarkably differs.[26]

Regarding specifically collective redress mechanisms, it is argued in the legal literature that careful consideration as to whether and in which areas a soft EU initiative should be developed is required not only to respect national procedural autonomy and the principles of subsidiarity and proportionality, but also to ensure that the possible risks of collective redress procedures are not overlooked and do not outweigh the potential advantages.[27]

Has Poland retained its national procedural autonomy regarding collective civil proceedings? Has the Commission's Recommendation had any impact on Polish procedural law?

---

23 Zampia Vernadaki, 'Civil Procedure Harmonization in the EU: Unravelling the Policy Considerations' (2013) 9(2) *Journal of Contemporary European Research* 308.

24 Cf. Cafaggi, above note 4, pp. 255–256. See also Rui Tavares Lanceiro, 'The implementation of EU law by national administrations: Executive federalism and the principle of sincere cooperation' (2018) 10(1) *Perspectives on Federalism* 77.

25 Oana Ştefan, 'Soft Law and the Enforcement of EU Law' <https://kclpure.kcl.ac.uk/portal/files/49209194/Soft_Law_Enforcement_Stefan.docx>, p. 13.

26 Ibid, pp. 242–243.

27 Sara Benedi Lahuerta, 'Enforcing EU Equality Law through Collective Redress: Lagging behind?' (2018) 55 *Common Market Law Review* 784.

3.1. HISTORY

As a matter of fact, the first (and so far only) Polish statute related mainly to collective civil proceedings is the 2009 Act on the Pursuit of Claims in Group Proceedings (in Polish *ustawa o dochodzeniu roszczeń w postępowaniu grupowym*), hereafter referred to as the APC;[28] therefore, it is a statute adopted long before the Commission's Recommendation.

The history of the discussion on collective redress in Poland dates back to at least 2005 when the Commission's Green Paper – Damages actions for breach of the EC antitrust rules[29] – was published. It promoted collective actions as saving time and money. In response, the Polish government took a position on this suggestion in which they were opposed to the introduction of collective actions, even though they supported the introduction of some solutions intended to facilitate 'collective' redress for consumers (e.g. joint attorneys).[30] However, the Commission did not stop there and in 2007–2008 this initiative was followed by numerous events and debate.

The Polish government, exposed to this huge debate going on about collective redress, changed its position in 2008 and began working on the draft APC. This initiative was already underway when the Green Paper of 27 November 2008 on consumer collective redress was published by the Commission.[31] The Commission presented four policy options therein and the last option (judicial collective redress procedure) was accompanied by the list of issues to be decided. Although this checklist was known to the Polish government, they remained quite independent in their attitude towards this EU-inspired initiative. Not all the issues referred to in the checklist were resolved in the APC. However, in its response of 2 March 2009 to the Green Paper, the Polish government supported the last option and took a position that the EU could issue a

28 See further Anna Piszcz, '"Class Actions" in the Court Culture of Eastern Europe' in Laura Ervo and Anna Nylund (eds), *The Future of Civil Litigation – Access to Courts and Court Connected mediation in the Nordic Countries*, Springer International Publishing Switzerland, Cham 2014, pp. 357–379.

29 Commission, 'Green Paper – Damages actions for breach of the EC antitrust rules' COM (2005) 672.

30 In Polish, available at: <http://ec.europa.eu/competition/antitrust/actionsdamages/files_green_paper_comments/permanent_representation_of_the_republic_of_poland.pdf>.

31 Commission, 'Green Paper on consumer collective redress' COM (2008) 794 final.

directive regarding collective redress.[32] It also mentioned that in Poland the works on the introduction of the collective redress mechanisms were underway.

The EU support for the collective redress mechanisms was mentioned in some documents accompanying the Polish legislative works.[33] However, the explanatory notes to the draft APC did not clearly define the sources of inspiration of the Polish government and did not mention any EU documents. The creators of a proposed bill are required to provide assurance of its compliance with EU law in the explanatory notes (and they did) but not to describe a source of inspiration. As a result, Polish legal drafters usually do not exceed the required minimum as regards this information.

The APC was adopted on 17 December 2009 and came into force on 19 July 2010. On 4 February 2011, the Staff Working Document – Public Consultation: Towards a Coherent European Approach to Collective Redress[34] – was published by the Commission. When responding to it, the Polish government emphasised that collective redress mechanism should exist in all the Member States but only with regard to consumer claims and informed that Poland had already introduced the collective redress mechanism.[35]

It can be assumed that the above-mentioned soft initiatives of the EU inspired the Polish decision makers to adopt the 'hard' legislation on collective civil proceedings. However, the Commission's Recommendation, which recommended that all Member States should have national collective redress systems with respect to rights granted under Union law based on a number of common European principles implemented till 26 July 2015 at the latest, has not been followed by Poland in

---

32 In Polish, see Permanent Representation of the Republic of Poland to the European Union in Brussels, 'Odpowiedzi Rządu RP na poszczególne pytania zawarte w *Zielonej Księdze w sprawie dochodzenia zbiorowych roszczeń konsumentów (COM(2008)794)*' ['Replies of the Government of the Republic of Poland to individual questions contained in *Green Paper on consumer collective redress (COM(2008)794)*'], dated 02.03.2009, on file with author.

33 Opinions of the Bureau of Research at the Chancellery of the Sejm of 25.06.2009 and 21.10.2009. In Polish, available at: <http://orka.sejm.gov.pl/rexdomk6.nsf/Opdodr?OpenPage&nr=1829>.

34 Commission, 'Commission Staff Working Document – Public Consultation: Towards a Coherent European Approach to Collective Redress' SEC (2011) 173 final.

35 In Polish, available at: <http://ec.europa.eu/competition/consultations/2011_collective_redress/ministry_of_justice_poland_pl.pdf>.

certain important aspects.[36] The Commission should have assessed the implementation of the Recommendation on the basis of national practical experience by 26 July 2017 at the latest. To this end, in August 2017, the Commission closed a 12-week public consultation conducted with the aim of collecting evidence on the operation of collective redress arrangements in Member States and prepared a report.[37] The assessment has been carried out against the background that several years after the adoption of the Commission's Recommendation the risks of cross-border or even EU-wide infringements affecting a multitude of citizens or businesses have further increased, particularly but not exclusively as a result of greater internet use and online shopping.[38] A range of risks were identified, such as the risk of forum shopping, of double compensation or of conflicting decisions.[39] It clearly results from the Commission's Report that the Commission's Recommendation has not been followed by some of the Member States at all; Poland, however, is not in this group.[40]

The APC is still in force and it has been amended only once since its enactment. The changes implemented by the 2017 Act Amending Certain Acts to Facilitate the Recovery of Debts entered into force on 1 June 2017.[41] Although the legal drafters were well aware of the Commission's Recommendation, the end result proves that it was treated at least superficially in the course of legislative works. The amendments do not mean that decision makers wanted to implement the Commission's Recommendation; changes have, apparently, been introduced only in order to remove the drawbacks of the pre-existing legal framework identified in practice. And it becomes clear that Polish courts have gained

---

36 Cf. Piszcz, above note 1, pp. 116–119.

37 Report of 25 January 2018 from the Commission to the European Parliament, the Council and the European Economic and Social Committee on the implementation of the Commission Recommendation of 11 June 2013 on common principles for injunctive and compensatory collective redress mechanisms in the Member States concerning violations of rights granted under Union law (2013/396/EU), COM(2018) 40 final, hereinafter, the Commission's Report.

38 Ibid, p. 3.

39 Ibid, p. 12.

40 A brief diagnosis of the Polish system of collective redress mechanisms can also be found therein. Various pieces of information can be found when browsing the Commission's Report and they do not differ from what will be presented below; see the Commission's Report, pp. 4, 5, 7, 8, 9, 14, 16 and 17.

41 For more see, Anna Piszcz, 'Compensatory Collective Redress: Will It Be Part of Private Enforcement of Competition Law in CEE Countries?' (2017) 10(15) *Yearbook of Antitrust and Regulatory Studies* 234.

practice in handling the collective actions. Since the APC came into effect in 2010 to the end of 2017 there have been collective statements of claim submitted to courts in 242 cases, i.e. civil (234) and commercial (8) cases (2015 – 33, 2016 – 30, 2017 – 17 cases).[42] In 48 cases, the action was rejected for formal reasons. And as the Ministry of Development commented in 2016,

> after around six years of the functioning of collective redress, one can clearly see practical problems causing that the mechanism cannot be effectively used in accordance with its intended purpose. The best proof of this is the fact that so far none of 'big' group cases has been concluded with a final decision, even though some of them were filed in 2010.[43]

At some point in the legislative works, the Polish legal drafters noted that the amendments are justified in the light of the Commission's Recommendation.[44] In fact, however, provisions diagnosed by academics, judges and other practitioners as ineffective or counterproductive and improved by the legal drafters in 2017, as a rule, are not the same as the ones that, as badly missing from the Polish legal framework compared to the Commission's Recommendation, have needed inserting. If the Polish legal drafters believed that improvements could be achieved by means of the approximation to the solutions recommended by the Commission, there would be a chance to Europeanise the Polish legal framework for collective civil proceedings spontaneously. To the contrary, it is still hard to envision a situation in which Polish decision makers cease to believe that the only solution that remains is waiting for a directive and, for the time being, ignoring the Commission's Recommendation to a certain extent. Already in 2011, Poland's response to the Staff Working Document – Public Consultation: Towards a Coherent European Approach to Collective Redress[45] – featured an idea for reform of consumer collective redress mechanisms in Europe consisting of an EU directive

---

42 See *Pozwy zbiorowe w latach 2010–2017* (*Collective actions in 2010–2017*), in Polish, available at: <http://isws.ms.gov.pl/pl/baza-statystyczna/opracowania-wieloletnie/>. Also, cf. Piszcz, above note 1, p. 119.

43 'Package for creditors' of 2016, p. 1. In Polish, available at: <https://www.mr.gov.pl/media/21040/Pakiet_wierzycielski.pdf>.

44 Since 11.07.2016 it has been stated in the Explanatory Notes to the draft Amending Act. In Polish, available at: <http://orka.sejm.gov.pl/Druki8ka.nsf/0/B9D80E83748EE247C125809D004C3CB5/%24File/1185-uzasadnienie.docx>.

45 Commission, 'Commission Staff Working Document – Public Consultation: Towards a Coherent European Approach to Collective Redress' SEC (2011) 173 final.

setting minimum standards for Member States.[46] Certain Polish solutions were offered to the Commission as a possible model that could be reproduced in such a directive. There is no evidence that Polish decision makers have changed their position, so it may be that they wish to avoid double legislative works.

Differences between the Commission's Recommendation and Polish procedural rules regarding collective civil proceedings are presented below.

3.2. A COMPARISON OF THE EU RECOMMENDATION AND POLISH PROCEDURAL LAW

The first sentence of paragraph 2 of the Commission's Recommendation recommends that Member States should have collective redress mechanisms at a national level for both injunctive and compensatory relief. However, taking into account declaratory relief and other remedies (in the legal literature interim remedies[47] and restitution[48] are mentioned separately), in fact there seems to be more than just injunctive and compensatory collective redress referred to in the Commission's Recommendation. It must be admitted that already in 2009 the Polish legislature created a system in which not only injunctions, compensation and restitution but also declaratory relief were and are available in group proceedings.[49] And, so far, the most popular type of remedy claimed in group proceedings in Poland has been declaratory relief. Before the 2017 amendments, it was not clear how to interpret provisions on compensatory redress in group proceedings due to their vagueness, and it was quite risky to go through this type of proceeding. In particular, the requirement that the amounts claimed must be identical in sub-groups to at least two members of the overall group 'taking into account the common circumstances of the case' (the so-called

46 In Polish, available at: <http://ec.europa.eu/competition/consultations/2011_collective_redress/ministry_of_justice_poland_pl.pdf>.

47 Sebastian Peyer, 'Private antitrust litigation in Germany from 2005 to 2007: Empirical evidence' (2012) 8(2) *Journal of Competition Law & Economics* 350.

48 Cf. Cafaggi, above note 4, p. 239.

49 Articles 1–2 of the APC. According to Article 2, the APC applies to selected areas: product liability, tort liability, liability for non-performance or improper performance of a contract, liability for unjust enrichment, and, in relation to consumer claims, also in other matters.

standardisation of claims)[50] used to deter potential group members from participating in the action or lead them to reduce their claims to be eligible. Therefore, claimants used to require that courts declare that the defendant was liable for the infringement[51] and, by means of such a judicial decision, make the defendant settle with them or, eventually, file individual actions aiming at further remedies. However, individual proceedings involving individual group members conducted just after group proceedings multiply court proceedings instead of reducing them and the costs incurred may exceed the ones that would be incurred if one of these two modes of proceedings was in fact eliminated. The 2017 amendments include, first, the clarification that the standardisation of claims is an equalisation of the amounts of claims of group members or subgroup members (no common circumstances of the case needed therefor), and, secondly, the improvement of the rules regarding declaratory relief.

In the next step, it is necessary to define *locus standi* (legal standing), an issue falling within the scope of national procedural autonomy – even if indeed, there are some provisions relating to standing in the Commission's Recommendation. In the legal literature[52] it is argued that when Member States define *locus standi* according to their own legal systems, they must respect the well-known principles of equivalence and effectiveness, and the principle of effective judicial protection.[53] The Commission's Recommendation covers aspects of both group and representative collective actions.[54] It must be stressed that, in spite of the

50 Article 2 paras 1–2 of the APC. Its narrow interpretation is provided in, among others, the decision of the Court of Appeals in Cracow of 07.12.2011, I ACz 1235/11, in Polish available, at: <http://classaction.pl/case_law/28-postanowienie-sadu-apelacyjnego-w-krakowie-wydzial-i-cywilny-z-dnia-7-grudnia-2011-r/>.

51 Based on Article 2 para 3 of the APC.

52 Cf. Lahuerta, above note 26, p. 797.

53 The right to an effective judicial remedy is guaranteed by Article 47 of the European Charter of Fundamental Rights.

54 Elisabetta Silvestri says, however, that in the Commission's Recommendation 'standing to sue is granted only to "representative entities" identified in advance by Member States or to public authorities'; Elisabetta Silvestri, 'Towards a Common Framework of Collective Redress in Europe? An Update on the Latest Initiatives of the European Commission' (2013) I(1) *Russian Law Journal* 49. Obviously, the 'body' of the Commission's Recommendation with respect to legal standing contains – in Chapter III ('Principles common to injunctive and compensatory collective redress') – only the subchapter 'Standing to bring a representative action'. But recital 17 of the preamble to the Commission's Recommendation gives an insight into the broader range of available collective actions. See also para 10 sentence 2.

title of the APC, not only group collective actions but also representative collective actions are available in Poland.[55] However, the status quo gives the impression that the former are supplemented by a very narrow scope of representative collective actions. Every group of claimants needs to consist of at least ten persons with claims of the same kind and with the same or similar factual basis thereof, not necessarily consumers.[56] The group must be represented by one of its members, that is a lead claimant,[57] who needs to be, in turn, represented by a barrister or a legal advisor unless the lead claimant is not a barrister or a legal advisor herself/himself.[58] A representative collective action can be brought by the regional (municipal) consumer ombudsman,[59] who is a public authority. Crucially, a non-governmental organisation (including a consumer organisation) does not have standing to bring representative collective actions, unless it is a member of the group, and there are no minimum criteria of eligibility applicable modelled on paras 4–6 of the Commission's Recommendation.[60]

Poland exclusively applies the 'opt-in' principle in the national collective redress schemes, which is recommended regarding compensatory collective redress by paras 21–24 of the Commission's Recommendation. The result of the 'Package for creditors', published by the Ministry of Development in 2016, was that a discussion was also required on the introduction of an opt-out system.[61] Finally however, there have been no continuation of this issue and it is not clear whether it is

55 Article 4 of the APC.

56 Article 1 para 1 of the APC. See also Piszcz, above note 41, p. 234.

57 Article 4 paras 1–3 of the APC.

58 Article 4 para 4 of the APC.

59 In Polish *powiatowy (miejski) rzecznik konsumentów*. Article 4 para 2 of the APC. Article 4 para 4 of the APC applies. See also para 7 of the Commission's Recommendation.

60 Anna Piszcz, 'A few remarks on standing to bring a collective redress action' in Anna Budnik (ed.), *Locus standi across legal cultures. Białystok Volumes on Law & Culture 3*, Temida2, Białystok 2015, p. 74.

61 See in Polish <https://www.mr.gov.pl/media/21040/Pakiet_wierzycielski.pdf>. Also <https://bip.kprm.gov.pl/kpr/wykaz/r302158777046,Projekt-ustawy-o-postepowaniu-grupowym.html> and <https://legislacja.rcl.gov.pl/docs//2/12287513/12366041/12366042/dokument231430.pdf>. On the discussion of the opt-in vs opt-out model see, among others, Laura Ervo, 'Opt-in is out and opt-out is in: Dimensions based on Nordic options and the commission's recommendation' in Burkhard Hess, Maria Bergström and Eva Storskrubb (eds), *EU civil justice: Current issues and future outlook*, Hart Publishing, Oxford-Portland 2016, pp. 186ff; Ken Daly, *The Growth of Collective Redress in the EU: A Survey of Developments in 10 Member States*, U.S. Chamber Institute for Legal Reform, Washington 2017, p. 39.

going to take place in the nearest future at all. Paragraph 21 of the Commission's Recommendation states that any exception to the recommended principle, by law or by court order, should be duly justified by reasons of sound administration of justice. It is not clear, however, whether what is 'sound administration of justice' is different in various Member States (like legal traditions are different) or whether there is, in fact, only one standard thereof for all Member States (the 'average', a common denominator for e.g. Swedish and Polish administrations of justice).[62]

There is a kind of a certification of group proceedings at the early stage of litigation. The court decides that cases which do not meet the conditions for collective actions are not continued,[63] which is compliant with paras 8–9 of the Commission's Recommendation. The examination of the admissibility of collective action results in a specific decision on this matter. The practice, however, has shown the reverse side of this phase of group proceedings, as it used to make the whole procedure lengthier, and thereby restrict access to this procedure as a whole. In numerous competent courts, the certification phase used to take at least 1.0–1.5 years after the action was filed. In particular the requirement of holding a public hearing in this phase and the appealability of a certification decision contributed to the prolixity of this stage of group proceedings. The 2017 amendments introduced the certification of group proceedings in chambers instead of at a public hearing, and some changes making appeal procedures more effective.[64] These changes allow claimants the chance to save time due to the reduced duration of group proceedings.

Later on, after the certification decision becomes final, the court determines modalities of spreading information on group proceedings (including the dissemination method),[65] which is compatible with paras 10–12 of the Commission's Recommendation. In the case of actions filed before the 2017 amendments, unless all potential group members joined the class already, announcements needed to take place in a popular nationwide newspaper; only in particular cases could the court have ordered an announcement to be published in the local press.

---

[62] For more, see Sofia Oliveira Pais and Anna Piszcz, 'Package on Actions for Damages Based on Breaches of EU Competition Rules: Can One Size Fit All?' (2014) 7(10) *Yearbook of Antitrust and Regulatory Studies* 222.

[63] Article 10 para 1 of the APC.

[64] Article 10 paras 1–2a of the APC.

[65] Article 11 paras 1–4 of the APC.

After the amendments, a way to publicise group proceedings is chosen with a view to its expediency. In particular, the information may be published on the websites of the competent court, on the websites of the parties or their lawyers, as well as in nationwide or local press.

Courts apply exactly the same 'loser pays' principle[66] to collective actions as they do to individual civil proceedings. In this context, the level of deterrence from bringing frivolous actions is the same. Modalities applicable to collective redress concern a lower level of court registration fees and the lack of legal aid to assist group members.[67] Moreover, there is an exemption from court registration fees for regional (municipal) consumer ombudsmen in consumer cases, but it is not limited to group proceedings.

Clearly, Poland does not follow paras 14–16 and 32 of the Commission's Recommendation. From the beginning of the APC, there have been no specific rules on funding, and decision makers do not seem eager to introduce them. The APC allows for self-financed actions as well as actions funded by third parties without scrutiny by the court. The recognised sources do not point to any rationale as to why the Polish legislature has not deployed the above concept in this context.

The APC allows for some form of contingency fee to be paid to the lawyer.[68] There is a specific provision on the operation of such remuneration in collective redress actions.[69] It is a performance fee in the form of a success fee, with the amount ranging up to 20% of the value of the award.[70] However, according to available information, this system of lawyers' remuneration is hardly applied in Poland.[71] It is clear that contingency fees, naturally, cannot be applied in the case of group actions for declaratory relief that have dominated all collective actions, as there is no awarded amount. And in the case of other actions, it has become quite the trend to require up-front fees from represented claimants. Therefore, it may be assumed that Polish provisions on the lawyers'

---

66 Recommended in para 13 of the Commission's Recommendation.

67 Article 24 para 2 of the APC.

68 Which seems contrary to paras 29–30 of the Commission's Recommendation.

69 Article 7 of the APC.

70 See also Žygimantas Juška, 'The Impact of Contingency Fees on Collective Antitrust Actions: Experiments from Lithuania and Poland' (2016) 41 *Review of Central and East European Law* 387–389; Piszcz, above note 41, p. 237.

71 Magdalena Tulibacka, 'Class Actions in Poland 2016: Lingering problems and reform proposals. Report for the Conference "Empirical Evidence on Collective Redress in Europe", at the University of Oxford, 12–13 December 2016' [2016] <https://www.law.ox.ac.uk/sites/files/oxlaw/poland_-_tulibacka.docx>, pp. 10–12.

remuneration do not create incentives to unnecessary litigation. Interestingly, so far contingency fees have not been steeped in legal traditions of Poland.

One of the missing pieces from the Polish legal framework can also be seen in the lack of an equivalent to para 33 of the Commission's Recommendation. Outside the scope of the newly implemented Directive 2014/104/EU,[72] its principles have not been followed with regard to the priority to be given to the decision of the public authority and to limitation periods.[73] The general line of Polish jurisprudence considers administrative decisions only as evidence which may be assessed in civil proceedings along with any other material brought by the parties.[74] Administrative decisions in cases of practices infringing collective interests of consumers have been treated as binding on a court in civil cases; however, first, it does not result from legal provisions but the Supreme Court's jurisprudence,[75] and, second, the latter has not been inspired by the Commission's Recommendation but the earlier jurisprudence of the Supreme Court preceding Directive 2014/104/EU, relating to competition law and drawing inspiration from EU competition law (Regulation 1/2003[76]).

Next, there are no means of alternative dispute resolution specifically tailored for collective actions.[77] The APC only states that at every

---

72 Directive 2014/104/EU of the European Parliament and of the Council of 26.11.2014 on certain rules governing actions for damages under national law for infringements of the competition law provisions of the Member States and of the European Union, OJ L 349, 05.12.2014, p. 1. See Anna Piszcz and Dominik Wolski, 'Poland' in Anna Piszcz (ed.), *Implementation of the EU Damages Directive in Central and Eastern European Countries*, University of Warsaw Faculty of Management Press, Warsaw 2017, pp. 211ff.

73 Of all the types of litigation regarding tort liability only in damage litigation in competition cases are the following solutions present: the binging effect of administrative authorities' decisions, five-year limitation period suspended when administrative proceedings are commenced, rules on disclosure of evidence in favour of a claimant. Consequently, civil procedural rules in place have become more fragmented. This approach of the Polish legislature proves its general unwillingness to exceed the requirements of EU legislation when transposing directives into national law (to 'gold-plate'). Implementation goes beyond the minimum necessary to comply with directives, by extending the scope, quite rarely.

74 Resolution of the Supreme Court of 09.10.2007, III CZP 46/07.

75 Ruling of 23.04.2015, III SK 61/14.

76 Council Regulation (EC) No. 1/2003 of 16.12.2002 on the implementation of the rules on competition laid down in Articles 81 and 82 of the Treaty, OJ L 1, 04.01.2003, pp. 1–25.

77 Recommended in paras 25–28 of the Commission's Recommendation.

stage of the case, the court may refer the parties to mediation.[78] Moreover, general provisions on out-of-court dispute resolution apply. By-the-by, to date only scarce collective civil proceedings have ended with a settlement. At least one of the cases brought against an insurance company ended with a settlement at the preliminary stage of the certification.[79]

The above analysis shows that there is no wide realisation of the Commission's Recommendation in Poland. A couple of lacunae can be identified in the Polish legal framework for collective civil proceedings, that is: (1) the lack of legal standing of non-governmental organisations (NGOs); (2) the lack of provisions on funding; (3) the lack of provisions with regard to the priority to be given to the decision of the public authority and to limitation periods; and (4) the lack of means of alternative dispute resolution specifically tailored for collective actions. Maintaining these lacunae may be attributed to the use of the procedural autonomy by the legislature. The decision makers only took care to ensure that Poland was not in breach of EU law but did not pay attention to EU soft law.

Also, the design of the certification phase, modalities of spreading information on group proceedings and the (unintended) preference for declaratory relief might have been considered to be within the national procedural autonomy. However, in this author's opinion, attention should be drawn to para 2 of the Commission's Recommendation stating that '(…) Member States should ensure that the collective redress procedures are fair, equitable, timely and not prohibitively expensive'. It might not only have been disputed whether the listed solutions complied with these soft law requirements. There might also have been room for concerns over whether they respected the principle of effective judicial protection binding on Member States. The 2017 update of the APC embracing changes to the listed solutions aimed at making group proceedings faster and cheaper, not only clarified areas of doubt but, in the context of the national procedural autonomy, it also made Polish civil procedural law more 'functionalised' to the requirements of effective judicial protection.

---

78 Article 5 of the APC.

79 Agnieszka Trzaska, 'Poland. The Class Actions Law Review – Edition 2' [2018] <https://thelawreviews.co.uk/edition/the-class-actions-law-review-edition-2/1169583/poland>.

4. ATTEMPT AT AN ASSESSMENT AND PERSPECTIVES

Europeanisation of civil proceedings resulting from the EU 'hard' legislation has not occurred very often so far. There have been several sector-specific directives (regarding enforcement of claims arising under a given sector of EU law) and horizontal directives limited to specific aspects of civil procedure ('piecemeal' directives).[80] Where directives require to harmonise certain rules applicable to resolving cross-border disputes, Poland, as a rule, introduces identical provisions to deal with purely internal proceedings. The decision makers do not opt for the separation of the two categories of disputes from each other. It may be assumed that with regard to collective civil proceedings the scenario would be the same. Traditionally, the use of procedural autonomy seems steeped in and dependent upon interactions of various kinds; the Polish legislature seems to prefer maintaining the existing procedural differences even if it results in relatively little correlation with EU soft law, but not at any price. Polish legal provisions become closer to the EU soft-law model as a result of spontaneous Europeanisation when it is evidently more practical. It is hard to say for sure whether there is full awareness or 'premeditation in resistance' where decision makers tend to maintain procedural autonomy as far as possible.

The four lacunae in the Polish legal framework for group proceedings identified in the previous section have not been filled in on the occasion of the amendments of the APC. In this respect, there is neither cumulative nor serious progressive realisation of the EU's vision for collective civil proceedings. There has been no considerable loss of Poland's procedural autonomy in this area so far. However, the amendments regarding solutions such as the design of the certification phase and modalities of spreading information on group proceedings, as well as the facilitation of actions other than the ones for declaratory relief, may be considered as making the Polish legal framework more compliant with the Commission's Recommendation. As a result, the actual scope of procedural autonomy remains smaller.

---

80 Rafał Mańko, 'Europeanisation of civil procedure: Towards common minimum standards?' (2015) European Parliament <http://www.europarl.europa.eu/RegData/etudes/IDAN/2015/559499/EPRS_IDA(2015)559499_EN.pdf>, p. 4. See e.g. Directive 2008/52/EC of the European Parliament and of the Council of 21 May 2008 on certain aspects of mediation in civil and commercial matters, [2008] OJ L136/3. The legislation in this field is not only concerned with cross-border disputes.

The problem of a relative inertia of the Polish legislature may be related to the fact that the new government formed in November 2015 after the last parliamentary election has been very engaged with other changes to legislation. The other causes may be exclusively practical. The Polish decision makers may be waiting for a directive on collective redress mechanisms suggested by the European Economic and Social Committee[81] in order to avoid double legislative works which may be contradictory and counterproductive if the contents of a directive are different from the contents of the Commission's Recommendation. Second, the Polish decision makers usually do not seem very eager to voluntarily introduce solutions that are far from Polish procedural 'classics' and seem alien to the Polish system such as provisions on funding, sophisticated means of alternative dispute resolution, the binding effect of administrative decisions or the suspension of limitation periods in new instances (contingency fees are an exception to this approach). It is also appropriate, at this stage, to add that this approach is proven via the frequent adoption of minimum solutions in the case of minimum harmonisation clauses contained in directives (here, a sample of this is Directive 2014/104/EU). Third, the lack of legal standing of NGOs may be explained in a different yet simple way. Poland used to have quite a long tradition regarding legal standing of NGOs, in particular in the area of the abstract control of standard forms of agreements concluded with consumers. Those cases were free from court registration fees. On the other hand, a winning party represented by a professional lawyer (an advocate or an attorney-at-law) could have received the costs of legal aid resulting from the tariffs provided for by law and not from the actual expenditure. This resulted in cost pathologies. The consumer organisations being in fact 'factories' of such actions appeared in Poland; they used to copy the same template of an action regarding the same clauses from the same standard form of agreements concluded with different, numerous consumers in order to win as much lawyers' fees 'reimbursement'

81 European Economic and Social Committee, 'Opinion on the Communication from the Commission to the European Parliament, the Council, the European Economic and Social Committee and the Committee of the Regions Towards a European Horizontal Framework for Collective Redress' COM (2013) 401 final, [2014] OJ C170/68. See point 3.3 where the Committee states that only a directive would ensure a solid core of harmonisation while at the same time giving the Member States enough leeway for accommodating the particularities of their national legal systems; hereafter, the draft Directive.

from the infringer as possible.[82] From 2008 to 2013 the annual number of filed actions increased from 325 to 41,016. Finally, the legislature decided to move those cases from civil proceedings to administrative proceedings initiated only *ex officio* as of 17 April 2016. It may be that decision makers are afraid of the extension of legal standing in group proceedings for very similar reasons. And unless a directive requires it, such an unpopular solution will not appear with regard to group proceedings.

It seems that only a directive may take things a step further, whether horizontal or sector-specific.[83] A proposal for a directive of the European Parliament and of the Council on representative actions for the protection of the collective interests of consumers, and repealing Directive 2009/22/EC[84] is already in place, as one of the key planks of the EU's New Deal for Consumers legislative reforms. To a certain extent, it takes into account the Commission's Recommendation.[85] However, some procedural elements from the Recommendation are not reproduced in the draft Directive due to its more targeted scope.

The draft Directive is not going to replace existing national collective redress mechanisms. Taking into account their legal traditions, it leaves it to the discretion of the Member States whether to design the representative action set out by the directive as a part of an existing or future collective redress mechanism or as an alternative to these mechanisms, insofar as the national mechanism complies with the modalities set by the directive.[86] Anyway, the Commission believes that the absence of an EU-wide collective redress mechanism is of particular practical relevance to consumer protection, as shown by concrete cases,

---

82 For more, see Paulina Korycińska-Rządca, 'Review of the New Polish Model of Abstract Control of Standard Forms of Agreements Concluded with Consumers' (2016) 9(14) *Yearbook of Antitrust and Regulatory Studies* 247–264.

83 Especially that the preamble to the Commission's Recommendation, Recital 7 lists consumer protection, competition, environmental protection, protection of personal data, financial services legislation and investor protection as areas where supplementary private enforcement of rights granted under EU law in the form of collective redress is of value.

84 COM(2018) 184 final.

85 From this perspective it seemed disappointing that according to the Commission's Report, the Commission was only oriented towards strengthening the redress and enforcement aspects of the Injunctions Directive (Directive 2009/22/EC of the European Parliament and of the Council of 23 April 2009 on injunctions for the protection of consumers' interests, OJ L 110, 01.05.2009, pp. 30–36) in appropriate areas.

86 Recital 24 of the preamble to the draft Directive.

including the diesel emissions case. The directive is going to be applied to representative actions brought against infringements by traders of provisions of the EU law listed in Annex I that harm or may harm the collective interests of consumers.

Keeping in mind the identified lacunae in the Polish legal framework and the scope of the draft Directive, it needs to be concluded that, if the draft Directive is adopted, all the lacunae will need to be filled in with regard to representative actions aimed at the protection of the collective interests of consumers. Qualified entities, in particular consumer organisations, will need to be designated.[87] Provisions on funding will also need to be added.[88] Solutions with regard to the effects of final decisions of the public authority and the suspension of limitation periods, that are not available at the moment, will need to be introduced.[89] National decision makers will also need to respond to the fact that the draft Directive promotes collective out-of-court settlements.[90] The existing Polish legal provisions on out-of-court settlements are not sufficiently tailored for collective actions.

On 26 March 2019, the European Parliament's first reading of the draft Directive has been closed.[91] The European Parliament legislative resolution, among others, deleted from the draft Directive the possibility for courts to issue a declaratory decision instead of a redress order and introduced the prohibition of contingency fees for lawyers' remuneration (the sum that is paid only if the case is won). These are some of the issues that are regulated in Poland in a different way, too.

The resolution also made it very clear that the draft Directive aims at minimum harmonisation and that Member States remain free to adopt or maintain provisions that are more favourable to consumers. Certainly, the minimum harmonisation would better comply with the principles of subsidiarity and proportionality, respect the Member States' autonomy, allow to fully respect their legal traditions and give them a freedom to propose more innovative and far-reaching solutions.[92]

---

87 Article 4 of the draft Directive.

88 Article 7 of the draft Directive.

89 Articles 10–11 of the draft Directive.

90 Article 8 of the draft Directive.

91 P8_TA(2019)0222, available at: <http://www.europarl.europa.eu/sides/getDoc.do?type=TA&reference=P8-TA-2019-0222&language=EN>.

92 Maciej Gac, *Group litigation as an instrument of competition law enforcement – analysis based on European, French and Polish experience*, University of Warsaw Faculty of Management Press, Warsaw 2017, pp. 441 and 460.

It remains to been seen what the final word of the EU legislature is. It is clear that the file cannot be concluded by the parliamentary end of term. However, votes on the draft Directive taken by the European Parliament in plenary on 26 March 2019 will remain legally valid for the next Parliament. After the elections, the files will continue once the new Parliament has been formed. Provided that the draft Directive is adopted in this, or similar, design, one thing can be assumed with some degree of certainty. While implementing the draft Directive, most probably Polish decision makers will not be eager to establish the same principles for other sectors. In such a case, the (further) fragmentation of procedural rules will occur. After all, the implementation may also allow to check out whether decision makers are oblivious of the principle of procedural autonomy or, being aware of its limits, they take in procedural solutions above the minimum required by the directive or, to the contrary, there is nothing more offered by them than that minimum.

PROCEDURAL AUTONOMY BETWEEN EU LAW AND THE SLOVENIAN LAW OF CIVIL PROCEDURE

Aleš Galič

1. INTRODUCTION

There have been significant developments since the European Court of Justice (hereinafter: ECJ) established the doctrine of procedural autonomy and the principles of effectiveness and equivalence restricting the scope of this doctrine.[1] The doctrine had roots in time, when EU law was concerned

[1] Procedural rules of each Member State generally apply to cases of EU law. Under the principle of effectiveness Member States must ensure that the remedies and procedural rules available to enforce rights arising from EU law do not render them impossible in practice or excessively difficult to enforce. The principle of equivalence obliges them to ensure that remedies and procedural rules concerning enforcement of EU law must not be less favourable than those attaching to analogous claims of a purely domestic nature. See e.g. ECJ judgments of 16.12.1976, C-33/76, *Rewe-Zentralfinanz eG and*

primarily with rights in substantive law and the doctrine of procedural autonomy was focused on the issue of how (substantive) rights, existing under EU law, are enforced in proceedings in national courts, pursuant to national procedural law. Nowadays however, the EU law itself – although often in a fragmented and in sectoral manner – extends deep into the domain of procedural law. Important EU instruments which affect civil procedure, perhaps even to a greater extent than the 'judicial co-operation in civil matters' can be found in those areas of EU law that are primarily concerned with substantive, not procedural law (e.g. alternative dispute resolution of consumer disputes, unfair contract terms in consumer contracts, collective redress, effective protection of IP rights, private enforcement of antitrust). In addition, starting with the adoption of so-called 'second generation regulations' even the core area of European civil procedure (i.e. judicial cooperation in civil matters) has slowly started to detach itself from traditional domains of international private law. Certain – though still fragmented – areas of 'pure' civil procedure are now subject to regulation on the community level. These developments do not *per se* diminish importance of procedural autonomy of Member States, *in casu* Slovenia, however the interface between EU law and national procedural law becomes more far reaching and more complex, thus opening doors for more uncertainty and tensions. Undoubtedly, the influence of EU law on Slovenian civil procedure is growing. This however does not mean that the issue of procedural autonomy has itself gained sufficient attention in Slovenian academic circles or in case law of Slovenian courts. In fact, the author could not find one single source, either in legal writing (either by authors specialising on the EU law or by authors specialising in civil procedure) or in case law even mentioning the issue of 'procedural autonomy'. Though issues relating to the interface between national civil procedure law and EU civil procedure have been discussed, they have focused on different, usually more pragmatic aspects. On a positive side, examples from EU law were often invoked as an

---

ReweZentral AG v. Landwirtschaftskammer für das Saarland, ECLI:EU:C:1976:188, and, more recently 15.03.2017, C-3/16, *Aquino*, ECLI:EU:C:2017:209: '48 It should be recalled here that, according to settled case-law of the Court, in the absence of EU rules on the matter, it is for the national legal order of each Member State to establish procedural rules for actions intended to safeguard the rights of individuals, in accordance with the principle of procedural autonomy on condition, however, that those rules are not less favourable than those governing similar domestic situations (principle of equivalence) and that they do not make it excessively difficult or impossible in practice to exercise the rights conferred by EU law (principle of effectiveness)'. See also: 20.09.2018, C-448/17, *EOS KSI Slovensko*, ECLI:EU:C:2018:745.

argument in favour of possible reform of corresponding legal instruments in national law. On a negative side, attention focused on lack of clarity and predictability resulting either from poor or hasty drafting of EU Regulations or from 'insufficient implementation measures'. No concerns on the level of fundamental principles and policy issues (relating to a possible perceived need of protection of national procedural autonomy) have been raised though. This is another consequence of the mentioned pragmatic approach: provided that a quality of EU law is ensured and provided that the application of EU law and its interface with national law does not produce more uncertainties and tensions than application of exclusively national law, the prevalence of national procedural law is not perceived as a value *per se*.

2. MORE EFFECTIVENESS, LESS PROCEDURAL AUTONOMY, LESS COHERENCE OF NATIONAL LEGAL SYSTEM?

In recent years the emphasis in the discourse surrounding the interface between national laws on the one hand and the EU law on the other hand has clearly been shifting from the principle of national procedural autonomy to the requirement of effectiveness of EU law. The number of cases where national procedural law had to (and will have to) 'step back' in order to ensure effective exercise of rights under EU law is increasing.[2] The practical result thereof is that it is, in reality, often easier for litigants in national courts to enforce rights under EU law than rights under national law. This is contrary to concerns which led to the adoption of the principle of equivalence. These developments to a certain extent led to systemic distortions in the national justice system since certain categories of litigants (typically consumers) are treated, concerning procedural issues, entirely differently and enjoy preferential treatment compared to all other parties, who are equally 'weaker' and 'vulnerable', but their cases do not involve reliance on EU law. The requirement of *ex officio* application of consumer law, combined with the principle of effectiveness,

---

2 E.g. Case C-243/08, *Pannon*, ECLI:EU:C:2009:350, 04.06.2009; Case C-49/14, *Finanmadrid EFC*, ECLI:EU:C:2016:98, 18.02.2016; Case C-169/14, *Juan Carlos Sánchez Morcillo and María del Carmen Abril García v. Banco Bilbao Vizcaya Argentaria SA*, ECLI:EU:C:2014:2099, 17.07.2014; Case C-448/17, *EOS KSI Slovensko*, ECLI:EU:C:2018:745, 20.09.2018.

led to far-reaching adaptations concerning how proceedings (litigation,[3] payment order,[4] arbitration,[5] enforcement proceedings[6]) involving consumers are conducted (extending to entirely passive consumers, who have not entered appearance, consumers who entered appearance without contesting jurisdiction and consumers who did use available remedies). Particularly far reaching are positions where consumer law on unfair clauses always constitutes a part of public policy (and can thus be invoked as late as in action for setting aside an arbitration award[7]) or that a consumer, who did not file a statement of opposition against a payment order, can still rely on the court, dealing with enforcement of judgment, to assess whether a term in a contract concluded between a trader and a consumer is unfair.[8] In addition, in *Pénzügyi Lízing* the ECJ imposed the requirement that the national court must investigate of its own motion whether a term conferring exclusive territorial jurisdiction in a contract concluded between a seller or supplier and a consumer, which is the subject of a dispute before it, falls within the scope of Directive 93/13 and, if it does, assess of its own motion whether such a term is unfair.[9] The requirement seems very far reaching – especially in light of the Brussels I Regime, where the obligation of the court extends merely to informing the consumer of the consequences of entering appearance without contesting jurisdiction (Article 26(2) of the Regulation No. 1215/2012[10]). It is difficult to see why safeguards for consumers concerning jurisdiction agreements in a purely national context should be more stringent than safeguards for consumers who are exposed to agreements conferring jurisdiction to courts of the country, which is not the country of their domicile. But this is a question of a coherence of EU law itself. There is

---

3 Joined Cases C-240/98 to C-244/98, *Oceano*, ECLI:EU:C:2000:346 and Case C-137/08, *Pénzügyi Lízing*, ECLI:EU:C:2010:659, 09.11.2010.

4 Case C-243/08, *Pannon*, ECLI:EU:C:2009:350, 04.06.2009; Case C-49/14, *Finanmadrid EFC*, ECLI:EU:C:2016:98, 18.02.2016.

5 Case C-40/08, *Asturcom Telecomunicaciones SL v. Cristina Rodríguez Nogueira, Mostaza Claro*, ECLI:EU:C:2009:615, 06.10.2009.

6 Case C-169/14, *Juan Carlos Sánchez Morcillo and María del Carmen Abril García v. Banco Bilbao Vizcaya Argentaria SA*, ECLI:EU:C:2014:2099, 17.07.2014; Case C-40/08, *Asturcom Telecomunicaciones SL v. Cristina Rodríguez Nogueira*, ECLI:EU:C:2009:615.

7 Case C-40/08, *Asturcom Telecomunicaciones SL v. Cristina Rodríguez Nogueira, Mostaza Claro*, ECLI:EU:C:2009:615.

8 Case C-49/14, *Finanmadrid EFC*, ECLI:EU:C:2016:98, 18.02.2016.

9 C-137/08, *Pénzügyi Lízing*, ECLI:EU:C:2010:659, 09.11.2010.

10 Regulation (EU) No 1215/2012 Of the European Parliament and of the Council of 12 December 2012 on jurisdiction and the recognition and enforcement of judgments in civil and commercial matters (recast).

another, probably more controversial issue, namely that of the impact of these developments on the coherence of national procedural law.

A question arises whether it fits into the principles of a national justice system in a systemic way that it is merely a specific and a single category of weaker parties that 'enjoy' much broader procedural protection – amounting to an outright paternalism – than any other – more than e.g. employees in unlawful dismissal disputes, creditors of maintenance claims, tenants (including vulnerable tenants) in eviction cases, victims of body injury harm, to some extent even minor children in family law cases. It is not problematic that the ECJ requires national courts to assess *ex officio* whether contract clauses in consumer contracts are null and void. This requirement, *per se* is entirely in line with the principle *iura novit curia* (Article 180 of the Slovenian Civil Procedure Act). However, it is a general rule of civil procedure in Slovenia that if the defendant enters appearance without contesting jurisdiction (and there is no exclusive jurisdiction concerned), this constitutes a tacit jurisdiction (or arbitration) agreement. Equally, no defences in substantive law are admissible in the stage of enforcement of a judgment. Such a situation negatively affects the overall coherence of the justice system.[11]

Would it be a viable solution to adjust all procedural rules affecting vulnerable parties to the requirements that the ECJ has imposed for consumer cases? It is not uncommon that procedural rules of EU law in narrow sectoral legislation have triggered more far-reaching legislative changes in Member States, thus resulting in overcoming fragmentation. The latest such example in Slovenia regards the disclosure of documents mechanism of the Antitrust Damages Directive.[12] This has recently triggered and has been used as a model for a ground-breaking reform to disclosure of documents in the Civil Procedure Act, thus not restricted merely to private enforcement of antitrust.[13] Here, the reform was indeed needed since the previous system, in line with the outdated 19th-century

---

11 A lack of systematic coherence is evident even within the 'class of consumers'. It is merely consumers acting as defendants, who benefit from the safeguards, established by the ECJ, but not consumers in the position of claimants (e.g. a consumer who relied on a jurisdiction clause in the contract, not knowing that it is null and void, and brought proceedings against the trader in the place of the trader's domicile).

12 Directive 2014/104/EU of the European Parliament and of the Council of 26 November 2014 *on certain rules governing actions for damages under national law for infringements of the competition law provisions of the Member States and of the European Union* [2014] OJ L 349.

13 Amendment of the Civil Procedure Act, ZPP-E, Official Gazette No. 10/17.

approach in civil law systems, provided for an extremely narrow scope of disclosure obligations.

It is doubtful whether the Slovenian legislature would be willing to adopt another far-reaching reform of procedural law, which would extend the above-mentioned procedural requirements concerning consumers to all other categories of vulnerable parties. This would namely, to a great extent, dismantle the principle of party autonomy and the individual's primary responsibility for his actions and omissions, thus the most fundamental principles of national civil procedure. Thus, 'upgrading' the ECJ's standard for consumer cases to general procedural regime for all cases involving weaker or vulnerable parties (insofar it is at all possible to establish, at least in light of the circumstances of the case at hand, who is the weaker party) would amount to an undesired spontaneous harmonisation. In addition, one should also be mindful of the fact that the requirements, promoted by the ECJ case law, concern foremost consumers as defendants. It is difficult to apply the same standards to cases, where the weaker parties are typically in a position of a claimant (as is the vast majority of labour law disputes).

3. CHANGING LIMITS OF PROCEDURAL AUTONOMY: A POLICY DECISION OR A CIRCUMSTANTIAL BY-PRODUCT?

3.1. GENERAL

The European Commission has an ambition to 'Europeanise' civil procedure – not merely under the title of 'judicial co-operation in civil matters'. This would, it is assumed, diminish the differences between national procedural laws of Member States and, by extension, diminish the importance of national procedural laws. There is hardly any area of EU law where the legislative activity of the EU is more accelerated and more ambitious than in the area of judicial cooperation in civil matters, whereas community rules with a clear procedural impact are increasingly adopted in other areas of EU law also. One would logically expect that when the EU 'civil procedure law' is expanding, that goes hand in hand with diminishing importance of national procedural law, at least in a cross-border context. However, the practical effects of the 'accelerated Europeanisation of procedural law' are not as straightforward and one-sided as it could be expected. Paradoxically, in certain areas of EU law, the importance of national procedural laws (and of differences between these national laws!) has actually gained on importance due to the accelerated (perceived) Europeanisation. This is, one would submit, often not a result of a deliberate policy decision. Rather, it is a collateral by-product. It can be a result of a (political) compromise reached in a legislative process. It can be an inevitable consequence of the inability of the European legislator to regulate all aspects of proceedings in matters that it aspires to 'Europeanise'. Hence, an increasing number of instances, where a reference to the national law is made in the regulations, is understandable. But it can also simply be a matter of a poor quality – an unwanted, but inevitable by-product that goes hand in hand with the speed in adopting the new legislation.

3.2. EXAMPLE NO. 1: NEW PROCEDURAL REMEDIES IN THE BRUSSELS I *BIS* REGULATION

The most telling example of the unexpected (and, from the viewpoint of EU legislature, undesired) reaffirmation of national procedural law of the Member States can be found in the new system of remedies against enforcement of foreign judgment in the Brussels I *bis* Regulation.[14] The compromise solution between the (aspired) full abolition of exequatur on the one hand and retaining the old system on the other resulted in a well-known compromise – a 'reverse exequatur'. On the application of the person against whom enforcement is sought, the enforcement of a judgment shall be refused where one of the grounds referred to in Article 45 of the Brussels I *bis* Regulation is found to exist (Article 46). The procedure for refusal of enforcement shall, in so far as it is not covered by this Regulation, be governed by the law of the Member State addressed (Article 47). The result of the reform is that to a certain extent the divergences between the manner the Regulation is applied in Member States has increased compared to the regime which was in place before the recast. Furthermore, inevitably national law shall be applicable (although this is nowhere stated explicitly in the Regulation) also with regard to issues which do not constitute 'procedure for refusal of enforcement', e.g. suspension of enforcement, making it conditional on the provision of security or limiting it to protective measures (Article 44) and 'adaptation'

14 Regulation 1215/2012 on jurisdiction and the recognition and enforcement of judgments in civil and commercial matters.

measures (Article 54). Another crucial issue is left to the national law of the Member States, namely whether it should be possible to invoke defences of 'national enforcement law' within the proceedings concerned with the application for refusal of enforcement. Pursuant to Recital 30 of the Regulation a party challenging the enforcement of a judgment given in another Member State should, *to the extent possible and in accordance with the legal system of the Member State addressed*, be able to invoke, in the same procedure, in addition to the grounds for refusal provided for in this Regulation, the grounds for refusal available under national law and within the time-limits laid down in that law. In Slovenia all above issues remain controversial and it is, in absence of any case law, uncertain how the new system will be applied. Certain authors advocate the view that it should indeed be possible to invoke defences of 'national enforcement law' within proceedings concerned with application for non-enforcement under Article 46 of the Brussels I *bis* Regulation.[15] In the author's opinion however this standpoint is not convincing – already for the reason that it would lead to an unwanted splitting of jurisdiction. In Slovenia, namely, local courts are vested with jurisdiction to decide on a debtor's objections against enforcement (thus: when defences under national enforcement law are invoked, e.g. that the judgment debt has already been paid or that certain property is exempt from enforcement). Appeals against these decisions go to the appellate court. On the other hand, different courts (namely: district courts) decide on applications for refusal of enforcement under Article 46 Brussels I *bis*. Appeals against their decisions go to the Supreme Court. A similar problem exists as to the question whether it is possible to decide defences under Article 46 Brussels I *bis* (e.g. public policy, exclusive jurisdiction …) as a preliminary question within enforcement proceedings or only as a main question in proceedings brought by an application pursuant to Article 45 Brussels I *bis*. The Brussels I *bis* does not give an explicit answer and here as well, approaches in Member States (pursuant to their national laws) differ. Slovenia – in the author's view correctly and in line with the intention of the new Brussels I *bis* regime – opted for the latter solution: the debtor who wishes to invoke defences set out in Article 46 Brussels I *bis* must bring an application for refusal of enforcement (in the district court). The debtor cannot expect that grounds for non-enforcement set out in Article 46 Brussels I *bis* will

---

15 See e.g. A. Ekart and V. Rijavec, *Zakon o izvršbi in zavarovanju z novelo ZIZ-L*, GV Založba, Ljubljana 2018, p. 206.

be decided *incidenter* (i.e. as a preliminary question) in enforcement of judgment proceedings in a local court. Not everyone agrees with this solution, however.[16] Moreover, even concerning notification of competent courts the situation is not as straightforward as it used to be. In the old system it was left to the national courts simply to notify courts having jurisdiction in the first instance, jurisdiction to decide the debtor's objection and the jurisdiction on the appellate level. It was however clear ('euro-uniform') that the first stage was *ex parte* proceedings, the opponent party (then: the judgment debtor would only subsequently be entitled to oppose the court decision) and merely formalities were checked by the court in the first stage. In the new system however, it is left to the Member States, whether they set out an adversarial procedure already in the first stage, or whether the opponent party (here: the judgment debtor) would be given opportunity to be heard only through a statement of opposition against the first decision on application for refusal of enforcement is given. Most countries have indeed opted for such a system, but not all (Slovenia, the UK and Lithuania, to the author's knowledge). With the latest amendment of the Law on enforcement[17] of judgments this system was changed and as of last year, the proceedings are immediately adversarial.

It would exceed the purpose of this chapter to scrutinise in detail the new system of remedies in the Brussels I *bis* Regulation. The examples above are given in order to demonstrate that the importance of national procedural law has increased (compared to the system in the old Brussels I Regulation) or that at least uncertainties accompanying the dilemma to what extent national law can apply have considerably increased.

3.3. EXAMPLE NO. 2: CROSS-BORDER TAKING OF EVIDENCE

The CJEU has already confirmed that the European Evidence Regulation (EER) is not of a mandatory character and that a court may rely on its national law in order to obtain evidence located abroad. In *Lippens*,[18] the CJEU confirmed that the EER is only to be used when the court of the first Member State *decides* to take evidence in one of the two ways provided by the EER. The Regulation does not determine *when* the taking

16 Ibid.

17 Article a42.b of the amended Law on enforcement of judgments (Zakon o izvršbi in zavarovanju), Official Gazette, No. 11/2018.

18 C-170/11, *Lippens*, ECLI:EU:C:2012:540.

of evidence abroad must be carried out in the first place. It is left to the national law of each contracting state to define when evidence needs to be taken abroad. Thus, a judge may summon a witness who lives abroad to appear before it. In *ProRail*,[19] the CJEU extended its position as regards the non-binding character of the EER to expert evidence.

The *Lippens* case concerned a specific situation where a person who was at the same time a party to proceedings was summoned and examined as a witness. The EER does not provide for a difference in treatment based on the status of the persons heard as witnesses depending on whether or not they are parties to proceedings.[20] The question is therefore posed whether the standards set by the CJEU in this case can be extended to proper witnesses. What makes it all the more complicated is that some national laws do not distinguish between the examination of the parties and of witnesses (e.g. of the UK and the Netherlands), other national laws perceive these as two distinct means of evidence (e.g. Slovenia and Austria), whereas some national laws have traditionally prohibited the examination of parties for the purpose of taking evidence altogether (e.g. Italy). The main finding in *Lippens* is that the EER does not enjoy exclusivity and does not prevent the court from applying the methods provided by its own national law. It is, this author believes, safe to conclude that this finding applies to proper witnesses as well.

The second important finding in *Lippens* is that a court applying its national law may use coercive measures if the summoned person does not comply. It is doubtful whether this position can be automatically extended to proper witnesses. It should be noted that the situation concerning parties summoned as witnesses (which was the case in *Lippens*) is specific. In such cases, genuine coercive measures are usually not necessary – and they were not contemplated in the given case. It suffices that the court can draw adverse inferences from the party's refusal to testify. The situation is usually different when it comes to uncooperative proper witnesses. The major dilemma when it comes to such measures, if applied against a witness residing abroad, is whether they are compatible with the principle of territoriality. A court of one state can validly exercise its sovereign powers (of which the taking of evidence is an element) only within its boundaries. Of course, measures involving physical coercion in the territory of a foreign state are not

19 C-332/11, *ProRail*, ECLI:EU:C:2013:87.

20 Opinion of AG Jääskinen delivered on 24.05.2012, C-170/11, *Lippens*, ECLI:EU:C:2012:311 at [63].

an option (i.e. imprisonment or bringing the witness forcibly to the court). The third one, however, i.e. imposing fines against a witness who fails to appear in court for no valid reason, could be relevant. What is specific in summoning a witness from one country to appear in the court of another country is that the contemplated procedural act takes place exclusively within the court's jurisdiction (including the effect of possible fines). On the other hand, the 'evidentiary material' is – when the summons is issued – located abroad. Many commentators posit that imposing such fines against a person located abroad would violate the other state's sovereignty (even if they were only enforceable within that jurisdiction). As observed by AG Jääskinen, some governments of EU Member States shared this view as well, after the CJEU invited them to express their position.[21] One can, however, also argue that imposing fines on a witness residing abroad does not infringe the sovereignty of the foreign state. The court does not regulate what the witness should do in that other country, but only in the country of the court's jurisdiction (i.e. appear before that court and testify). In addition, the fines also do not have an extraterritorial effect – they can only be enforced in the country of the court that imposed them (thus, they can only be effective if the person affected has assets within that jurisdiction). Thus, in this view, such orders do not have any extraterritorial effects. It is true, however, that when the foreign witness is summoned, he or she is not within the jurisdiction. Summoning him or her presupposes that he or she is expected to travel to the country where the proceedings are to take place. But this could also be considered merely a 'preparatory step' in order to take evidence and does not amount to exercising sovereign power.

In its judgment the CJEU made no reference whatsoever to the issue of state sovereignty. It merely imposed the condition that coercive measures should be in accordance with EU law. What this means exactly remains unclear. AG Jääskinen noted that EU law does not contain any rules governing the matter, however, general principles, such as the principle of proportionality can limit the discretion available to Member States in this area.[22] This would rather support the view that such measures are not already, *per se*, inadmissible, but that a proper balance must be sought. The interpretation that the reference to EU law actually amounts to a reference

---

21 Ibid, at [54].

22 Opinion of AG Jääskinen delivered on 24.05.2012, C-170/11, *Lippens*, ECLI:EU:C:2012:311 at [55].

to international law (since it is a principle of EU law that international law must be respected) is not convincing. If that were the CJEU's intention, it would be much simpler just to make reference to compliance with international law.

What is crucial, from the viewpoint of the topic of 'procedural autonomy' is that if no fines can be imposed against uncooperative foreign witnesses, the ability of a court to summon a foreign witness to appear before it would remain, while recognised on paper, ineffective in practice. The provisions of national law governing the consequences of non-appearance form a part of national law concerning summoning witnesses. The latter without the former remains ineffective. In such a case, the benefits of the possibility of summoning foreign witnesses – confronting them with the statements of other witnesses, assessing their credibility, gaining a personal impression – are lost. The court would namely need to resort to the taking of evidence through a requested court under the EER, as that would remain the only court with the power to apply coercive measures against an uncooperative witness (Article 13 EER). But in that case, both the efficiency and promptness of the taking of evidence as well as the benefits of the principle of immediacy (in law of evidence) are lost. It should thus be argued that if the CJEU confirmed that the national court can apply the methods provided under its national law in order to hear witnesses located abroad, it presupposed that this also includes the application of measures that are a necessary precondition for the effectiveness of such methods. In other words, if the national law on taking of evidence can apply, it can only apply 'in a package' – together with those provisions which ensure its effectiveness.

3.4. EXAMPLE NO. 3: CROSS-BORDER SERVICE OF JUDICIAL DOCUMENTS

A reference should be made to the other area of traditional international judicial assistance – cross-border service of documents. Here, the approach of the CJEU concerning the mandatory nature of the applicable EU Regulation is exactly the opposite to the one discussed in the preceding paragraph. In *Alder*,[23] the CJEU held that the use of the Cross-Border

---

[23] C-325/11, *Alder*, ECLI:EU:C:2012:824.

Service Regulation is binding if the addressee resides abroad. Therefore, rules of domestic laws, providing for more or less fictitious methods of service within jurisdiction to persons not physically present in the same state, thus making it possible to avoid service abroad, are not compatible with Article 1 of the Regulation. At first sight it is difficult to see why the approach as to the relation between the EU Regulation and the national law concerning two related issues is exactly the opposite: for the cross-border service of documents, the judge is precluded from relying on his or her national law and must use the methods provided in the applicable Cross-Border Service Regulation, whereas for the cross-border taking of evidence, the judge is still free to apply his or her national law and make the EER effectively inoperable. By invoking only a grammatical interpretation one should come to identical results. As the CJEU pointed out in *Lippens* and *ProRail*, the EER only applies '*where* the court [...] requests,' but does not determine where such a request must be made in the first place. Exactly the same, however, is also the case in the Cross-Border Service Regulation. It applies '*where* a judicial or extrajudicial document has to be transmitted from one Member State to another for service there' (but it does not define when service must be made abroad in the first place).

A closer look at the arguments offered by the CJEU, however, reveals that the approach is consistent, if not entirely convincing. Concerning both Regulations, the main concern of the CJEU was to ensure the maximum possible respect for fundamental procedural guarantees. Use of fictitious methods of service (in order to avoid the need to serve documents abroad) jeopardises a party's right to be heard and therefore it cannot be regretted that such methods are no longer admissible. On the contrary, the possibility of the continued use of methods of, for example, summoning foreign witnesses to be heard in the court where proceedings on the merits are pending, as the CJEU convincingly explains, can add to the effectiveness of the taking of evidence and to the better procedural position of the parties.

What remained overlooked by the ECJ, though, is a different aspect. In *Alder* the ECJ has (in practical consequence) required those Member States whose national laws required foreign litigants to appoint representatives authorised to accept service of judicial document within the jurisdiction, to abolish such rules. Therewith however, the ECJ has – unintentionally – increased, not decreased the differences in how the Regulation operates in the context of national law. In many Member States the question of how all subsequent (i.e. all except the claim) documents are served on the parties abroad is not posed at all. This goes on account of a national system of procedure that provides for a mandatory representation by lawyers. Since the party is required to be represented by a lawyer with a right of audience before the national court (thus, in practical terms, a local lawyer), all documents will be served within the jurisdiction – on the lawyer. The problem of how to serve all documents in proceedings on a foreign party thus remains relevant only for the systems, such as the Slovenian one, which do not provide for a mandatory representation by lawyers. It is difficult to see why the system that requires a (foreign) party to appoint a lawyer within the jurisdiction is compatible with human rights standards, whereas the system that requires a (foreign) country to appoint a representative to accept service within the jurisdiction (which can of course also be, and it often was, also a local lawyer) infringes fundamental procedural guarantees. True, the mandatory representation by lawyers affects all parties, not just foreigners, whereas the rule that a party must appoint a representative, authorised to accept service, affects merely parties, residing abroad. This can be an issue of possible indirect discrimination, but this was not the ECJ's assessment.

It seems that the EU legislature has realised that in *Alder* the ECJ has gone too far. Article 7a of the draft Proposal for a new Cross-Border Service of Documents Regulation[24] namely overrules the *Alder* judgment. Member States shall, if the draft is adopted, again be free to apply its national rules requiring foreign litigants to appoint representatives authorised to accept service. It remains to be seen how this possibility will apply in Slovenia, where the rule of national procedural law has already been changed following the ECJ's judgment in *Alder*.

Turning to another issue related to the mentioned draft new Cross-Border Service of Documents Regulation, this chapter attempts to show that the changing limits of national procedural autonomy can sometimes be just a matter of bad drafting of legislation. The impact on the national procedural law can however be much bigger than anticipated and acknowledged by the EU legislature.

---

24 Article 7a of the Proposal for a Regulation of the European Parliament and of the Council amending Regulation (EC) No 1393/2007 of the European Parliament and of the Council on the service in the Member States of judicial and extrajudicial documents in civil or commercial matters (service of documents). Brussels, 31.05.2018, COM(2018) 379 final, 2018/0204(COD).

The draft new Regulation changes the scope of its application. It is no longer envisaged that the Regulation is applied 'when a document needs to be served abroad' (thus leaving substantial room for application of national law). Instead draft Article 1 of the new Regulation provides as follows: '1. This Regulation shall apply [...] to the service of: (a) judicial documents *on persons domiciled in a Member State other than the one* where the judicial proceedings take place.' The explanatory memorandum to the draft explains the change as follows:

> However, as regards judicial documents, the proposal clarifies that the Regulation applies in all situations where the domicile of the addressee is in another Member State. In doing this, the Regulation tries to put an end to the current bad practice in which defendants in another Member State are served in the territory of the Member State of origin through alternative or fictitious methods of service of documents, as permitted by the procedural law of the Member State of origin, irrespective of the information on the foreign address of the defendant at the disposal of the court or judicial authority seized with the proceedings. With the new scope wording, courts would not be able to carve such situations out of the scope of the Regulation by simply qualifying the service of the documents as "domestic".

In the view of the drafters of the proposal, the obligation always to apply the Regulation when the addressee is domiciled abroad constitutes a 'higher standard'. But this is a case merely when the domestic service, used in order to avoid applying the Regulation, is fictitious. It is however wrong to assume that every service not effected in the state of the addressee's *domicile* (!) is fictitious. To start with, the place of domicile (as a legal concept, depending on national law) is not necessarily the place of the real address where the addressee lives. Thus, under the proposed new system, even if the addressee has a habitual residence or a temporary residence in the country where proceedings were brought, the court would not be able to serve the document in the place where the addressee actually lives. In this case serving the documents to the country of the addressee's domicile would clearly be much more fictitious than the 'domestic service'. The drafters have obviously confused the concept of domicile with the concept of 'real address', which would be the proper standard if one genuinely wished to ensure the ultimate goal of fair service – namely that the addressee really receives the document. It should be noted that in numerous countries, Slovenia included, the court may actually not serve the document at all in the place of the defendant's registered domicile if the defendant (a physical person) does not actually live in the place of his registered domicile (which is, for different reasons, not a rare occurrence in Slovenia).[25] The court must make genuine attempts to find the addressee and may not already in the first step simply leave the document on the registered address of the defendant's domicile although it is clear that the addressee does not live there. How this can fit into the new regime, if it is established that the person who is still registered as being domiciled in Slovenia, has actually moved to another country is not clear. Moreover, under the new proposed system it would not be admissible to serve the claim in the addressee's workplace (Article 139(1) of the Slovenian Civil Procedure Act, hereinafter CPA) if the addressee's domicile is in another Member State (e.g. daily migrant workers or employees who acquired temporary residence in the country where proceedings were brought). It would also no longer be possible for process-servers to serve the claim 'wherever they find the addressee' (Article 139(3) of the CPA). These are not fictitious methods, but methods that guarantee to the greatest possible extent (much greater than leaving the document in the place of the addressee's domicile, which he might not have any factual contact with) that the addressee receives the document. The place where the document is served on the defendant should not be confused with the place of the defendant's domicile. The latter is a general criterion for establishing jurisdiction (but courts in other Member States can have jurisdiction by virtue of special or exclusive or protective rules of jurisdiction). Thus, serving a claim on a person who is temporarily present in the state's territory is an exorbitant (and explicitly prohibited) ground for jurisdiction. This however does not mean that if the court, which is not the court in the place of the defendant's domicile, has jurisdiction by virtue of the Brussels I Regulation, should be prevented from serving the document on the defendant who is temporarily present (or even habitually resident) in the territory of that state. Finally, under the new proposed regime it would not be possible to serve a claim against the foreign company on its domestic registered legal representative (the company's director). True, under the Cross-border Service of documents it is admissible to serve a document on the party's legal representative. But if the addressee (the company) is domiciled abroad, the Regulation imposes the obligation to serve abroad (to the domicile of the addressee) and prohibits the 'substitute' domestic service – although in the explained case it would not at all be fictitious.

---

25 Judgment of the Slovenian Constitutional Court No. 278/08 of 09.07.2009.

It is welcome that the EU legislature wishes to put an end to fictitious methods of domestic service and thereby diminish the scope of applicability of national procedural law on service of judicial documents. The EU legislature however did not also intend to put an end to those methods of domestic service which are not fictitious, but quite on the contrary, aim to ensure to the greatest possible extent that the addressee receives the document, instituting the proceedings. Exactly this will nevertheless be the result – a far-reaching 'putting to an end' of rules of national law on service of documents, even those aimed to ensure real and not fictitious service. The given example thus demonstrates that far-reaching changes concerning procedural autonomy (either expanding or – as in this case – narrowing it) of Member States are often not a matter of a deliberate policy decision but rather of a poor drafting and lack of sufficient attention given to the complex nature of law of procedure.

To conclude, this example (as in fact also all other examples discussed above) shows that the relation between EU instruments in the field of judicial cooperation on the one hand and the national procedural autonomy on the other, is increasingly becoming a question of how far the (desired) euro-autonomous interpretation of rules set in these instruments reaches. It is not that much at issue whether a certain piece of national legislation prevents the effective application of EU law,[26] which used to be the main concern of the initial approach to the topic of procedural autonomy.

4. AN ADDITIONAL REMARK: POSSIBLE FUTURE DEVELOPMENTS

A new important player has entered the arena of EU law; namely the Charter of Fundamental Rights of the EU. It can be expected that principles of effectiveness and equivalence shall gradually cease to be perceived as independent principles, and shall instead be assessed as a

26 This issue was detected in Slovenia, e.g. with regard to Article 8 of the Brussels II Regulation (Regulation No. 2203/2001) which provides that courts of the child's habitual residence have jurisdiction over matters of parental responsibility. Slovenian law however provides that the court pronouncing the divorce must *ex officio* also decide matters of custody over the child and of access to the child (Article 421 of the CPA). Quite some persuasion was needed before Slovenian judges realised that they may, in order to ensure effective application of EU law, not apply this rule if the child is habitually resident abroad (except if both parents agree – Article 12 of the Brussels II Regulation).

part of fundamental guarantees as enshrined in Article 47 of the Charter.[27] If such development indeed occurs it can be expected that the principle of procedural autonomy shall gradually be replaced by a kind of a fourth instance doctrine along with recognising that the Member States enjoy a 'margin of appreciation', thus allowing for a broad discretion of Member States within the limits of the requirements of EU law. If the focus shifts to overriding and broadly framed fundamental rights, such as the right of access to court, the right to effective legal remedy and the right to a fair trial (with several 'limbs', e.g. the right to be heard and the guarantee of equality of arms) it is, in the long term, inevitable that the procedural autonomy remains merely a myth since practically every procedural rule of the national law can, at least to some extent, be relevant from the viewpoint of these guarantees. It can be expected though that practical considerations will trigger new doctrines to develop, perhaps similar to the so-called 'fourth instance doctrine' and the concept of the margin of appreciation developed by the European Court of Human Rights.[28] This should concern the interface both between EU law and national laws as well as the interface between the ECJ and national courts. Uniformity of procedural laws of EU Member States or replacing these laws by the EU instruments altogether should not be a desired goal per se, but only insofar as otherwise rights and freedoms protected by the EU law would be infringed.

---

27 Cf. C-93/12, *Agrokonsulting*, ECLI:EU:C:2013:432, 27.06.2013: 'Article 47 of the Charter, it is apparent from the Court's case-law that that provision constitutes a reaffirmation of the principle of effective judicial protection, a general principle of European Union law stemming from the constitutional traditions common to the Member States.'

28 See e.g. ECtHR, *Tautkus v. Lithuania*, No. 29474/09, 27.11.2012, *Perlala v. Greece*, 17721/04, 22.02.2007.

AUTONOMY OF THE SPANISH LEGISLATOR IN THE REGULATION OF PROCEDURAL LAW

The Borders of European Case Law

Jordi NIEVA-FENOLL

'Procedural autonomy' of the Member States does not exist in a sense that could be understood before the creation of the European Communities, i.e. sovereignty. In the framework of the current EU it is impossible to conceive that States enjoy full freedom to legislate in any area, not only the procedural one, because their conventional commitment to the implementation of European law prevents a national legislator from issuing its norms as if that law did not exist. The commitment of the States is with all the institutions of the EU, and also with the European Court of Justice.

Assuming this situation, rather than 'procedural autonomy' (a very ambiguous expression), freedom of procedural regulation conditioned by European law could be a better description. Therefore, national norms cannot prevent the implementation of European law. The most relevant question, however, is not trying to mark the borders of both legislations, but rather those of the Court of Justice at the time of conditioning, with its case law, this national freedom of regulation mentioned before.

Despite this conclusion, the work of the European Court of Justice may not have really tangible limits. So far it has usually tried to relate its decisions in this regard with the protection of the rights of citizens, especially those in a more sensitive position. In addition, its task up to now has been to declare the inapplicability of national norms, and not to create others in order to take their place. Even in relation to the controversy about the acts of the judge on his/her own motion, the ECJ has acted this way as well, although sometimes it was apparently not the case.

However, obviously there is a lack of better predictability of the decisions of the ECJ, clarifying the sectors in which it will intervene. But this predictability is hardly conceivable since all legal orders – including the European one – are essentially evolutionary. Therefore, the possibility of establishing some basic procedural rules for the entire EU could guarantee greater legal security.

In Spain there have not been many situations in which the concept of procedural autonomy has opened an important debate. The only remarkable situation was *ex officio* control of unfair character of contractual terms, claimed by the ECJ, which did not exist in Spanish law and forced an important legal reform.

1. INTRODUCTION

The normative competences of the institutions of the EU are well known, as well as the controversies about these legal acts, especially regarding the normative freedom of the Member States based on these provisions. This general problem belongs to the field of European constitutional law and therefore will not be the subject of this chapter.

However, it is probably much more interesting to consider the possibility that it is not the European Commission, Council or Parliament, but rather the European Court of Justice that might object to the national legislative sovereignty, particularly in procedural matters, or at least influence the case law of the national courts on the interpretation of the procedural norms.

This issue cannot be settled by proclaiming a mere obedience to the Court of Justice of the European Union by national judges and legislators.

First of all, the Court of Justice of the European Union is not always transparent in its conclusions. Second, case law, by its very nature, is constantly being modified and often appears to be contradictory or simply surprising, as shall be seen. Third, case law is just a set of reasoned resolutions that – in principle – do not create procedures, but at the most make recommendations on the regularity of national regulations and their compatibility with Union law.[1] Fourth, if procedural law is based on unstable legal acts such as judgments, some kind of legal uncertainty is created, which is not desirable at all taking into account that a judicial process is precisely conceived to give legal certainty to the parties. And fifth, because this reality, despite the current state of the European law after several decades of direct effect[2] and primacy,[3] still poses a serious problem of sovereignty of the Member States.

Therefore, the possibilities of legislative influence of the Court of Justice through its case law should be explored. This chapter will focus on its positive and negative effects. It shall also consider an attempt of alternative solution that could provide greater legal certainty in the future than currently exists.

2. THE BORDERS OF THE CASE LAW OF THE COURT OF JUSTICE OF THE EUROPEAN UNION

The judgments of the Court of Justice of the European Union on preliminary ruling try to be quite short and exhaustive so as not to cause more problems of interpretation. But those problems are finally created when transposing the solution of the concrete case to similar ones of different Member States. Sometimes, in the first case itself the solution is not as clear as hoped.

Although the origins of the question that is being analysed were a long time ago, as is well known, in *Van Gend en Loos* (1963) with the direct effect, and more specifically in *Costa v. Enel* (1964) with the principle of primacy, since ancient times there has existed[4] and still exists the notion

1 Case C-32/12, *Duarte Hueros v. Autociba SA, Automóviles Citroën España SA*, ECLI:EU:C:2013:637. See also F. Gascón Inchausti, *Derecho europeo y legislación procesal civil nacional: entre autonomía y armonización*, Marcial Pons, Madrid 2018, p. 111.

2 Case C-26/62, *Van Gend & Loos v. Nederlandse administratie der belastingen*, ECLI:EU:C:1963:1.

3 Since Case C-6/64, *Costa v. ENEL*, ECLI:EU:C:1964:66.

4 Case C-45/76, *Comet BV v. Produktschap voor Siergewassen*, ECLI:EU:C:1976:191 at [13].

of 'procedural autonomy' of the Member States.[5] According to this autonomy each State, without violating the law of the Union, can freely enact procedural rules taking into account that the legislative competence in this matter – and in the vast majority of the rest – remains in the hands of the Member States. The two conditions[6] – not exclusive for the procedural matter[7] – were defined in *Delena Wells*:[8] *principle of equivalence* (the procedure established to execute European law shall not create more unfavourable conditions than for the claims of domestic law) and the *principle of effectiveness* (the procedure should not render impossible or excessively difficult the exercise of the rights granted by European law), which came to summarise what the Court of Justice had already said piecemeal on several occasions.[9]

However, jurists do not agree on determining exactly when that 'procedural autonomy'[10] was born. In some languages, the terminology designated to refer to it is not even peaceful.[11] But apart from that, authors do not succeed in defining a single point, which is the important one: in which precise situations does the ECJ exercise its competence in the context of the preliminary rulings, in more concrete terms than those indicated in *Delena Wells*?

And no wonder about that. The Court of Justice has no superior court above it and it is, in fact, the supreme interpreter of European law,[12]

---

5 Quoting for the first time this very expression, Case C-201/02, *Delena Wells v. Secretary of State for Transport*, ECLI:EU:C:2004:12 at [65].

6 See D.-U. Galetta, *L'autonomia procedurale degli Stati membri dell'Unione europea: Paradise Lost?*, Springer, Milano 2009, p. 20. C. Krönke, *Die Verfahrensautonomie der Mitgliedstaaten der Europäischen Union*, Mohr Siebeck, Tübingen 2013.

7 See Case C-387/16, *Valstybinė mokesčių inspekcija prie Lietuvos Respublikos finansų ministerijos v. Nidera BV*, ECLI:EU:C:2018:121 at [22].

8 Case C-201/02, *Delena Wells v. Secretary of State for Transport*, ECLI:EU:C:2004:12 at [67].

9 M. Bobek, 'Why there is no principle of "procedural autonomy" of the Member States' in B. De Witte and H.-W. Micklitz (eds), *The European Court of Justice and the Autonomy of the Member States*, Intersentia, Antwerp-Cambridge 2011, p. 6.

10 See Galetta, above note 6. p. 3. Case C-300/17, *Hochtief AG v Budapest Főváros Önkormányzata*, ECLI:EU:C:2018:635, 07.08.2018, C-234/17, *XC and Others v. Generalprokuratur*, 24.10.2018. C-54/16, *Vinyls Italia SpA v. Mediterranea di Navigazione SpA*, ECLI:EU:C:2017:433, 08.06.2017.

11 The notion seems to have been created by J.V. Louis, *L'ordre juridique communautaire*, Office des publications officielles des Communautés Européennes, Brussels, 1993, p. 179.

12 As Article 31 of the Treaty establishing the European Coal and Steel Community said, and as was also remembered by the ECJ in its first judgment, it is bound 'to ensure that the interpretation and application of the treaty'. Case C-1/54, *France v. ECSC High Authority*, ECLI:EU:C:1954:7.

and therefore it exercises its own competence as it deems appropriate,[13] this being automatically adequate because it is confirmed by the Court itself. The Court of Justice's judgments constantly try to balance and delimit its function, but its way of working is sometimes erratic, like that of any other high court in difficult points like this one. It is very hard to be completely coherent when a court gathers almost 30 judges coming from different legal systems. Furthermore, judgments are different in every specific case, and they tend to be formulated in general terms.

As will be justified later in this chapter, sometimes judgments seem to have a political rather than a legal background, but this makes it very difficult to predict[14] on which specific items the Court of Justice will intervene and in what way.[15] The Court of Justice does not work as a legislator would do, in the sense that it often lacks clarity and specificity in its assertions. As any other tribunal, it acts case by case.[16] Therefore, finding general lines of its work that could be considered 'legislative', is not always easy for the Court of Justice itself.[17] This poses obvious problems when it comes to establishing these lines.

3. THE CONSTANT, THOUGH ERRATIC, CASE LAW ABOUT PROCEDURAL AUTONOMY

The idea – not the expression – of procedural autonomy appeared in 1960 with *Humblet*.[18] In those first words of the Court of Justice, the

---

13 Bobek, above note 9, p. 12.

14 Galetta, above note 6, p. 135.

15 J.S. Delicostopoulos, 'Towards European Procedural Primacy in National Legal Systems' (2003) 9(5) *European Law Journal* 603. A. Arnull, 'The principle of Effective Judicial Protection in EU law: An Unruly Horse?' (2011) February *European Law Review* 51.

16 B. Krans, 'EU Law and National Civil Procedure Law: An Invisible Pillar' (2015) 4 *European Review of Private Law* 581.

17 See E. Hofmann, 'Der Abschied von der (ohnehin meist falsch verstandenen) Verfahrensautonomie der Mitgliedstaaten? Anmerkung zu EuGH v. 15. 10. 2015, Rs. C-137/14' (2016) 51(2) *Europarecht* 188. M. Kramme, 'Verfahrensautonomie der Mitgliedstaaten im Zivilverfahrensrecht – Grundsatz des Unionsrechts oder Phantom?' in C. Behme et al (eds), *Perspektiven einer europäischen Privatrechtswissenschaft, Jahrbuch Junger Zivilrechtswissenschaftler*, Nomos, Munich 2017, p. 407. W. Schroeder, 'Nationale Maßnahmen zur Durchführung von EG-Recht und das Gebot der einheitlichen Wirkung: Existiert ein Prinzip der „nationalen Verfahrensautonomie"?' (2004) 129(1) *Archiv des öffentlichen Rechts* 3.

18 Case C-6-60, *Humblet v. Belgian State*, ECLI:EU:C:1960:48.

judges affirmed – repeatedly – that 'it has no jurisdiction to annul legislative (…) measures of one of the Member States (…) it may merely record (…) such a failure',[19] indicating that the State itself had to carry out this annulment when the national rules were contrary to Community law.[20] In fact, in those phrases is contained the essence of everything that has been said in the following almost 60 years, and that was later developed in the aforementioned direct effect and primacy.

In the *Fleischkontor* case (1971),[21] the Court indicated what it would later say with regard to procedural autonomy: Member States should establish procedures to enforce the rights established by Community law, in order to avoid differences of treatment between the different States.[22] This constitutes the embryo of the aforementioned principle of effectiveness, and also of the principle of equivalence.

But it was with the *Comet* case (1976)[23] that the Court of Justice directly referred to procedural matters for the first time, deriving its assertions from the principle of primacy. It argued that national courts could not submit the rights deriving from the Community law to exigences of national law that would damage the direct effect.[24] Four days later, in the *Rewe* case,[25] the Court began to mark the outlines of 'procedural autonomy', saying that Member States should designate courts and create procedures to safeguard the direct effect, no less advantageously than the protection of lawsuits based on national law. In other words, there is procedural autonomy, but the Court of Justice points out the areas of the Member State's action.[26]

Perhaps in the case in which the Court of Justice began to vary its statements in an ascending expansion line, especially in procedural

---

19 Case C-6-60, *Humblet v. Belgian State*, ECLI:EU:C:1960:48 at I, 2.

20 Ibid at III, 6.

21 Case C-39/70, *Norddeutsches Vieh- und Fleischkontor GmbH v. Hauptzollamt Hamburg St Annen*, ECLI:EU:C:1971:16.

22 Case C-39/70, *Norddeutsches Vieh- und Fleischkontor GmbH v. Hauptzollamt Hamburg St Annen*, ECLI:EU:C:1971:16 at [5]–[6].

23 Case C-45/76, *Comet BV v. Produktschap voor Siergewassen*, ECLI:EU:C:1976:191.

24 See Case C-45/76, *Comet BV v. Produktschap voor Siergewassen*, ECLI:EU:C:1976:191 at [9], [10].

25 Case C-33/76, *Rewe v. Landwirtschaftskammer Saarland*, ECLI:EU:C:1976:188.

26 See also Case C-208/90, *Emmot v. Minister for Social Welfare*, ECLI:EU:C:1991:333.

matters, was in the well-known case *Simmenthal* (1978),[27] initiating a tendency that would be developed in the years to come. It literally said that

> a national court which is called upon, within the limits of its jurisdiction, to apply provisions of community law is under a duty to give full effect to those provisions, if necessary refusing of its own motion to apply any conflicting provision of national legislation, even if adopted subsequently, and it is not necessary for the court to request or await the prior setting aside of such provision by legislative or other constitutional means.[28]

The important point is set by the words 'own motion'. The Court of Justice was granting *ex officio* powers, non-existent in most national legal systems, in order to enforce Community law.[29] And this possibly supposes a work of creation of law that could exceed the limits of the expression 'procedural autonomy'.

Something similar, and even more obvious, happened in the *Peterbroek* case (1995), in which the Court of Justice created the possibility that a judge could invoke *ex officio* the breach of Community law in the context of an appeal.[30] But nevertheless in the *Van Schijndel* case,[31] whose judgment was issued on the same day as the previous one and with the same judges,[32] the Court modified what was said in *Peterbroek*, asserting that the judges could not use that *ex officio* power if this

> would oblige them to abandon the passive role assigned to them by going beyond the ambit of the dispute defined by the parties themselves and relying on facts and circumstances other than those on which the party with an interest in application of those provisions bases his claim,

---

27 Case C-106/77, *Amministrazione delle Finanze dello Stato v. SpA Simmenthal*, ECLI:EU:C:1978:49 at [22].

28 Case C-106/77, *Amministrazione delle Finanze dello Stato v. SpA Simmenthal*, ECLI:EU:C:1978:49 at [24]. See also Cases C-10/97 and C-22/97, *Ministero delle Finanze v. IN.CO.GE.'90 Srl*, ECLI:EU:C:1998:498 at [21]: 'the Court held that every national court must, in a case within its jurisdiction, apply Community law in its entirety and protect rights which the latter confers on individuals, setting aside any provision of national law which may conflict with it, whether prior or subsequent to the Community rule'. See also Case C-314/08, *Filipiak v. Dyrektor Izby Skarbowej w Poznaniu*, ECLI:EU:C:2009:719.

29 See Case C-497/13, *Faber v. Hazet*, ECLI:EU:C:2015:357.

30 Case C-312/93, *Peterbroeck v. Belgian State*, ECLI:EU:C:1995:437.

31 Cases C-430/93 and C-431/93, *Van Schijndel v. Stichting Pensioenfonds voor Fysiotherapeuten*, ECLI:EU:C:1995:441 at [22].

32 See A. Biondi, 'The European Court of Justice and Certain National Procedural Limitations: Not such a tough Relationship' (1999) 36 *Common Market Law Review*

making a call to the traditional *secundum allegata et probata* (*partium*) of the 12th to the 15th centuries,[33] i.e. when impartiality is broken by the judge going beyond the borders of the object of the judgment, and thereby violates the right of defence. These important statements are also creative, although they confirm the traditional procedural doctrine. In *Oceano* (2000) this *ex officio* activity was proclaimed for the *a limine* assessment of the unfair character of contractual terms.[34] Due to its relevance[35] – especially in Spain – the next section will focus on this important issue.[36]

The Court of Justice was more cautious in the *SpA San Giorgio* case (1983).[37] The Court stated that the judge should not apply presumptions or rules of burden of proof that would compromise the exercise of the rights of a party under Community law. However, the Court of Justice did not create alternative rules, but simply said that the judge should not apply them. Therefore, it did not go beyond insisting on the *ex officio* activity of the judge, although in this case the Court was considering a matter that is usually conducted by the judge on his/her own motion in the national systems.

However, in the *Verholen* case (1991)[38] the Court seemed to be creating law again. The Court of Justice recognised the procedural representation of a husband over his wife when she is not able to be party to the proceedings, even if it is not recognised in domestic law, in order to claim, of course, rights derived from European law. However, it can also be said that the Court of Justice is only ordering not to apply the rule

---

1277. S. Prechal, 'Community Law in National Court: the Lessons from Van Schijndel' (1998) 35 *Common Market Law Review* 681.

33 See J. Nieva-Fenoll, 'La actuación de oficio del juez nacional europeo' (2017) 9000 *Diario La Ley*, and J. Nieva-Fenoll, 'La cattiva reputazione del principio inquisitorio' (2014) 68 3 *Rivista Trimmestrale di Diritto e Procedura Civile* 943.

34 Cases C-240 and C-244/98, *Océano Grupo Editorial SA*, ECLI:EU:C:2000:346. Case C-40/08, *Asturcom Telecomunicaciones v. Cristina Rodríguez*, ECLI:EU:C:2009:615. Case C-76/10, *Pohotovosť s. r. o. v. Iveta Korčkovská*, ECLI:EU:C:2010:685. See also Bobek, above note 9, pp. 3–4.

35 A. Adinolfi, 'The "procedural autonomy" of member states and the constraints stemming from the ECJ's case law: is judicial activism still necessary?' in H.-W. Micklitz and B. De Witte (eds), *The European Court of Justice and the Autonomy of the Member States*, Intersentia, Antwerp-Cambridge 2011, p. 281.

36 See also Case C-94/14, *Flight Refund v. Deutsche Lufthansa AG*, ECLI:EU:C:2016:148.

37 Case C-199/82, *Amministrazione delle Finanze dello Stato v. SpA San Giorgio*, ECLI:EU:C:1983:318 at [14].

38 Cases C-87/90, C-88/90 and C-89/90, *Verholen v. Soziale Verzekeringsbank*, ECLI:EU:C:1991:314.

that prevents representation. As shall be underlined hereafter, this way of doing is far more relevant than it may seem at first.

Another interesting judgment came with the *Kapferer* case (2006).[39] The Court of Justice held that the infringement of Community law does not allow attacking a judgment having the force of *res judicata*. Therefore, the Court does mark the limits of *res judicata*, in the sense that it cannot be affected by future judgments on the same points already discussed in the first process. Again, although this is consistent with the usual procedural doctrine of the Member States, the Court was marking the subjective boundaries of *res judicata*.[40]

4. THE SPANISH CASE: THE INFLUENCE OF CASE LAW ON THE *EX OFFICIO* POWERS OF THE JUDGE

The Spanish legislator remained quite far from European case law on procedural autonomy until 2013. Since 2000[41] there had been a significant number of judgments affecting Spanish proceedings, as will be explained later on, but the legislator did not implement an important and immediate legislative reform until the judgment of the Court of Justice of the European Union of 14 March 2013 was issued.[42]

This preliminary ruling was a response to a question raised by a commercial court in Barcelona, which for the first time considered the compatibility with the European law of a very aggressive old procedure for debtors who had contracted a mortgage with a bank in Spain. This procedure allowed that as soon as a single, normally monthly instalment of the debt was not paid, the bank could initiate a very quick executive proceeding in which the debtor had nearly no opportunity of defence. After the proceeding was celebrated, the debtor could rapidly see how his property was auctioned for a very low price. After the auction, he still owed money to the bank for the part of the debt that could not have been paid with the money obtained in the auction. The procedure, which still

---

39 Case C-234/04, *Kapferer v. Schlank & Schick GmbH*, ECLI:EU:C:2006:178 at [21].

40 Case C-2/08, *Amministrazione dell'Economia e delle Finanze v. Fallimento Olimpiclub Srl*, ECLI:EU:C:2009:506.

41 Cases C-240/98–C-244/98, *Océano Grupo Editorial v. Rocío Murciano*, ECLI:EU:C:2000:346.

42 Case C-415/11, *Mohamed Aziz v. Catalunyacaixa*, ECLI:EU:C:2013:164.

exists, dates back to the 19th century and had always been described as being clearly abusive, but neither the Spanish Supreme Court nor the Constitutional Court had decided to deauthorise it.

The effects of this procedure were brutal after the crisis of 2008. Many people lost their homes very quickly. It also created a problem for the banks, because they accumulated an impressive surplus of real estate that could not be sold in the auctions at a minimally reasonable price, precisely as a consequence of the crisis. As a result, the banks kept the unsold houses as part of its actives. The effects of this situation are still being felt in the Spanish economy.

But in 2013 the Court of Justice of the European Union ruled, in compliance with the provisions of Council Directive 93/13/EEC of 5 April 1993 – and the case law that interprets it – that in this procedure the judge could determine *ex officio* the existence of unfair contractual terms, and that the parties could also claim this unfair character as a defence. And bearing in mind that the vast majority of mortgage bank contracts contained a good number of such terms, the debtors finally found a way to defend themselves properly in this proceeding.

It only took two months for the Spanish legislator to react with an important reform,[43] duly fulfilling the judgment. The response of the Spanish authorities to European requirements is usually swift. This is due to two completely sociological factors that are not very well known. In the first place, the European feeling of the population in general is still very strong in Spain.[44] As a result, there is a tendency for the authorities to properly follow the European dictates so as not to show a bad image to the population nor to the European authorities. These are the – benign – consequences of having been an isolated country that suffered from a fascist dictatorship for almost 40 years. After the death of its dictator, Spain found a path of openness and modernity with its incorporation in 1986 into the European Economic Community.

This ruling of 2013 showed that in Spain there is not too much political interest in preserving procedural autonomy. In fact, European intervention in this matter is in principle welcome, as it is usually considered to be high level. However, this ruling was only the consequence of the regular case law on a rather broader subject, which will be explained briefly below.

---

43 See Law 1/2013, 14.05.2013.

44 In the referendum over the European Constitution of 2005, the rate of affirmative votes was 77%, while it was rejected in France and the Netherlands.

The Court of Justice has only recognised that its intention was to improve consumer protection against unfair terms,[45] but in fact its judgments have gone much further,[46] since it seeks a deterrent effect for the entrepreneur, threatening with global annulments, not only of the unfair term, but of the entire contract.[47]

Since *Oceano* (2000), the judge can analyse *ex officio* an unfair term,[48] and currently in the framework of any procedure[49] and at any stage of it.[50] This is so even if a term of prescription is already precluded[51] and although the consumer did not allege it – which is unusual with prescription[52] – as soon as the judge had the data to do so,[53] always respecting the right of defence of the parties.[54] For this purpose it may even proceed *ex officio*,[55] but only in order to declare the term completely void, without being able to integrate or modify the unfair term,[56] as this

---

45 See E. Arroyo Amayuelas, 'No vinculan al consumidor las cláusulas abusivas: del derecho civil al procesal y entre la prevención y el castigo' in AAVV, Arroyo Amayuelas and A.S. de Nicolás (eds), *La europeización del derecho privado: cuestiones actuales*, Marcial Pons, Madrid 2016, p. 65.

46 See some important statistical information about case law in F. Gómez-Pomar and K. Lyczkowska, 'Spanish Courts, the Court of Justice of the European Union, and Consumer Law' (2014) October *InDret* 1.

47 About the German solution in a similar matter, M. Dellacasa, 'Judicial Review of "Core Terms" in Consumer Contracts: Defining the Limits – Judgement, C-26/13, Kasler' (2015) 11 *ERCL* 163.

48 See Cases C-240/98–C-244/98, *Océano Grupo Editorial v. Rocío Murciano*, ECLI:EU:C:2000:346.

49 Cases C-618/10, *Banco Español de Crédito v. Joaquín Calderón*, ECLI:EU:C:2012:349; C-415/11, *Mohamed Aziz v. Catalunyacaixa*, ECLI:EU:C:2013:164; C-537/12 and C-116/13, *Banco Popular Español v. María Teodolinda Rivas* and *Banco de Valencia v. Joaquín Valldeperas*, ECLI:EU:C:2013:759; C-377/14, *Radlinger and Radlingerová v. Finway a.s.*, ECLI:EU:C:2016:283; C-49/14, *Finannadrid v. Jesús Vicente Albán e.a.*, ECLI:EU:C:2016:98.

50 Cases C-397/11, *Erika Jőrös v. Aegon Magyarország Hitel Zrt.*, ECLI:EU:C:2013:340; C-415/11, *Mohamed Aziz v. Catalunyacaixa*, ECLI:EU:C:2013:164; C-169/14, *Juan Carlos Sánchez Morcillo y María del Carmen Abril García v. BBVA*, ECLI:EU:C:2014:2099; C-448/17, *EOS KSI Slovensko s.r.o.*, ECLI:EU:C:2018:745.

51 Case C-473/00, *Cofidis SA v. Jean-Louis Fredout*, ECLI:EU:C:2002:705.

52 Ibid.

53 Case C-243/08, *Pannon GSM v. Erzsébet Sustikné Győrfi*, ECLI:EU:C:2009:350. See also Case C-32/12, *Duarte Hueros v. Autociba SA, Automóviles Citroën España SA*, ECLI:EU:C:2013:637.

54 Case C-472/11, *Banif Plus Bank v. Csaba Csipai*, ECLI:EU:C:2013:88.

55 Case C-137/08, *VB Pénzügyi Lízing Zrt. v. Ferenc Schneider*, ECLI:EU:C:2010:659.

56 Cases C-32/12, *Soledad Duarte v. Autociba and Automóviles Citroën España*, ECLI:EU:C:2013:637; C-482/13, C-484/13, C-485/13, C-487/13/13, *Unicaja Banco v. José Hidalgo e.a. and Caixabank v. Manuel María Rueda*, ECLI:EU:C:2015:21.

could probably be counterproductive in order to achieve the deterrent effect.[57] In 2006,[58] the Court extended those powers to annul an arbitration clause unfair for the consumer.[59]

In 2012,[60] the Court established that the judicial assessment of an unfair term could benefit any other consumer to whom the same seller or supplier had applied the same term, even though it was not a party in that procedure, something that is certainly relevant in terms of 'res judicata'.[61] However, in 2009 and 2010 it reaffirmed its traditional case law when the Court of Justice stated that once the process was concluded with a final decision, *res judicata*[62] makes it unmodifiable.[63] Later on, the Court reaffirmed that if the judge has already ruled once about the unfair character of a term in an initial phase of the process, he/she cannot reconsider the question later in the course of the process,[64] which is completely logical.[65]

It also argued that *ex officio* activity was only possible if the procedural rules of national law allowed it, stating that the unfair character of a term was a question of public order,[66] as national law usually allows judges the *ex officio* assessment of the violations of public order.[67]

57 Case C-618/10, *Banco Español de Crédito v. Joaquín Calderón*, ECLI:EU:C:2012:349.

58 Case C-168-05, *Elisa María Mostaza v. Centro Móvil Milenium*, ECLI:EU:C:2006:675.

59 Case C-435/10, *Jana Pereničová, Vladislav Perenič v. SOS financ, spol. s r. o.*, ECLI:EU:C:2011:751. C-40/08, *Asturcom Telecomunicaciones v. Cristina Rodríguez*, ECLI:EU:C:2009:615.

60 Case C-472/10, *Nemzeti Fogyasztóvédelmi Hatóság v. Invitel Távközlési Zrt.*, ECLI:EU:C:2012:242.

61 See J. Nieva-Fenoll, *La cosa juzgada*, Atelier, Barcelona 2006, p. 203.

62 Cases C-40/08, *Asturcom Telecomunicaciones v. Cristina Rodríguez*, ECLI:EU:C:2009:615; C-76/10, *Pohotovosť s. r. o. v. Iveta Korčkovská*, ECLI:EU:C:2010:685.

63 See Case C-168/15, *Milena Tomášová v. Ministerstvo spravodlivosti SR and Pohotovosť s. r. o.*, ECLI:EU:C:2016:602.

64 Case C-421/14, *Banco Primus v. Jesús Gutiérrez García*, ECLI:EU:C:2017:60. See also M. Ebers, 'From Océano to Asturcom: Mandatory Consumer Law, Ex Officio Application of European Union Law and Res Iudicata' (2010) 4 *European Review of Private Law* 835.

65 See Nieva-Fenoll, above note 61, p. 25.

66 Case C-76/10, *Pohotovosť s. r. o. v. Iveta Korčkovská*, ECLI:EU:C:2010:685.

67 Article 1255 of the Spanish Civil Code, Article 11.2 of the Spanish Ley Orgánica del Poder Judicial and Article 247 of the Spanish Civil Procedure Code. See also Article 6 of the French Code Civil, Article 1229 of the Italian Codice Civile and §138 of the German BGB.

5. WHAT DOES THE COURT OF JUSTICE ACTUALLY DO?

So far this has been a summary of the case law. Even if not expressly acknowledged, the conclusion has long been clear. As Rodriguez Iglesias[68] stated, the main basis is the prevalence of European law, which means that the national order cannot have its effects if it causes discriminatory treatment for European law itself, or when the efficacy of European law could be compromised. In other words, equivalence and effectiveness.

It is completely useless defining the boundaries of such statements, which are not exclusively focused on procedural law.[69] They will never be more precise than the general definition of those two principles: equivalence and effectiveness. Moreover, these two principles are extremely vague since they depend on the decision of the Court of Justice in every specific case. Furthermore, the discussion goes beyond cross-border cases, since they affect, as can be seen, national law.[70]

However, up to now the Court of Justice has only been creative in terms of the *ex officio* powers of the judges, and partly about evidence and *res judicatai*,[71] although without saying anything different from what was already assumed by the comparative proceduralist doctrine, except in the matter of *ex officio* judicial powers.

Hence, in this last controversial question, it could be said that the Court of Justice is not creating law, but simply ordering not to apply rules that prevent the national judge from making an assessment *ex officio*. This is more or less the same conclusion that the Court has maintained since the beginning, that is, it does not annul national norms, it does not create them for the concrete case nor with a general vocation, but only identifies the obstacles that Member States create for the application of European law, ordering their removal.

68 G.C. Rodríguez Iglesias, 'Sui limiti all'autonomia procedimentale e processuale degli Stati membri nell'applicazione del diritto comunitario' [2001] *Rivista italiana di diritto pubblico comunitario* 27.

69 See C.N. Kakouris, 'Do the Member States Possess Judicial Procedural "Autonomy"?' (1997) 34 *Common Market Law Review* 1390.

70 B. Krans, 'The impact of EU Law on Dutch Civil Procedure Law' in A. Nylund and B. Krans (eds), *The European Union and National Civil Procedure*, Intersentia, Antwerp-Cambridge 2016, p. 89.

71 B. Krans, above note 16, p. 567. S. Wagner, 'Unionsrechtliche Rechtskraftdurchbrechung? – Zu den Grenzen der mitgliedstaatlichen Verfahrensautonomie auf dem Gebiet der Rechtskraft nach der Rechtsprechung des EuGH' (2014) 2 *ZeuS* 211.

This is absolutely true and would be consistent with the well-known Kelsenian function of negative legislator ascribed to the constitutional courts.[72] This conclusion could be doubtful considering the *ex officio* powers of the judge, but even in relation to them here it has been demonstrated that the only thing the Court of Justice has done is to return the dispositive principle – the principle that states that the parties to the procedure themselves are to determine the subject matter of proceedings – to its original conception,[73] from which over the centuries the doctrine was moving away in favour of a somewhat fetishist understanding of the borders of the judicial decision, which only sought to obtain some legal certainty that was lost precisely because of that too extensive understanding of the power of the parties.

Consequently, the Court of Justice is not creating law, but simply pointing out the obstacles to its application. Even in the thorniest case, that of the *ex officio* powers, the Court of Justice has only pointed out that the natural fulfilment of national law, together with a judge respecting too strictly the powers of the parties, would produce an ineffectiveness of European law. This is especially evident in the case of unfair terms, since consumers might not be individually in the best conditions to claim the unfair character, as demonstrated in *Ocean*. But something similar happened in the first case, in *Simmenthal*, in which it was intended to protect individuals bound by a tax, a matter similar to the one dealt with in *Peterbroek* and *Van Schijndel*, in which the rights of employees were clarified.

However, it is a quite rough way of doing, marking the boundaries of the Court of Justice by considering a sort of social commitment of the subject[74] in which there may be a lack of defence of individuals.[75] The Court of Justice has not expressly referred these boundaries in these terms. In the future it could decide to extend its powers to other cases not so socially sensitive in the same way. In fact, this way of doing could also be considered creative with good reasons.

---

72 H. Kelsen, 'Wesen und Entwicklung der Staatsgerichtsbarkeit' in *Veröffentlichungen der Vereinigung der Deutschen Staatsrechtslehrer, vol. V*, De Gruyter, Berlin 1929, p. 56.

73 Nieva-Fenoll, above note 33.

74 See Cases C-317/08, *Rosalba Alassini v. Telecom Italia SpA*, ECLI:EU:C:2010:146; C-75/16, *Livio Menini, Maria Antonia Rampanelli v. Banco Popolare Società Cooperativa*, ECLI:EU:C:2017:457; C-73/16, *Peter Puškár v. Finančné riaditeľstvo Slovenskej republiky, Kriminálny úrad finančnej správy*, ECLI:EU:C:2017:725.

75 See M. Hoskins, 'Tilting the Balance: Supremacy and National Procedural Rules' (1996) 21 *European Law Review* 365–376.

Therefore, the interesting study in this area should focus on which possibilities open the work of the Court of Justice of the European Union, and not so much in the delimitation of its borders[76] that, in a realistic sense, are objectively non-existent.[77]

6. THE DEROGATORY EFFECT OF CASE LAW

The question that must be asked is whether the case law of the European Court of Justice causes the immediate repeal of national procedural rules. The answer cannot be affirmative in terms of immediacy, since national sovereignty would be compromised, so that the system would no longer be that of a decentralised normative space,[78] not even that of a federal State,[79] but rather that of a centralist State which, of course, is not the European Union.[80]

However, a certain derogatory effect in the short-medium term is inevitable. The national judge, as is well known, must declare the inapplicability of the national rule contrary to European law, but cannot repeal it, since this is the exclusive competence of the national legislator. Which means that even if a national judge has declared the aforementioned inapplicability, another judge could continue to apply the rule, as in fact has already happened in the past.

That is why the intervention of the legislator becomes urgent, since otherwise the State could run the risk of going through a process to declare the failure to fulfil obligations under EU law. Consequently, the national legislator must adapt to European regulations,[81] legislating as suggested by the Court of Justice. Nevertheless, the Court does not make legislative recommendations with positive content. Therefore, the national legislator

76 See D.-U. Couronne, 'L'autonomie procédurale des États membres de l'Union européenne à l'épreuve du temps' (2010) 3–4 *Cahiers de droit européen* 275.

77 C.N. Kakouris, above note 69, p. 1411.

78 C. Matusescu and C. Gilia, 'Aspects regarding the EU Member States competence in the enforcement of the European Legislation' [2011] *Challenges of the Knowledge Society* 540.

79 Galetta, above note 6, p. 132.

80 X. Arzoz Santisteban, 'La autonomía institucional y procedimental de los Estados Miembros de la Unión Europea: mito y realidad' (2013) 191 May–August *Revista de Administración Pública* 160.

81 H. Mayer, 'Der Vorrang des Unionsrechts und die Rechtskraft Nationaler Individualrechtsakte' [2012] *Zbornik Radova* 433.

will draft a rule that contains exactly the opposite content to that declared contrary to European law, adjusting the new provision to the terms desired by the Court of Justice.

Everything would be much simpler if European law contained rules of procedural law, but this is not usually the case. The Court of Justice used to deduce procedural law from substantive law, although formulated in a negative sense. This does not exclude, of course, that the newly created national legislation is contrary, again, to European law.

If this happens, the way to repeal the new regulations will obviously be slow, since there will be no choice but to wait for the legislator to become aware of the problem – for which a non-Eurosceptic political will is needed – or that a judge may ask for a preliminary ruling, which could perfectly well not happen. The contrasts in forensic customs in this regard on the part of the Member States are great.

Adapting national law to European law, especially in procedural matters, is not easy. However, the political functioning of the European Union does not allow to act with greater speed. This lack of agility provokes a certain paralysis, a great unpredictability and differences between Member States which, of course, are contrary to legal certainty and to the aims of the European Union. But the current scheme offers no bigger chances, as has already been said. The EU is not a state, and a change in this matter would mean that it would begin to behave as such.

7. DOES THE COURT OF JUSTICE OF THE EUROPEAN UNION DETERMINE THE WORK OF THE NATIONAL LEGISLATOR?

A different question, although very related to the previous one, is whether the Court of Justice can predetermine the work of the national legislator. Do its judgments force national legislators to implement reforms of the procedural laws?

It is certainly a curious case. This situation is unusual in the civil law systems, in which it is not often peacefully accepted that case law is a source of law. Whatever it might be, at European level case law of the Court of Justice is a powerful engine that does produce law, although obviously in a mediate sense.

The question is whether the national legislator is obliged by the case law of the Court of Justice, and the answer is obviously positive.[82] The national legislator cannot act against the judgments of the Court,[83] for the same reason expressed above: the avoidance of failure to fulfil European law, which could give rise to a case against the state.

But this does not mean that the possibilities of the national legislator are definitively limited, or even suppressed in part by the case law. On the contrary, all that case law has an influence only in a few occasions, whose number is not even big. It is true that case law has influenced in very varied areas of the procedural order,[84] but this does not mean that a whole Law of Civil Procedure, for example, is relevant to European law. On the contrary, the matters affected by the case law are extraordinarily limited and, therefore, the vast majority of the procedural provisions will continue to be as the national legislator desires.

The problem, which has already been pointed out, is that nobody ever knows which will be the next point the case law will affect. But the normative work is never complete. The legal system is a living entity, and therefore not only is it positive for the Court of Justice to intervene indirectly in the legislative work, but it is reasonable so that the national legislator does not only take into account the transposition or adaptation to directives, but it is also aware that European law as a whole requires the national legislative work in coherence with its guidelines common to all Member States.

In fact, far from being some kind of nuisance, it is an embryonic mechanism, one more, of approaching the different European legislations towards a codifying work that perhaps will come someday. The only obstacles to this work can be sentimental or even worse, nationalist. But it is certainly magnificent for community purposes that the laws of the Member States are also approaching in procedural matters. Procedural law is no longer something purely national and coined by the traditions of each state.

---

82 K. Kowalik-Bańczyk, 'Procedural Autonomy of Member States and the EU Rights of Defence in Antitrust Proceedings' (2012) 5(6) *Yearbook of Antitrust and Regulatory Studies* 230. N. Zingales, 'Member State Liability vs. National Procedural Autonomy: What Rules for Judicial Breach of EU Law?' (2010) 20 *German Law Journal* 430.

83 Galetta, above note 6, p. 135.

84 See E. D'alessandro, 'L'incidenza dell pronunce della Corte di Giustizia sulla portata delle pronunce italiane in punto di giurisdizione. I casi Interedil e Gothaer' (2019) 1 *Revista Ítalo-Española de Derecho Procesal* 1–15.

It is difficult to conceive a branch of law that is more transnational and transversal than procedural law. Not only because all legal systems – also the Anglo-Saxon legal systems[85] – come from a common procedural tradition, that of the last post-classic Roman process, which was transmitted to most European States through the teachings of Bologna since the 11th century, and from there to most of the world. It must also be borne in mind that regardless of the legal tradition, a judge is a judge anywhere, like a witness, a document or an expert. Evidence, as a concept, does not change its consideration in the different cultures of the world, differing only in its concrete regulation, but taking into account a unique conceptual reality that can be seen in the vast majority of procedural institutions.

Perhaps in the future more contributions will come from the Court of Justice, but it has to be said that so far, they have served to correctly update the procedural rules in several states in some areas, such as the one highlighted above of the dispositive principle.

The legislative capacity of the Member States to build their own procedural system,[86] as well as the possibilities of the national courts to develop it, continues to exist.[87] Now the Court of Justice is walking this path with us simply by giving reference guidelines when the national peculiarities of the national regulations hinder the work of the EU. The Court is not something alien to the States. It certainly has a guiding role for the Member States.

8. A UNIFORM EUROPEAN CIVIL PROCEDURE?

Perhaps it would be positive someday to have at least a single model procedure for all of Europe[88] for civil matters.[89] This would undoubtedly make things much easier in transnational cases, but also in communication between lawyers and judges in the various instruments of cooperation that

85 See P. Brand, *The Making of the Common Law*, Hambledon Press, London 1992. About the Roman influence over H. Bracton, *De Legibus et Consuetudinibus Angliae*, ca. 1235.

86 Delicostopoulos, above note 15, p. 601.

87 See A. Afilalo, 'Towards a Common Law of Europe: Effective Judicial Protection, National Procedural Autonomy, and Standing to Litigate Diffuse Interests in the European Union' [1998] *Suffolk Transnat'l L. Rev.* 349.

88 See Gascón Inchausti, above note 1, p. 56.

89 See M. Storme, 'A Single Civil Procedure for Europe: A Cathedral Builder's Dream' (2005) 22 *Ritsumeikan Law Review* 87.

already exist. It should not be so difficult to agree on at least some points about the basic procedural structure of that model.

There is an initiative already in this regard with the European Parliament Resolution of 4 July 2017, which contains recommendations to the Commission on the minimum common standards of a civil process for the EU.[90] However, although it includes a text with some articles, it is still a set of guidelines like those of any other directive, formulated even on a more general level than is sometimes observed. But this is a beginning, in line with the work of the European Law Institute and UNIDROIT.

Can these provisions really go beyond the establishment of basic principles and rights? We have some experience, not always positive, in the criminal procedural field,[91] and it certainly was not something as ambitious as a code. Perhaps we should act in the future with a greater courage, although with the necessary prudence in politically sensitive aspects. The establishment of a basic civil procedure should not be one of them.

90 2015/2084(INL). <http://www.europarl.europa.eu/sides/getDoc.do?pubRef=-//EP//TEXT+TA+P8-TA-2017-0282+0+DOC+XML+V0//EN&language=EN>.

91 See the wide set of Directives on this regard: 2010/64/EU; 2012/13/EU; 2012/29/EU; 2013/48/EU; 2014/41/EU; 2014/42/EE; 2016/343/EU; 2016/800/EU.

PROCEDURAL AUTONOMY IN SWEDEN

Is *Materielle Prozessleitung* the Answer?

Anna Wallerman Ghavanini*

According to a statement from an influential procedural law textbook in Sweden, the consequences of Europeanisation of civil procedure in consumer cases can largely be handled by courts through active engagement with the parties on defining the scope of the dispute: so-called *materielle Prozessleitung*. The chapter argues that while *materielle Prozessleitung* can indeed ensure compliance, to a significant degree, with EU legal requirements within the ordinary procedure, it can have only very limited effects on procedures initiated outside the ordinary courts, such as arbitration and summary procedures. Furthermore, achieving these effects would require judges to take a significantly more active role than what is

* I am grateful to my colleagues Jakob Heidbrink and Sebastian Wejedal, as well as to the editors, for their valuable comments on earlier versions of this chapter. All remaining errors are, of course, my own.

currently regarded as common and proper. It can be questioned whether judges are prepared and equipped to take on this role, without a mandate from the legislature and considering the workload and pace in the lower courts, where the opportunities for successful *Prozessleitung* are best. The chapter also raises a principled concern as to the appropriateness of far-reaching *materielle Prozessleitung* as a general solution to the problem of Europeanisation, seeing that it would significantly alter the balance between party autonomy and court passivity. The chapter concludes with a call for a principled approach to procedural autonomy, which reserves some flexibility for the Member State legal orders.

1. THE PROBLEM – AND A SOLUTION?

Europe is, as was recently noted by the editors of the present volume, 'in a period of increasing Europeanisation of civil procedure.'[1] When, in 1976, the Court of Justice of the European Union (CJEU) delivered its seminal *Rewe* and *Comet* rulings establishing the principle of national procedural autonomy,[2] it may have been a matter of pragmatism. EU law at the time contained few, if any, procedural provisions or competences of consequence. In the decades that have passed since, that has changed significantly; partly through sectoral harmonisation, partly through the establishment of an area of freedom, security and justice including the judicial cooperation in civil matters, and partly as a result of the Court's own activity. As so many other fields, civil procedure is increasingly turning into a melting pot for multilevel and multisource legal norms.

Yet, a student of civil procedure in Sweden may be forgiven for thinking that Europeanisation does not carry any innovations of consequence for domestic civil procedure. None of the main textbooks on civil procedure devote more than a few pages to EU law implications.[3] Even in scholarly

---

1 A. Nylund and B. Krans, 'The European Union and National Civil Procedure – A Rocky Road or a Smooth Process?' in A. Nylund and B. Krans (eds), *The European Union and National Civil Procedure*, Intersentia, Antwerp-Cambridge 2016, p. 1.

2 Case 33/76, *Rewe-Zentralfinanz eG and Rewe-Zentral AG v. Landwirtschaftskammer für das Saarland*, ECLI:EU:C:1976:188; 45/76, *Comet BV v. Produktschap voor Siergewasse*, ECLI:EU:C:1976:191.

3 P.O. Ekelöf, H. Edelstam, L. Heuman and M. Pauli, *Rättegång I*, 9th ed., Norstedts, Stockholm 2016, pp. 81–84; P.O. Ekelöf, H. Edelstam, and M. Pauli, *Rättegång II*, 9th ed., Norstedts, Stockholm 2015, p. 143; B. Lindell, *Civilprocessen: Rättegång samt skiljeförfarande och medling*, 3rd ed., Iustus, Uppsala 2017, pp. 61–71; P. Westberg, *Civilrättskipning*, 2nd ed., Norstedts, Stockholm 2013, pp. 123–126.

literature, the divide between European measures for cross-border dispute resolution, on the one hand, and general domestic civil procedure, on the other, remains profound. As a consequence, the effects of EU law on the ordinary civil procedure in Sweden remain unexplored in numerous significant aspects.[4]

The most reputable textbook of civil (and criminal) procedure in Sweden is *Rättegång*, which was originally authored by the late professor Per Olof Ekelöf – indisputably the grand old man of civil procedure in Sweden – and is currently being revised and updated by a team of experts. It appears in five volumes and now in its ninth edition.[5] An age-mate of the Treaty of Rome, it has shaped and continues to shape (it is mandatory reading at six of the seven LL.M. degree programmes in Sweden) generations of Swedish lawyers. Within those five volumes, national procedural autonomy receives the attention of two paragraphs – one of which is set in fine print. At its first mention, the principle of national procedural autonomy and the requirement of effective enforcement of substantive EU legal rights, as specified by the principles of effectiveness and equivalence, are acknowledged.[6] It is also noted that these principles 'may occasionally require that a provision in the Code of Judicial Procedure is applied in a particular way'.

The second mention is more interesting. There, it is noted that consumer procedures present a particular problem in relation to the Europeanisation of civil procedure.[7] The problem stems, as the authors correctly observe, from the fact that consumer procedures under Swedish law are governed by the party autonomy principle, which leaves the court

---

4 With a few notable exceptions, in particular T. Andersson's works *Rättsskyddsprincipen*, Iustus, Uppsala 1997, *Dispositionsprincipen och EG:s konkurrensregler*, Iustus, Uppsala 1999, and 'Ex Officio Application of the Unfair Terms Directive Cases Against Consumers: A Swedish Perspective' in A. Nylund and M. Strandberg (eds), *Civil Procedure and Harmonisation of Law*, Intersentia, Antwerp-Cambridge 2019, pp. 153–170. See also K. Nordback, *Interimistiska åtgärder i EU-rättsliga mål*, Iustus, Uppsala 2005; L. Ervo, 'Group Actions in Sweden: A Moderate Start' in V. Harsági and C.H. van Rhee (eds), *Multi-party redress mechanisms in Europe: squeaking mice?*, Intersentia, Antwerp-Cambridge 2014, pp. 243–259; L. Ervo and A. Persson, 'The Finnish and Swedish legislation in the light of the "ARD" directive: boards and ombudsmen' in E. Lein, D. Fairgrieve, M. Otero Crespo and V. Smith (eds), *Collective redress in Europe: why and how?*, British Institute of International and Comparative Law, London 2015, pp. 455–478.

5 P.O. Ekelöf et al., Rättegång III, 8th ed., Norstedts, Stockholm 2018, pp. 97–99; 218–221, 247–248.

6 Ekelöf, Edelstam, Heuman and Pauli, above note 3, pp. 81ff.

7 Ekelöf, Edelstam and Pauli, above note 3, p. 143.

in principle unable to take *ex officio* action. However, the paragraph is concluded by the assertion that these challenges 'can probably be resolved by the court through *materielle Prozessleitung*, by which the consumer can be induced, for example, to invoke an alternative ground for his claim.'[8] *Materielle Prozessleitung* (in Swedish: *materiell processledning*) denotes the court's competence and duty to manage the subject matter of the dispute, particularly by entering into dialogue with the parties in order to ensure that their submissions are clear, complete, and a true representation of their respective positions.[9] Thus, what Ekelöf et al propose is that the challenges of Europeanisation of consumer procedure can be solved through (more or less) informal communications between the courts and the parties, without the need for legislative amendments.

This thought should be viewed against the background of the legal situation in Sweden. The Swedish legislature has, as this author has explained elsewhere,[10] reacted to the Europeanisation of civil procedure with almost complete inertia, even in the face of legal developments at the CJEU that are difficult to accommodate within Swedish civil procedure *de lege lata*.[11] Thus, it falls largely on the judiciary – which, following the principle of sincere cooperation laid down in Article 4(3) of the Treaty of the European Union (TEU), must take any action available to ensure the effective enforcement of EU law in its jurisdiction[12] – to adapt national procedures to European requirements. This, naturally, limits the scope of possible responses, as courts are not at liberty to promote judicial reforms as freely as the legislature; this is particularly true for Swedish courts, which are known for their judicial restraint and loyalty to the legislative and executive powers.[13] The Supreme Court has so far never

8 Ekelöf, Edelstam and Pauli, above note 3, p. 143. This and all other quotes from Swedish sources are translated by the author, unless otherwise specified. For a similar, but more extensively reasoned, proposition regarding Norwegian law, see H. Haukeland Fredriksen and M. Strandberg, '*Ex Officio* Application of EU Consumer Protection law in Norwegian Courts' in A. Nylund and M. Strandberg, (eds), *Civil Procedure and Harmonisation of Law*, Intersentia, Antwerp-Cambridge 2019, pp. 171–191 at 176–181.

9 See further section 2 below.

10 A. Wallerman, 'The Curious Incident of the Dog in the Night-Time: Europeanisation of Civil Procedure in Sweden' in A. Nylund and B. Krans, (eds), *The European Union and National Civil Procedure*, Intersentia, Antwerp-Cambridge 2016, pp. 147–160.

11 For examples see section 3 below.

12 See e.g. Case C-249/11, *Hristo Byankov v. Glaven sekretar na Ministerstvo na vatreshnite raboti*, ECLI:EU:C:2012:608.

13 See e.g. M. Wind, 'The Nordics, the EU and the Reluctance Towards Supranational Judicial Review' (2010) 48 *Journal of Common Market Studies* 1039, 1046.

ruled on procedural implications of the Unfair Terms Directive[14] or on the effects of the principles of effectiveness and equivalence in consumer cases. Consequently, there is little or no guidance for lower courts as to how to exercise their *ex officio* powers, or the extent of such powers, in EU consumer law cases. Lower instance courts remain, of course, free – and indeed obliged – to themselves assess and apply the requirements of EU law in cases that come before them. However, a previous study shows that Swedish lower courts only exceptionally cite CJEU case law in consumer disputes.[15]

Against this backdrop, the proposition made in *Rättegång* has the merit of being pragmatic and optimistic. It does away with the need to set aside national legislation, which Swedish courts are traditionally reluctant to do. Instead it builds on the tools already available in the Code of Judicial Procedure (CJP),[16] which judges are already used to applying. Thereby, it integrates European procedural requirements into the Code, making it a *development of*, rather than a *break from*, current principles and traditions. In this sense, the proposition is testament to a belief in the adaptability of national rules and the flexibility of the European ones. If it is indeed true that the problem of court activity in consumer procedure – arguably the greatest challenge Swedish civil procedure faces as an effect of Europeanisation – can be dealt with through *materielle Prozessleitung*, it would be fair to say that there is still room for national autonomy and originality in European civil procedure.

The remainder of this chapter will be devoted to analysing whether this assertion holds true, and what, if that is the case, this implies for procedural autonomy in Sweden and beyond. The analysis proceeds as follows. Section 2 will briefly examine the law and practise of *materielle Prozessleitung* in Swedish civil procedure. Section 3 will be devoted to a number of case studies of EU consumer procedure law and whether reliance on *materielle Prozessleitung* will indeed allow Swedish courts to comply with the requirements set up by CJEU case law. Section 4 will summarise the findings of the case studies and put them in a broader institutional context. Section 5 concludes with a discussion as to whether and to what extent it is still warranted to talk about national procedural autonomy.

---

14 Council Directive 93/13/EEC of 5 April 1993 on unfair terms in consumer contracts [1993] OJ L91/29.

15 See M. Derlén and J. Lindholm, 'Från Champagne till Ramlösa: EU-domstolens rättspraxis i svenska underinstanser' [2017] *Europarättslig tidskrift* 695, 713ff.

16 Rättegångsbalken (1942:740).

2. *MATERIELLE PROZESSLEITUNG* IN SWEDISH CIVIL PROCEDURE

The duty of *materielle Prozessleitung* is codified in Chapter 42, Section 8, paragraph 2 of the CJP:

> During the preparation, the court shall proceed, depending upon the nature of the case, the issues in dispute to be elucidated and the parties to state everything that they wish to invoke in the case. By questions and observations the court shall attempt to remedy unclear and incomplete statements made by the parties.[17]

This provision should be viewed in the context of other rules reinforcing the party autonomy principle, such as the prohibition on the court to give judgment for 'something else or more than that properly demanded by a party' or to base its judgment on 'circumstances other than those pleaded by a party as the foundation of his action' (CJP 17:3) and the parties' exclusive responsibility to present evidence (CJP 35:6).[18] The rules apply without distinction to all kinds of commercial disputes, including consumer disputes.[19] *Materielle Prozessleitung* does not offer dispensation from these requirements of party initiative, but charges the court with ensuring that the parties do take the initiatives needed in order to pursue their actions. The judge's influence is limited to offering opportunities to the parties to take actions that may be beneficial to them.

In practice, *materielle Prozessleitung* is typically exercised through a written request for clarification and/or supplementing information (particularly at the early stages of litigation), or through questions and dialogue during an oral hearing. The legislative provision uses the language of a mandatory requirement ('the court *shall* ...'), and it is not unusual for appeal courts to quash a lower instance ruling on account of insufficient *Prozessleitung*. Still, the forms for and extent of such activity are left to the discretion of the court, which has to negotiate its way between the Scylla of rejecting well-founded claims and the Charybdis of inquisition and (perceived) partiality.

---

17 Translation by A. Brunzelius, R. Bader Ginsburg and K. Thelin, published in Promemoria of the Ministry of Justice, Ds 1998:65, available at <www.regeringen.se>.

18 Except in cases not amenable to out-of-court settlement; however, consumer procedures can, according to long-established tradition, be finally settled out of court and thus are not covered by the exception.

19 Cf. Government Bill 1994/15:17, p. 21, where it is explicitly noted that the CJP 17:3 applies also in cases that fall under the Unfair Terms Directive.

In this balance, judges will find little concrete guidance in literature. It has long been established that *materielle Prozessleitung* can be relied upon not only where there is a need to clarify the parties' positions, but also – albeit under great caution – where there are indications that the parties (or one of them) are overlooking a certain course of action, such as entering a particular defence or bringing a certain piece of evidence.[20] Generally, commentators have drawn a line in the sand where the court's actions would amount to either counselling[21] or pursuing independent inquiries. Still, these are vague restrictions and opinions differ as to their meaning. For instance, as regards bringing potentially relevant but not formally invoked facts or means of evidence to the parties' attention, one influential commentator argues that this is only permissible if a party has previously alluded to the fact or material, albeit in an insufficient or unclear fashion,[22] whereas the authors of another textbook hold that the court may enquire about factual circumstances typically present in a certain type of dispute, even without indications that the parties to the dispute at hand intended or wished to invoke them.[23]

As regards consumer and small claims disputes in particular, some guidance can be found in the preparatory works of the extensive 1987 CJP reform, which saw the short-lived small claims procedure abolished and small claims disputes brought under the scope of the general civil procedure rules of the CJP. In those works, the drafters of the amendments advocate more active *materielle Prozessleitung* in small claims disputes in order to compensate, to some extent, for the expected lack of legal representation.[24] In a similar vein – and of particular importance for consumer procedures – it was noted that *materielle Prozessleitung* would help create a level playing field and even out imbalances between the parties.[25] It was also held that the existence of mandatory rules of private law – such as the consumer protection legislation – should have the same effect, i.e. more active and far-reaching *materielle Prozessleitung*.[26]

---

20 P.O. Ekelöf, H. Edelstam and M. Pauli, *Rättegång V*, 8th ed., Norstedts, Stockholm 2011, pp. 45ff; Westberg, above note 3, pp. 335ff.

21 Cf. however E. Eldjarn, *Materiell prosessledelse*, Cappalen Damm Akademisk, Oslo 2015, p. 3, who prefers the term 'guidance' over 'management' (Norwegian: *veiledning* over *prosessledelse*) as providing a more adequate idea of the concept.

22 Lindell, above note 3, p. 294.

23 Ekelöf, Edelstam and Pauli, above note 20, p. 50.

24 Government Bill 1986/87:89, p. 107.

25 Public Inquiry Report SOU 1982:26, p. 122.

26 Government Bill 1986:87/89, p. 106.

In later CJP reforms, however, the trend seems to have been reversed, with the drafters emphasising the parties' responsibilities rather than those of the court.

3. EUROPEANISATION THROUGH *MATERIELLE PROZESSLEITUNG*: CASE STUDIES

This section will examine the proposition described above: that *materielle Prozessleitung* can function as a method for the implementation of EU law requirements on Swedish civil procedure in consumer cases. The analysis will focus on five case studies based on the case law of the CJEU: examining unfair prorogation clauses; courts going beyond the scope of the dispute as defined by the parties; examining facts of the case, in particular in relation to the applicability of the Unfair Terms Directive; disapplying unfair arbitration awards; and protecting consumer rights in summary and default procedures. These cases have two things in common. First, the problem brought before the CJEU, or a very similar problem, might have occurred before Swedish courts. Cases focusing on procedural mechanisms and characteristics with no equivalent in Swedish civil procedure have been excluded. Second, the CJEU's judgment in all these cases are, at least on a *prima facie* examination, difficult to reconcile with the CJP as it is normally interpreted.

For reasons of space, the analysis of each problem will be brief and focus only on the points of interest for the purposes of this chapter. It should in particular be noted that the analysis focuses on *materielle Prozessleitung* as a means of Europeanisation and therefore does not take into account other potential avenues to ensure EU law compliance, such as harmonious interpretation of national law.

3.1. UNFAIR PROROGATION CLAUSES

In *Océano*,[27] the CJEU ruled on the effects of an unfair prorogation clause in a consumer agreement. It held that such clauses must not be binding

[27] Joined Cases C-240/98 to C-244/98, *Océano Grupo Editorial SA v. Roció Murciano Quintero and Salvat Editores SA v. José M. Sánchez Alcón Prades and Others*, ECLI:EU:C:2000:346.

on the consumer, and that the Directive empowered the national court to assess and set aside an unfair clause of its own motion. In *Pannon*,[28] it reinforced that decision by holding that the national court had indeed a duty to carry out such *ex officio* assessment of potentially unfair clauses, including (but not limited to) prorogation clauses. It further held that the court must refrain from applying clauses that have been found unfair, unless the consumer has been aware of their unfair nature and expressed his willingness to be bound by it.

According to the CJP, the court is in principle able to decline jurisdiction only following an objection by the defendant (CJP 10:18). *Ex officio* examination of a prorogation clause upon which the claimant bases his choice of court is possible only in two situations: where competence is exclusive by law (which would only apply exceptionally in consumer cases) and where the defendant remains entirely passive. If a defendant consumer enters a defence in substance without objecting to the court's competence, or fails to lodge an objection within the prescribed time limits (CJP 34:2 establishes that an objection to the court's competence must be lodged in the first, and timely, submission in the case), the court would be bound to proceed with the case without examining its competence or the fairness of the prorogation clause. The requirements of *Océano* and *Pannon* thus seem difficult to fulfil.[29]

Could this problem be addressed by way of *materielle Prozessleitung*? First, as the legal requirement of party activity remains unaltered, the time limit described above implies that any *Prozessleitung* must occur before the consumer enters his first appearance in court (orally or in writing); otherwise any objection incited would be time-barred. It would certainly be possible for the court to notify the consumer, when issuing the law suit, of his right to contest the court's competence and the potentially unfair nature of a prorogation clause, in the same way as is already done in cases falling under the scope of the Brussels I Regulation.[30] If the consumer 'takes the hint' and lodges an objection – or if he remains completely passive – the court is at liberty to perform a full review of the clause.

---

28 Case C-243/08, *Pannon GSM Zrt. V. Erzsébet Sustikné Győrfi*, ECLI:EU:C:2009:350.

29 For a more thorough discussion of this problem and possible solutions see Andersson, above note 4, pp. 158–162. As he points out, it may be possible to solve the problem by reading a mandatory jurisdiction provision into the Act on Unfair Terms in Consumer Contracts; this, however, falls outside the scope of the current study.

30 Regulation (EU) No 1215/2012 of the European Parliament and of the Council of 12 December2012 on jurisdiction and the recognition and enforcement of judgments in civil and commercial matters [2012] OJ L 351/1, Art. 26(2).

Conversely, if the consumer explicitly accepts the court's jurisdiction, this is also acceptable.[31]

If, however, the consumer fails to take a stand on the competence issue, the problem persists: EU law demands that the court examines the grounds for its competence and, as the case may be, declares the action inadmissible, whereas Swedish law prohibits such *ex officio* activity. The likelihood of this situation materialising depends, of course, on the manner in which the consumer is informed of his rights. If the court explicitly asks whether the consumer accepts the jurisdiction of the court, the risk may be minor. However, it is doubtful whether judges would be willing to take so active a role, and more generally held information notices may fail to alert the consumer to the course of action needed.

Lastly, it may be noted that if the judgment in *Océano* is, as has been suggested, interpreted as requiring the dismissal of the action without even notifying the defendant,[32] compliance naturally cannot be achieved by way of *materielle Prozessleitung*, as this method by definition presupposes interaction between the court and the parties.

3.2. GROUNDS NOT RELIED UPON AND REMEDIES NOT SOUGHT

In *Duarte Hueros*,[33] the CJEU held that national law precluding the court from granting a price reduction (to which the consumer was entitled, but which he had not requested) where a consumer had brought an action for rescission (which the consumer was not entitled to under substantive law) was contrary to the principle of effectiveness. The Court noted that under the applicable national law, the court was bound by the remedy sought by the party, and that remedy could not be altered once an action had been filed. This, it held, made the consumer protection offered by the Consumer Sales and Guarantees Directive[34] excessively difficult to enforce, as the consumer could be expected neither to anticipate the court's assessment as regards the severity of the fault, nor to bring

31 C-243/08, *Pannon GSM Zrt. v. Erzsébet Sustikné Győrfi*, ECLI:EU:C:2009:350 at [33].

32 T. Andersson, 'EG-domstolens avgörande i Océano-målet samt konsumenträtt och forumregler i Sverige' (2001) 4 *Europarättslig Tidskrift* 565, 572.

33 Case C-32/12, *Soledad Duarte Hueros v. Autociba SA and Automóviles Citroën España SA*, ECLI:EU:C:2013:637.

34 Directive 1999/44/EC of the European Parliament and of the Council of 25 May 1999 on certain aspects of the sale of consumer goods and associated guarantees [1999] OJ L 171/12.

alternative claims. Similarly, in *Asbeek Brusse* and *Banif Plus Bank*, the CJEU found that the effectiveness of EU consumer protection requires that national courts be able to establish the unfairness of a contract clause and all consequences flowing from that unfairness, 'without waiting for the consumer [...] to submit a statement requesting that that term be declared invalid'.[35] This requirement applies even where the consumer has been fully informed of his rights.

As was described in the previous section, Swedish law provides that the court is neither permitted to award the claimant a remedy other than that sought, nor to base its reasoning on grounds other than those duly relied upon by the parties (CJP 17:3). Changing or amending the claim is, according to the main rule, not permitted, although exceptions are provided for (CJP 13:3). Additional grounds may be added in the first instance, as long as they do not have the effect of changing the subject matter of the procedure (CJP 13:3(3)). Thus, the Swedish rules on changing the action appear to be more generous towards the claimant than the Spanish provisions applicable in *Duarte Hueros*. Yet, they do not provide a possibility for the court to grant a consumer the appropriate remedy, where the consumer himself has failed to identify it. Nor do they, as appears to have been the case in *Asbeek Brusse* and *Banif Plus Bank*, allow the court to grant any relief based on the unfairness of a contractual clause, unless the consumer has relied upon that unfairness in court.[36]

Still, it is conceivable that a circumspect judge through questions and observations may induce the consumer to amend his claim or the grounds for it. This would be possible as long as the problem is discovered and handled during the preparatory stage of the procedure (as regards the remedy sought) or generally in the first instance (as regards the grounds). Again, this solution presupposes that the judge's questions or remarks are clear enough for the consumer to understand what actions are required of him, and that the judge feels that such clarity is possible without overstepping her competence and risking her impartiality. Assuming that can be achieved, however, it appears that compliance with this requirement can indeed be ensured through *materielle Prozessleitung*.

---

35 Case C-472/11, *Banif Plus Bank Zrt v. Csaba Csipai and Viktória Csipai*, ECLI:EU:C:2013:88 at [28]; Case C-488/11, *Asbeek Brusse and de Man Garabito v. Jahani BV*, ECLI:EU:C:2013:341 at [50].

36 It would be possible to achieve this effect by considering the unfairness to be a matter outside the scope of party autonomy (cf. C-488/11, *Asbeek Brusse and de Man Garabito v. Jahani BV*, ECLI:EU:C:2013:341 at [45]). Again, however, this discussion falls outside the scope of this chapter.

3.3. EXAMINATION OF FACTS

In *Pénzügyi Lízing*,[37] the CJEU held that when the applicability of the Unfair Terms Directive is in doubt, the national court must investigate this matter of its own motion. At first glance, this may seem like a simple reference to the *jura novit curia* principle, which is recognised in Swedish civil procedure. However, the Court also stated that this obligation entails that the national court 'in all cases and whatever the rules of its domestic law [must] determine whether or not the contested term was individually negotiated between a seller or supplier and a consumer.'[38] If the drafting of the contract has not been alluded to by the parties, complying with this requirement would entail going beyond the scope of the dispute as determined by CJP 17:3 (cited above). As it includes the establishment of facts, it possibly also requires the court to bring evidence of its own motion, which would be contrary to CJP 35:5.

However, again it seems likely that a timely exercise of *materielle Prozessleitung* may provide a cure. Indeed, that solution appears to have been prescribed by the CJEU itself in its related ruling in *Faber*, in which it established that a national court must determine *ex officio* whether an individual qualifies as a consumer under the Unfair Terms Directive as soon as the court 'has at its disposal the matters of law and of fact that are necessary for that purpose or *may have them at its disposal simply by making a request for clarification*'.[39] If the consumer can be prompted to invoke the fact that the unfair clause in question had not been individually negotiated, this would presumably often be sufficient to enable the court to rule on the matter (as this point is unlikely to be disputed by the defendant). Compared to the situations discussed above, this also seems to be a relatively unobtrusive and therefore less controversial case of *Prozessleitung*, particularly as standard clauses must be considered to be typical elements of consumer contracts.[40]

---

37 Case C-137/08, *VB Pénzügyi Lízing Zrt. v. Ferenc Schneider*, ECLI:EU:C:2010:659.

38 Ibid, at [51].

39 Case C-497/13, *Froukje Faber v. Autobedrijf Hazet Ochten BV*, ECLI:EU:C:2015:357 at [46] (emphasis added).

40 Cf. above at note 23. I. Bach, 'The Role of the Judge in Consumer Cases: A German Perspective' in A. Nylund and M. Strandberg, (eds), *Civil Procedure and Harmonisation of Law*, Intersentia, Antwerp-Cambridge 2019, pp. 139–151 at 147ff, reaches a similar conclusion on the basis of German law.

3.4. ENFORCEMENT OF ARBITRATION AWARDS

According to the Swedish Arbitration Act (AA),[41] consumer arbitration clauses are not valid unless negotiated after the dispute arose (AA section 6). Arbitral awards delivered despite the dispute not being covered by a valid arbitration agreement can be wholly or partially set aside in a subsequent procedure before the ordinary courts (AA section 34). This, however, is not possible if the consumer participated in the arbitration; in this case he is considered to have waived his right to invoke the invalidity of the arbitration clause (AA section 34(2)).

This appears to be at least partially incompatible with the requirements of the Unfair Terms Directive, as interpreted by the CJEU. According to the ruling in *Mostaza Claro*:

> a national court seized of an action for annulment of an arbitration award must determine whether the arbitration agreement is void and annul that award where that agreement contains an unfair term, even though the consumer has not pleaded that invalidity in the course of the arbitration proceedings, but only in that of the action for annulment.[42]

This appears to be in direct contradiction of the Swedish rules. The problem, furthermore, cannot be addressed by means of *materielle Prozessleitung*; once the arbitration proceedings have been brought to a close, the original invalidity of the arbitration clause can no longer be invoked and is in fact considered fully remedied through the consumer's participation in the arbitration procedure. *Prozessleitung* can (to some extent) compensate for party passivity but cannot supplement legal grounds in substance.

The same goes for the ruling in *Asturcom*,[43] according to which the court must refuse to uphold an arbitration award having arisen pursuant to an unfair arbitration clause, even if the consumer has not even brought an action to have the award set aside. Granted, if the case is brought before courts and the consumer has not lost his right to invoke the unfairness of the arbitration clause (for instance by, as was the case in *Asturcom*,

---

[41] Lag (1999:116) om skiljeförfarande.

[42] Case C-168/05, *Elisa María Mostaza Claro v. Centro Móvil Milenium SL.*, ECLI:EU:C:2006:675, operative part.

[43] Case C-40/08, *Asturcom Telecomunicaciones SL v. Cristina Rodríguez Nogueira*, ECLI:EU:C:2009:615.

complete passivity during the arbitration process), a judge could presumably resort to *materielle Prozessleitung* to induce the consumer to make the relevant objections, thereby relieving herself from the necessity of assessing the validity of the arbitration clause, and subsequent award, of her own initiative. However, this presupposes that the case is brought before the courts at all. If the defendant consumer does not bring action, enforcement of arbitration awards is normally handled by the Enforcement Authority, where the procedure is in writing and in principle not contradictory and where, consequently, there is very little opportunity for *materielle Prozessleitung*.

3.5. SUMMARY AND DEFAULT PROCEEDINGS

Most claims against consumers are not brought before the ordinary courts under the rules of civil procedure, but before the Enforcement Authority by way of an application for an order for payment.[44] This is a summary procedure that, in principle, does not allow for contradiction. If the defendant contests the claim, the proceedings are either dropped or, at the request of the applicant, transferred to an ordinary court. If the defendant does not contest, or does not reply at all, the claim is in principle presumed to be well founded, unless the claim lacks basis in law (Order for Payment Act (OPA)[45] section 23) or is based on manifestly incorrect facts (OPA section 39). Consequently, the opportunities for *materielle Prozessleitung*, in particular in favour of the consumer, who is most often the defendant, are extremely limited.

In *Banco Español*,[46] the CJEU held that the obligation of national courts – and in this case the Enforcement Authority must be considered to fulfil the same functions as a court[47] – to assess the unfair nature of consumer contract clauses applies also in summary proceedings. Furthermore, in

---

44 See further Andersson, above note 4, p. 163.

45 Lag (1990:746) om betalningsföreläggande och handräckning.

46 Case C-618/10, *Banco Español de Crédito, SA v. Joaquín Calderón Camino*, ECLI:EU:C:2012:349.

47 For a similar conclusion see Andersson, above note 4, p. 165. In fact, order for payment applications were until 1990 processed by the ordinary courts. When they were reallocated to the Enforcement Authority's competence, the legislature made clear that the reform was motivated by practical and economic reasons, which outweighed principled concerns about moving a judicial operation – which the assessment of orders for payment was clearly considered to be – to an executive authority (see Government Bill 1989/90:85, pp. 26–32).

Finanmadrid, the CJEU observed that where national law may lead to a situation where a consumer is faced with an order for payment without ever having had the benefit of an *ex officio* examination of the terms of the contract, 'such a procedural arrangement is liable to undermine the effectiveness of the protection intended by Directive 93/13.'[48] Consequently, at some point before an order for payment is enforced against a consumer, it must have been placed before a body competent and permitted to examine *ex officio* the legality of the claim against him. Since Swedish order for payment procedures are finally decided and enforced by the Enforcement Authority and a more thorough assessment can be achieved only if the consumer contests the claim, it seems that this procedure falls short of the effectiveness requirements. Possibly, the Enforcement Authority could engage in *materielle Prozessleitung* when serving the application for an order for payment on the consumer, thus trying to induce him to contest the order. However, because of the summary nature of the procedure which lends itself badly to in-depth assessments of individual cases, this would in practice be both difficult and impractical.

There is also a related problem concerning the information available to the court (including, in the case of summary procedures, the Enforcement Authority). As the CJEU has repeatedly pointed out, the obligation to examine the unfairness of a contract term occurs as soon as the court has available to it all the factual and legal circumstances necessary for such an assessment.[49] Since, in the Swedish order for payment procedure, the applicant does not need to submit the contract on which the claim is based,[50] the Enforcement Authority clearly does not have access to sufficient information, and may thus appear to be 'off the hook'. (Although one might question whether, in a situation where a court that has access to information would violate EU law by not using it, a Member State can avoid infringement by ensuring that the necessary information never even reaches the court.[51]) A similar problem may occur in relation to default judgments against consumers, where, according to the judgment in *Karel de Grote* the obligation to act *ex officio* still applies.[52]

48 Case C-49/14, *Finanmadrid EFC SA v. Jesús Vicente Albán Zambrano and Others*, ECLI:EU:C:2016:98 at [45]–[46].

49 See e.g. C-243/08, *Pannon GSM Zrt. v. Erzsébet Sustikné Győrfi*, ECLI:EU:C:2009:350 at [32]; C-618/10, *Banco Español de Crédito, SA v. Joaquín Calderón Camino*, ECLI:EU:C:2012:349 at [43].

50 Cf. OPA sections 11–12 and further Andersson, above note 4, p. 165.

51 Cf. on a similar question Bach, above note 40, pp. 143–145.

52 Case C-147/16, *Karel de Grote – Hogeschool Katholieke Hogeschool Antwerpen VZW v Susan Romy Jozef Kuijpers*, ECLI:EU:C:2018:320.

In both of these situations, there is in principle a competence for *ex officio* action on the part of the court (OPA sections 23 and 39 and CJP 44:8 respectively). However, there is also a presumption in favour of the claimant and the bar for finding a claim unfounded is relatively high, covering claims arising from criminal activities or manifestly unreasonable tort claims, but typically not flaws rendering invalid otherwise perfectly legitimate contracts. *Materielle Prozessleitung* is, as has already been discussed, difficult in summary procedures and by definition not an option in the default situation, where there is no communication between the court and the defendant. While the CJEU is yet to clarify what information it considers necessary in order to carry out an *ex officio* assessment, it is arguable that the current standard makes it too easy to enforce unfair contracts; a problem that could perhaps be addressed through harmonious reinterpretation of national provisions, but not by means of *materielle Prozessleitung.*

4. PROBLEMS, PRACTICE AND PRINCIPLES

The case studies in the previous section show that it is possible, at least in principle and in theory, to achieve many of the results prescribed by CJEU case law through *materielle Prozessleitung* in the early stages of a consumer dispute. An important exception, however, concerns cases that never reach the ordinary courts but are settled by proceedings before the Enforcement Authority.[53] As these cases, by a wide margin, make up the majority of consumer disputes, this exception is no mere trifle; already this finding effectively rebuts the proposition that Europeanisation of Swedish consumer procedure can be implemented by *materielle Prozessleitung.*[54] Clearly, legislative intervention is needed in order to fulfil the requirements of Europeanisation of civil procedure, either by extending the ordinary courts' mandate or by providing for supplemental safeguards in the summary and executive procedures.

However, even in the ordinary procedure – i.e. in the situations where *materielle Prozessleitung* could potentially provide a solution – resorting to

53 *Materielle Prozessleitung* also appears to be ineffective when it comes to judicial review of arbitration awards, but cases of this kind are considerably less frequent, and the problem is thus of lesser practical importance.

54 In fairness, it should be pointed out that the textbook by P.O. Ekelöf et al only covers ordinary procedure. Summary procedures are not dealt with at all, nor is arbitration.

Prozessleitung as the sole means of guaranteeing procedural consumer protection is associated with problems both in practise and in principle. This section will explore two: first, the demands that extensive, effective and fair *materielle Prozessleitung* places upon the judges responsible for carrying it out, and second, the constraints that are inherent in the concept and the effects that stretching them would have on the basic principles of civil procedure in Sweden.

As regards the first objection, one might wonder if Swedish judges are prepared to take on the responsibility that *materielle Prozessleitung* of the kind and extent discussed above would entail. During the consultation procedure for the legislative reform that originally introduced CJP 42:8(2), a Swedish first instance court rightly observed that '*materielle Prozessleitung* often is highly demanding on the judge, not only as regards legal expertise but also with regard to practical skills, imagination and the ability to quickly register discrepancies between the parties' submissions'.[55] In order to be able to achieve the results required, the judge first needs to pick up on the fact that there may be an EU consumer right at stake. In a legal tradition where the judges typically do not have any responsibility to investigate the case more than is warranted by the parties' claims, already this may be a stumbling block – although an analogy to those civil disputes where the courts actually are responsible for ensuring a legal and appropriate solution, such as custody disputes or (some) competition law cases, could be helpful in this regard.

Having noticed a (potential) violation of consumer substantive rights, the judge must then find a way to bring this to the parties' attention. She must do so in a way that fulfils the CJEU's requirement of balancing out the disadvantage, particularly as concerns legal knowledge, that the consumer finds himself in, taking into account also that the consumer often will appear in person and without legally qualified counsel before the court. She must make the consumer understand which actions are required of him in order to protect his rights. This will often go against the professional instinct of Swedish judges, who have been trained in the tradition of court passivity and party autonomy. Furthermore, she must achieve this without giving the other party, the opposing seller or supplier, reason to question her impartiality. This requires considerable diplomatic skills.

---

55 Government Bill 1971:45, p. 64. Cf. also Public Inquiry Report SOU 1982:26, p. 120, where the expert committee noted that successful *materielle Prozessleitung* requires 'considerable experience and a good psychological skill-set'.

All this must largely be achieved in the first instance; partly because the possibilities to amend a claim or present new facts are significantly circumscribed in the second instance (CJP 13:3(2) and 50:25(3)), and partly because of the leave to appeal system, which entails that most consumer disputes will not reach the appeal courts at all. Furthermore, consumer cases often concern small claims. If the claim is lesser than approximately SEK 23,000 (€2,300), the case will typically be decided under the rules for simplified procedure. This means that the cases will be decided by a single judge, and that judge may be a law clerk (i.e. a junior judge with less than two years of judging experience).[56] In other words, the complex and delicate task of *materielle Prozessleitung* in these cases is to be carried out by the least experienced judges, in the courts with the highest caseloads. One may be forgiven for wondering – and it is not an expression of distrust in the Swedish judges – whether the Swedish district courts are ready to take on the task of single-handedly, on a case-by-case basis,[57] adjust Swedish consumer procedure to the requirements of Europeanisation as described above.

Secondly, even if courts were to take on this challenging responsibility, the appropriateness of the solution is open to questioning. Is the extent of court activity necessary to achieve the result conceptually compatible with the idea of *materielle Prozessleitung*, or would it effectively entail overthrowing the party autonomy principle entirely?

The rules providing the legal basis for *materielle Prozessleitung* are discretionary in nature. Although the expert committee behind the most thorough exploration of the topic to date held that a judge is under duty to engage in *materielle Prozessleitung* as prescribed by law and consequently not at liberty to follow her own inclinations on the subject, it also noted that it ultimately is for the judge herself to decide what the law requires in any given situation.[58] Furthermore, the decisive matter for the judge would normally be what *actions* the judge considered warranted by and compatible with her responsibilities towards the parties, not the *results*

56 Act with Instructions to the District Courts (Förordning (1996:381) med tingsrättsinstruktion), section 18.

57 The government emphasised in Government Bill 1986/87:89, p. 105, that the judge engaging in *materielle Prozessleitung* must 'in every moment [...] carefully consider what is compatible with the requirement of efficient procedure, on the one hand, and with the court's reputation, on the other', keeping in mind that 'an action that may be acceptable in one situation may, in a slightly different setting, be less defensible.'

58 Public Inquiry Report SOU 1982:26, p. 120.

expected from those actions. Consequently, while *materielle Prozessleitung* may turn out beneficial for a consumer, he cannot demand such court intervention as a matter of right and, even where it does take place, it does not create any legal rights for him.

Relying on *materielle Prozessleitung* to ensure compliance with EU procedural consumer protection law seems to change this. The CJEU's case law is clearly result oriented, less concerned with the ways in which national procedure work (in Swedish doctrine usually termed the 'inner' or 'formal' side of procedure) than with the results obtained (the 'outer' or 'substantive' side). And in order to be able to obtain the 'correct' results, the judge would have to abandon her discretionary approach to *materielle Prozessleitung* and to keep at it until she obtains the invocations or objections needed to be able to offer effective (in the CJEU's understanding of the concept) legal protection of consumer rights.[59] In essence, the substantive consumer rights based on EU law would turn into a procedural consumer right to court guidance.

Such a development would undeniably alter the connection between party autonomy and court passivity. This, in and of itself, is however not necessarily an argument against it. In fact, there have been proponents for significantly more far-reaching *Prozessleitung* than what has become the norm in Swedish courts. In his addendum to the public inquiry of 1982, Professor Per Henrik Lindblom argued, with particular reference to consumer procedures, that an especially active *materielle Prozessleitung* is not only compatible with the party autonomy principle, but that 'on the contrary, party autonomy is one of the essential reasons that far-reaching *materielle Prozessleitung* can be recommended.'[60] The judge must under all circumstances, Lindblom pointed out, accept that a party may not wish

---

59 On the transformation of national procedural powers into EU legal obligations see Joined Cases C-430/93 and C-431/93, *Jeroen van Schijndel and Johannes Nicolaas Cornelis van Veen v. Stichting Pensioenfonds voor Fysiotherapeuten*, ECLI:EU:C:1995:441 at [14]; Case C-72/95, *Aannemersbedrijf P.K. Kraaijeveld BV e.a. v. Gedeputeerde Staten van Zuid-Holland*, ECLI:EU:C:1996:404 at [58]; Case C-2/06, *Willy Kempter KG v. Hauptzollamt Hamburg-Jonas*, ECLI:EU:C:2008:78 at [45]; C-40/08, *Asturcom Telecomunicaciones SL v. Cristina Rodríguez Nogueira*, ECLI:EU:C:2009:615 at [54]; Case C-397/11, *Erika Jőrös v. Aegon Magyarország Hitel Zrt.*, ECLI:EU:C:2013:340 at [30]; Case C-488/11, *Asbeek Brusse and de Man Garabito v. Jahani BV*, ECLI:EU:C:2013:341 at [45]–[46]; Case C-497/13, *Faber v. Autobedrijf Hazet Ochten BV*, ECLI:EU:C:2015:357 at [56]; and further A. Wallerman, 'Towards an EU law doctrine on the exercise of discretion in national courts? The Member States' self-imposed limits on national procedural autonomy' (2016) 53 *Common Market Law Review* 339.

60 Special opinion by P.H. Lindblom in Public Inquiry Report SOU 1982:26, p. 617.

to amend his claims or grounds. Speaking of *Prozessleitung* in terms of questions and information about mandatory law, Lindblom appears to have envisioned *materielle Prozessleitung* as an educational effort by the judge, followed by a question put to the consumer as to whether he, in light of the information just received, wish to change his plea.[61]

Such a conception of *materielle Prozessleitung* accords remarkably well with the case law of the CJEU. The Court has repeatedly held that where a national court finds of its own motion that a fact not relied upon is relevant for the outcome, the *audi alteram partem* principle requires it to invite both parties to submit observations on the matter.[62] It has also ruled that consumers remain free to accept to be bound by an unfair term or practise that goes against other mandatory law, as long as this represents an informed choice.[63] Thus, clear and extensive information followed by questions as to the consumer's informed choices appears to satisfy the European requirements; and should the consumer still remain passive, the CJEU has held that the principle of effectiveness does not require the national courts to make up for a consumer's 'total inertia'.[64]

Nevertheless, although *materielle Prozessleitung* of the required kind has been imagined in the Swedish context, such visions have failed to gain following; as a matter of fact, Lindblom's ideas were voiced as dissent in a public enquiry that took a more restrictive approach (which was later endorsed by the government, and would since appear to have been further restricted).[65] Although an extended use of *materielle Prozessleitung* may accommodate for the Europeanisation of Swedish civil procedure without the need for a revolutionary change, the increase in such court activity may in itself bring about a revolution of a different kind. It remains doubtful whether measures of this magnitude ought to be undertaken without legislative support in lower court case law and, consequently, whether

---

61 A similar view is proposed in the German context by Bach, above note 40, p. 150, who aptly observes that 'it is not the smartest party that should win, but rather the party that has the law on his side.'

62 Case C-472/11, *Banif Plus Bank Zrt v. Csaba Csipai and Viktória Csipai*, ECLI:EU:C:2013:88 at [31]–[36]; Case C-488/11, *Asbeek Brusse and de Man Garabito v. Jahani BV*, ECLI:EU:C:2013:341 at [52].

63 Case C-243/08, *Pannon GSM Zrt. v. Erzsébet Sustikné Győrfi*, ECLI:EU:C:2009:350 at [33].

64 Case C-40/08, *Asturcom Telecomunicaciones SL v. Cristina Rodríguez Nogueira*, ECLI:EU:C:2009:615 at [47]; Case C-34/13, *Monika Kušionová v. SMART Capital, a.s.*, ECLI:EU:C:2014:2189 at [56]; Case C-32/14, *ERSTE Bank Hungary Zrt v. Attila Sugár*, ECLI:EU:C:2015:637at [62].

65 See Section 2 above.

materielle Prozessleitung should be designated as the first, only or general solution to a challenge as significant as that of adapting Swedish civil procedure to European standards.

5. CONCLUDING REMARKS

The present volume invites us to rethink the principle of national procedural autonomy. Is there still autonomy for the Member States? If the word *autonomy* is taken seriously, then the answer arguably is no – and there is not even a 'still' about it, at least not unless we go to times before the existence of the EU.[66] Ever since its seminal rulings in *Rewe* and *Comet*, the CJEU has held that it is only 'in the absence of Union legislation' that Member States remain free to regulate their judiciaries, procedures and remedies as they see fit (subject, of course, to the principles of effectiveness and equivalence). This indicates that the Court believes that there could be Union legislation in the field, and that such legislation would constrain the Member States. This seems to be less of a conceptual autonomy than a deferral to practical realities.

Furthermore, *procedural* law seems to be losing its autonomy as a consequence of the CJEU's involvement. As has been discussed in this chapter, the Court's case law is based upon the premise of effectiveness; the effective enforcement of substantive rights. The effect is that procedural law becomes subordinate and expected to adapt to the requirements of substantive law.[67] In those Member States that, like Sweden, have long traditions of a civil procedure distinct from private law and with its own logic and principles, this change may offer significant systemic challenges.

A third question is whether any procedural autonomy that may (still) exist is a *principle*. Several commentators have made the observation that rather than having normative force, 'procedural autonomy' functions merely as a shorthand for the CJEU's case law on procedures and remedies

---

66 Similarly see e.g. M. Bobek, 'Why there is no principle of "procedural autonomy" of the Member States' in H.-W. Micklitz and B. de Witte (eds), *The European Court of Justice and the Autonomy of the Member States*, Intersentia, Antwerp-Cambridge 2012, pp. 305–322.

67 The author has discussed this elsewhere, see Wallerman, above note 59, p. 359. Cf. also J. Lindholm, *State Procedure and Union Rights: A Comparison of the European Union and the United States*, Iustus, Uppsala 2007, p. 331.

before national courts in EU law cases.[68] Referring to it as a principle, as the CJEU consistently does,[69] implies that it is not only descriptive of an actual state of the law, but a desired one. If the principle of national procedural autonomy is actually a principle in the normative sense of the word, this would entail that the EU legislature ought to refrain from enacting procedural harmonisation – and that the CJEU ought to, too. It might also entail that any exceptions to these principles – i.e. any EU harmonising measures in the field – should be construed restrictively.

Swedish literature, and in particular the work that has been under examination in this chapter, appears to have assumed that procedural autonomy is at least a reality, and that the room for manoeuvre is significant. The above analysis has shown that this may have been overly optimistic. However, this depends not only on national law and the construction of *materielle Prozessleitung*, its potential and its limits, but also on the interpretation of EU legal requirements. If understanding national procedural autonomy as a principle in the proper sense of the word, the effects produced by a *materielle Prozessleitung* more active than what is currently the norm in Swedish procedure, but within the limits of what may be considered legal and possible, may indeed be sufficient: after all, can it really be said that it is excessively difficult to get one's rights considered in court, when the court in question does all but raise them for you? If, however, the CJEU case law is taken literally as a requirement placed upon the Member States to guarantee that consumers are not bound by unfair clauses or other behaviour infringing their EU law rights, even in the complete absence of consumer action – that is to say, even in cases where the consumer after prompting fails to 'take the hint' – *materielle Prozessleitung* will not suffice.[70]

---

68 A. Arnull, 'The principle of effective judicial protection in EU law: An unruly horse?' (2011) 1 *European Law Review* 51, 52; S. Prechal, 'Community law in national courts: The lessons from *van Schijndel*' (1998) 3 *Common Market Law Review* 681, 682.

69 See e.g. Case C-550/07 P, *Akzo Nobel Chemicals Ltd and Akcros Chemicals Ltd v. European Commission*, ECLI:EU:C:2010:512 at [113] and [120]; Joined Cases C-378/07 to C-380/07, *Kiriaki Angelidaki and Others v. Organismos Nomarkhiaki Aftodiikisi Rethimnis and Dimos Geropotamou*, ECLI:EU:C:2009:250 at [159], [174] and [176]; Case C-604/12, *H.N. v. Minister for Justice, Equality and Law Reform and Others*, ECLI:EU:C:2014:302 at [41]; C-234/17, *Criminal proceedings against Generalprokuratur*, ECLI:EU:C:2018:853 at [21].

70 Cf. Case C-483/16, *Zsolt Sziber v ERSTE Bank Hungary Zrt*, ECLI:EU:C:2018:367, where, having failed to induce the consumer claimant to amend his claim in the relevant fashion, the national court felt itself obliged to inquire as to the EU law compatibility of national party autonomy rules (at [22]–[23]).

Lastly, it should be noted that none of the cases discussed here have been referred to the CJEU by Swedish courts. This silence should not be taken to indicate that the problem does not exist, as the above discussion makes clear. However, it implies that the Swedish legislation has not been considered by the Court, and that the solutions devised must be transplanted into the Swedish procedural order. While this chapter has focused on cases where the CJEU has stricken down on national procedural rules, there are also numerous examples of national procedural rules being held to be compatible with EU law, despite encroaching upon the effectiveness of Union rights. Perhaps, if Swedish courts were to join the conversation, a middle ground could more easily be found.

In Swedish civil procedure (and not only there[71]), 'flexibility' has been the highest fashion the last couple of decades. While this development can be criticised, one hardly wants the opposite. Flexibility inherently and inevitably leads to differentiation and discrepancy, but so does almost any application of law. It is submitted that the interests of (not only civil) justice would be better served by ensuring a certain room for national manoeuvre.

---

71 See M. Storme and B. Hess (eds), *Discretionary power of the judge; limits and control*, Kluwer, Mechelen 2003.

COMPARATIVE INSIGHTS ON PROCEDURAL AUTONOMY

Bart KRANS and Anna NYLUND

1. INTRODUCTION

This concluding chapter sets forth to answer the questions posed in the introductory chapter to this book. The book's aim was to explore whether there are any differences in the way procedural autonomy is conceptualised in the Member States, whether procedural autonomy is more limited in some countries than others; whether some doctrines, principles or pieces pose more problems for national civil procedure than others, and whether some type of issues are more easily integrated to national law directly. It is too soon to give definite answers to these questions, but the contributions in this book bring us a step further. There appear to be both similarities and differences among the Member States. In terms of EU law engendering challenges, the authors congregate to some extent around the obligation for courts to apply EU consumer law in their own motion. Additionally, the sectoral nature of EU civil procedure law (i.e. that it applies only to a specific category of cases) is identified as a problematic issue by several authors.

A discussion of features of EU law generating dissonance with national civil procedure constitutes a common core for the ten contributions in this book. Another shared element can be found in weaknesses in approaches to and implementation of EU law at the national level. Thus, this chapter will concentrate on these issues rather than 'ranking' countries or individual pieces of EU law. Section 2 will establish whether there are any differences to the conception of procedural autonomy. Then, a potential clash of procedural cultures will be discussed. Thereafter Section 4 will examine how differences between the EU approach and national approaches to civil procedural law are a source of tension and explain how the quality of EU law impacts national law. Section 5 will explore challenges that could be attributed to suboptimal implementation and awareness of EU law.[1] Section 6 discusses the role of multispeed integration and the final section (7) questions whether procedural autonomy is still a useful concept.

2. THE CONCEPTION OF PROCEDURAL AUTONOMY

The introductory chapter traced the genesis to ECJ case law addressing situations in the *absence of* EU procedural law, impelling national courts to apply the principles of effectiveness and equivalence, as well as the principle of efficient judicial protection. In the meantime, an extensive and variegated body of EU civil procedure law has emerged.[2] It 'extends deep into the domain of civil procedure'[3] of the Member States. Hence, issues

1 Introduction, in this volume, Section 3.
2 Introduction, in this volume, Section 2.
3 Galič, in this volume, Section 1.

related to the *presence* of the rapidly evolving body of EU civil procedure law are more pertinent, and the principle of effective judicial protection are briefly mentioned.

The density and diversity of rules, principles, and doctrines with civil procedural implications, some of which are hidden,[4] are a source of vexation for defining the nature and extent of 'procedural autonomy', as many of the authors in this volume notice.[5] The same applies to determining the leeway for national legislators and law.[6] Nevertheless, none of the contributions attempt at producing a comprehensive definition of the term or establishing the room for manoeuvre.

The limitations to procedural autonomy are, at least on the surface, tacitly accepted in the countries in this study, with the exception of Finland where academics have displayed a tepid response,[7] and Poland where the current government has challenged the limitations that EU civil procedure law poses on national law.[8] Limitations to procedural autonomy are accepted in Norway, where they emanate from the EEA Agreement.[9] Consequently, the narrowing room for manoeuvre appears to be accepted across Europe, perhaps because it could be perceived as an inevitable corollary of harmonisation and efficient enforcement of substantive law.

3. NO CLASH OF PROCEDURAL CULTURES ...

A few decades ago, some commentators claimed that civil procedure is deeply embedded in national (legal) culture, making it virtually immune to harmonising efforts and consequently, that such efforts would be futile.[10] This book's current research indicates the opposite: the absence of cultural clashes is striking. Both national and EU civil procedure law strive at combining justice and efficiency.[11]

4 Krans, in this volume, Section 3.
5 E.g. Nieva-Fenoll, in this volume, Sections 2 and 3; Wallerman Ghavanini, in this volume, Section 5; Introduction, in this volume, Section 2.
6 Introduction, in this volume, Section 2.
7 Ervo, in this volume, Section 3.
8 Piszcz, in this volume, Section 2.
9 Nylund, in this volume.
10 See e.g. R. Marcus, 'Putting American Procedural Exceptionalism into a Globalized Context' (2005) 53 *AmJCompL* 709–710, who rejects the notion, noticing how widespread it is particularly in the United States.
11 Hau, in this volume, Section 2.1.

Some incompatibilities are inevitably found at the cross-roads of 28 national legal systems and EU civil procedure law, but in the vast majority of cases, it is not a matter of a clash of deeply held, fundamental values where harmonisation would entail a landslide of changes and a transformation of the civil justice systems as such.

Belgium serves as an example. Member States opting for another solution than the EU could faces challenges, as the Belgian implementation of the IP Rights Enforcement Directive[12] demonstrates. Both Belgium and the EU recognise that legal costs are a hindrance for access to justice and efficient enforcement of rights. Belgian law attempts to curb the costs by applying maximum limits for recoverable costs, thus reducing the financial risk and by making decisions on costs more predictable. The EU has chosen a system to protect the prevailing party by guaranteeing full compensation of reasonable and proportionate costs. Neither system is as such superior to the other, at least when the fixed amounts are not unrealistically low: one protects the prevailing party, the other the opposite party. However, in terms of IP rights litigation, Belgian law is at least partly at odds with EU law. As Piet Taelman and Jarich Werbrouck argue, part of the Belgian system (i.e. experts' fees) is easily aligned with EU law, but the core issue of lawyers' fees is harder to resolve. The main problem is that EU law is sectoral: the fixed maximum system is as such compatible with EU law, the discrepancies are limited to IP rights.[13] The same problem has arisen in the Netherlands, where the Dutch legislator opted for applying the general rules also in cases falling under the Late Payment Directive,[14] but did the opposite – enacted a separate regime for legal costs – in cases concerning IP rights.[15]

Other examples of friction between EU and national civil procedure law emanate from procedural innovations, such as collective redress and court-connected mediation and other alternative dispute resolution processes.[16] Scepticism towards introducing these innovations may ensue *inter alia* from the fact that they challenge the idea of civil procedure offering adjudicative dispute resolution for disputes with two parties, not

12 EP and Council Directive (EC) 2004/48 of 29 April 2004 on the enforcement of intellectual property rights [2004] OJ L195/16.

13 Taelman and Werbrouck, in this volume, Section 2.4.

14 EP and Council Directive 2011/7/EU 16 February 2011 on combating late payment in commercial transactions [2011] OJ L48/1.

15 Krans, in this volume, Sections 4.1 and 6.

16 Piszcz, in this volume, Section 4.

facilitative processes or multi-party processes. The US American versions of these processes, at least as depicted in news media and popular culture, appear to clash with European civil procedure cultures.

Considering the absence of serious clashes between legal cultures, it is hardly surprising that the resistance towards the narrowing national leeway in the domain of civil procedure, is limited. The only contributor addressing this explicitly is Anna Piszcz, noting how the Polish government in its nationalistic efforts resists EU law, and thus also EU procedural law.[17] Spain is an example of the opposite attitude: it welcomes intervention, at least in general.[18] Norway is another example: although the EEA Agreement does not include civil justice, and the Norwegian government consistently rejects EEA relevance of EU law of a primarily procedural character, Norway has still implemented EU law voluntarily.[19]

4. ... BUT A CLASH OF APPROACHES TO CIVIL PROCEDURE

4.1. A CLASH BETWEEN BASIC TENETS OF CIVIL JUSTICE

Both EU and national procedural law aim at removing obstacles for substantive justice emanating from procedural law.[20] Yet, the foundations of EU civil procedure law differ significantly from national law. Differences in systems, or perhaps more accurately, the fact that EU civil procedure lacks a system,[21] is a source of friction – and frustration. The national civil procedural regulations aspire to be coherent, consistent systems guided by a set of principles, concepts and doctrines to resolve disputes and protect rights in fair and efficient proceedings. EU civil procedure law is not founded on such aspirations: it is primarily a set of tools to enable efficient enforcement of EU law and EU policies and to facilitate the proper functioning of the single market particularly in cross-border cases.[22] As a result, pivotal principles, concepts and doctrines remain underdeveloped.

---

17 Piszcz, in this volume, Section 2.
18 Nieva-Fenoll, in this volume, Section 4.
19 Nylund, in this volume, Section 4.
20 Nieva-Fenoll, in this volume, Section 5.
21 Krans, in this volume, Section 3.
22 For a more detailed account of the EU approach to civil procedure, see B. Hess, *Europäisches Zivilprozessrecht*, C. F. Müller, Heidelberg 2010, pp. 87–126.

Moreover, the primary objective of many EU law instruments is to remedy problems related to a specific group of cases, such as cross-border small claims, cross-border service of documents or consumer cases. Sectoral procedural law, which serves primarily as an extension of substantive law, is problematic for Member States where civil procedure law is independent from private law, where it constitutes a 'free-standing' set of rules.[23] In terms of equal treatment of citizens and the idea of the legal system as a coherent set of rules, it is problematic to render a higher level of protection to one group of litigants, such as consumers, but not to other litigants in a similar situation.[24] Additionally, EU civil procedure law is fragmented in the sense that they do not regulate all issues, leaving some issues to national law.

The ramification of the differences in these basic tenets is difficulties to align national law with the requirements of EU law and to assess the national room for manoeuvre. EU civil procedure law challenges the boundary between procedural and substantive law, and the quest for coherence. These differences are manifested in different approaches to procedural principles, sectoral and fragmented law. The dissonance of the foundational ideas could turn out to be highly disruptive for national civil procedure law.

To illustrate how the underlying 'ideology' and the underlying system of concepts, principles and doctrines – or the lack thereof, as well as the methods and quality of law are key factors challenging procedural autonomy of the Member States, four aspects of EU procedural law are examined in more detail. These are case law-based regulation; case law-based doctrines could destabilise the foundations of national civil justice systems; the sectoral nature of EU civil procedure; and fragmented regulation in EU law and impact of the methods of regulation.

4.2. THE TROUBLED WATERS OF CASE LAW AND POTENTIAL CONFLICT OF FUNDAMENTAL PRINCIPLES

ECJ case law obliging national courts to apply EU consumer law in their own motion illustrates several problems with EU civil procedure law.

23 Wallerman Ghavanini, in this volume, Section 5.
24 Galič, in this volume, Section 2.

One problem is inherent to doctrines developed by case law. The case-by-case method results in fluctuating development: two steps forward and one step back, hence, the next move is not fully predictable. This could be an issue particularly in Member States where courts have not been, and still are not, considered to produce law, i.e. case law is not a source of law. In his chapter, Jordi Nieva-Fenoll explores the troubles arising from case law, particularly in consumer law cases.[25]

Furthermore, the procedural and institutional differences among the Member States makes it difficult to determine whether and how a preliminary ruling concerning another Member State is relevant and how it would translate into one's own system. A thorough analysis would require in-depth knowledge of the civil justice systems in all Member States. The relative inclination of judges to engage in dialogue with the ECJ through preliminary rulings influences the degree of clarification of the relationship between national law and the requirements of EU law. By requesting preliminary rulings national judges have an opportunity to participate in the forming of EU law, as Laura Ervo argues.[26] Judges have, therefore, tools to elucidate the room for manoeuvre, but do not necessarily make use of them.

Another problem relates to the interpretation of the obligations of national courts as follows from the case law. The ECJ mandates national courts to apply EU consumer law on their own motion and to assume an active role in the proceedings by giving hints and feedback to the parties. However, some ECJ rulings can be interpreted to require courts to assume a quasi-inquisitorial role, which is at odds with the precepts of party proceedings and adversarial proceedings, shared by the Member States.[27] So far, the precise requirements for the role of courts in consumer cases have not been set firmly, thus, German and Swedish commentators believe active substantive case management suffices to fulfil the requirements arising from ECJ case law.[28]

The requirement of *ex officio* application of EU consumer law is furthermore discordant with the fundamentals of simplified proceedings for uncontested pecuniary claims in some countries. In many Member States, the claimant does not have to provide a copy of relevant documents, or the court does not have the power or time to review the

25 Nieva-Fenoll, in this volume, Sections 1–3 and 7.
26 Ervo, in this volume, Section 2.
27 Galič, in this volume, Section 2.
28 Hau, in this volume, Section 2.3, and Wallerman Ghavanini, in this volume.

documents attached, as Anna Wallerman Ghavanini notes.[29] She also stresses how *ex officio* application of EU law requires a highly knowledgeable judge, a prerequisite that *inter alia* the Swedish system for summary proceedings does not meet. Applying the same requirements to summary proceedings for an uncontested claim as for regular civil proceedings would on the one hand improve the protection of consumers, but on the other hand it is likely to require Member States to redesign the civil justice systems.

4.3. SECTORAL RULES CAUSE INCOHERENCE NATIONALLY

Most of EU civil procedure rules are sectoral – they apply only to a specific group of cases, such as consumer, competition or intellectual property rights cases, or only to cross-border cases. As the example on legal costs in Belgium demonstrates, the cost rules are as such compatible with EU law: they are only incompatible in cases on enforcement of IP rights. Operating with a higher maximum for IP cases results in fragmentation and discriminates against complex cases in other fields of law, note Taelman and Werbrouck.[30]

To overcome the fragmentation, the national legislator sometimes opts for spill-over (voluntary, follow-up, bottom-up) harmonisation by extending the sectoral norms to all civil cases regardless of the subject matter or whether they are cross-border or purely national cases. Although sectoral procedural rules formally limit national procedural only for a limited category of cases, EU law serves as a (gentle) push to harmonisation, argues Bart Krans.[31] From the national perspective it is to be hoped that it does not limit the leeway for national solutions in practice.

The aforementioned lack of coherent concepts and theories of EU civil procedure is a predicament to spill-over harmonisation. Wolfgang Hau demonstrates in his chapter how the inconsistent regulation of and terminology used in evidence law, as pertains to the standard and burden of proof, is at odds with the national, consistent approach.[32] The same

[29] Wallerman Ghavanini, in this volume, Section 3.5.
[30] Taelman and Werbrouck, in this volume, Section 2.4.3.
[31] Krans, in this volume, Section 7.
[32] Hau, in this volume, Section 5.

applies to collective redress where the rules differ among EU instruments.[33] Aligning national law with EU law is virtually unattainable, at least doing so in a comprehensive manner, if the rules lack coherent foundations. There are several other examples as well, *inter alia* that the rules on disclosure are regulated differently in the IP Rights Enforcement Directive and the Antitrust Damages Directive.

4.4. FRAGMENTED RULES AUGMENT DIFFERENCES AMONG MEMBER STATES

EU civil procedure hard law is often incomplete: it does not entail a comprehensive regulation of all issues but leaves certain issues to national law. Aleš Galič demonstrates using three examples – procedural remedies in the Brussels I *bis* Regulation, cross-border taking of evidence and cross-border service of documents – how fragmented regulation, where some issues are left to *lex fori* amplifies the legal-cultural and systemic differences among Member States.[34] By ending midway and leaping to national proceedings, fragmental hard law reduces the level of approximation and is in itself a source of unpredictability – the diametrical outcome of what was intended. Galič explicates how attempts at solving these problems have failed; how the amendments have created new, more severe problems rather than reducing the level of problems.[35] For instance, removing *exequatur* proceedings in the recognition and enforcement of foreign judgments appears at first sight to be a simplification, but at a closer look, it generates more problems. This is particularly true for situations where the defendant party contests enforceability. The result is an illusion of harmonisation and of uniform proceedings in cross-border cases.

Fragmental regulations that are not fully self-standing and independent of *lex fori* do not as such reduce procedural autonomy. However, this demonstrates how procedural autonomy can be an impediment in cross-border proceedings and add to unpredictability that is already tangible in these cases. Relying on *lex fori* does not facilitate improvement of national civil procedure law, either.

33 Piszcz, in this volume, Section 4.
34 Galič, in this volume, Section 3.
35 Galič, in this volume, Section 3.

5. CHALLENGES ARISING FROM THE IMPLEMENTATION OF EU CIVIL PROCEDURE LAW

5.1. INTERPLAY BETWEEN NATIONAL AND EU LAW

Factors shaping the leeway for national law emanate from both EU law and national law. Suboptimal implementation or lack of dialogue between national courts and legislators and the ECJ and EU legislators breeds tension between national law and EU law and inhibits fruitful interaction between the two. When national organs do not actively engage in shaping EU law, the outcomes are likely to be less satisfactory. Thus, some of the narrowing leeway must perhaps be attributed to national policies, rather than the EU itself. However, EU law could also serve as an impetus for benchmarking and reforming of national civil procedure law. The detrimental effects of minimum implementation could be far-reaching in terms of the amount of friction between national law and EU law, and the quality of national law. Factors related to national law are explored below.

5.2. LACK OF KNOWLEDGE OR INTEREST AS A FACTOR

Based on the contributions in this book, one can conclude that procedural autonomy is rarely discussed nationally, with few exceptions, such as Germany[36] and Poland.[37] Finland[38] and Slovenia[39] serve as examples of national silence on the topic. Vivid discussion among academics does not necessarily translate into a general discussion, as the example of Norway[40] illustrates. Consequently, the general knowledge of, and possibly interest in, procedural autonomy and EU civil procedure law in general, is low. This has, in turn, several adverse effects.

Nationally, one problem is that EU law is treated as 'technical' matters and that one implements EU law mechanistically and does not analyse potential pitfalls in terms of divergences between EU law and national law, or the need for bridging legislation to bridge the gap between fragmented

---

36 Hau, in this volume, Sections 1 and 2.

37 Piszcz, in this volume, Section 2.

38 Ervo, in this volume, Section 3.

39 Galič, in this volume, Section 1.

40 Nylund, in this volume, Section 2.

EU hard law and national law. If one does fully grasp the aims, content and structure of EU civil procedural law one is not able to implement it smoothly and correctly. Additionally, one might underestimate the extent and complexity of the EU civil procedure landscape.

Finland is an example where EU hard law, particularly law on judicial cooperation has been implemented as 'technical' law with no or very limited implications for Finnish law. Finns run things: rapid, piecemeal reforms are preferred over big reforms, which results in hardly any discussion on the interplay between EU law and national civil procedure law, and a risk of a 'homeward' interpretation of EU law.[41]

Swedish law does not fully comply with ECJ case law on *ex officio* implementation of EU consumer law, yet the legislature has not reacted. Implementation of the doctrine is left to the judiciary: judges must interpret the cases, draw the conclusions and adapt their practices accordingly. The results are unsatisfactory partly since relying on discretionary rules is not the optimal method of implementation and partly since Swedish lower courts seldom cite ECJ case law and thus their reasoning remains opaque.[42]

The Polish government, for instance, made minimal references to EU law when enacting rules on collective redress. Although EU soft law is by no means a binding source of law for interpretation of national law, it is still important for understanding the genesis of national rules inspired by soft law. It is also a source of information for assessing the functioning of national law and especially for remedying weaknesses in national rules.[43]

England is the paramount example of consistent application of a method of implementation that minimises the impact of EU law. The English use the method unless there is a perceived need for improvement and EU law is perceived to supply novelties. Implementation is done as *lex specialis* limited to cross-border cases, with almost no examples of voluntary harmonisation.[44] This approach results in maximisation of procedural autonomy.[45]

One should still bear in mind that voluntary over-implementation to harmonise national processes with cross-border processes is not necessarily

41 Ervo, in this volume, Sections 2, 4 and 5.

42 Wallerman Ghavanini, in this volume, Sections 1 and 4, and M. Derlén and J. Lindholm, 'Från Champagne till Ramlösa: EU-domstolens rättspraxis i svenska underinstanser' [2017] *Europarättslig tidskrift* 695, 713ff.

43 Piszcz, in this volume, Section 3.2.

44 Sorabji, in this volume, Section 1 and 2.

45 Sorabji, in this volume, Section 3.

a virtue, either. Successful spill-over implementation necessitates careful consideration of EU law. For instance, Belgium has over-implemented the Account Preservation Order Regulation[46] to create a corresponding system for national cases. However, the rules for purely national cases afford less protection than their European counterparts for cross-border claims do. Thus, national rules do not fully exploit the potential of the European innovation.[47]

5.3. EU LAW AND THE DEVELOPMENT OF NATIONAL LAW

EU civil procedure law has the potential of serving as an instrument to development of national law and for voluntary, bottom-up harmonisation of law. Benchmarking and bottom-up harmonisation has, however, several prerequisites.

First, it necessitates a high quality of EU law.[48] The examples discussed above in Section 4 illustrate some of the significant deficiencies of EU law. The Small Claims Regulation[49] is another example: it does not offer significant innovations for solving the enigma of access to a court for small claims. As John Sorabji notes, English law already had well-functioning national systems put in place. There was no utility in the European alternatives providing added value, thus no impetus for spill-over harmonisation.[50] Paradoxically, the European small claims proceedings served as a source of inspiration for the rules for electronic procedure in English law in the wake of Brexit.[51]

Collective redress was discussed in parallel on a European and a British national level, the national study arrived at the most pragmatic solution, and EU solutions would be resisted if they were not concordant, since they would be 'sub-optimal'.[52] Among Swedish lawyers the prevailing attitude

---

46 Regulation (EU) 655/2014 of the European Parliament and of the Council of 15 May 2014 establishing a European Account Preservation Order procedure to facilitate cross-border debt recovery in civil and commercial matters, [2014] OJ L189/59.

47 Taelman and Werbrouck, in this volume, Sections 3.2 and 3.3.

48 Hau, in this volume, Section 5.

49 European Parliament and Council Regulation No 861/2007 of 11 July 2007 establishing a European Small Claims Procedure [2007] OJ L199/1.

50 Sorabji, in this volume, Sections 1–3.

51 Sorabji, in this volume, Section 4.

52 Sorabji, in this volume, Section 4.

is that EU civil procedure law has 'no innovations of consequence for domestic law', and thus it is of little interest, Anna Wallerman Ghavanini observes.[53]

Second, it requires the legislator and other actors at the national level to be willing to use EU law to benchmark and develop national law.[54] The examples above are an indication of European law being dismissed too swiftly at the national level. There is a risk that a few pieces of EU law, be it hard law, case law or soft law, with subpar qualities could suffice to taint the reputation of all EU law. Finland is an example of a country without small claims proceedings at the national level. Nevertheless, the European rules were not used to reassess whether corresponding national rules should be enacted in parallel to implementing EU law for cross-border cases.[55]

Finally, soft law, such as recommendations, could serve as a 'gentle' method of approximation of laws. However, as Anna Piszcz argues, if legislators in many Member States do not seize the opportunity to acquaint themselves with European and global innovations and developments or to evaluate current regulation and practices, the EU may be tempted to use more powerful methods to attain both approximation and modernisation of laws.[56] Consequently, the leeway left to the Member States could be reduced.

5.4. NATIONAL DISINTERESTS AND THE INTERPLAY BETWEEN EU LAW AND NATIONAL LAW

The disinterested attitude towards EU law is detrimental for the quality of EU law and for procedural autonomy. When legislators, judges, policymakers, academics and other relevant groups often disregard developments in EU law, they do not engage in dialogue to identify the strengths and weaknesses in existing law or laws in-the-making. The lack of input lowers the quality of law and hinders identification of discrepancies in design or terminology between national law and EU law.

When EU policymakers identify obstacles to access to justice, the Member States could be proactive and examine whether their laws contain mechanisms hindering justice in general, in specific sectors or in cross-border cases. Perhaps EU law could be less invasive if the Member

53 Wallerman Ghavanini, in this volume, Section 1.
54 Hau, in this volume, Section 5.
55 Ervo, in this volume, Section 5.
56 Piszcz, in this volume, Sections 3.1 and 3.2.

States would take the initiative on their own. Perhaps the measures selected could more accurately address the underlying hindrances. Similarly, if all Member States would be receptive to novelties such as collective redress, disclosure and alternative dispute resolution, less efforts would be needed on a European level.

After all, harmonisation of laws has no value of itself. Legal diversity, on the contrary, is a fertile soil for innovation, as long as idiosyncrasies obstructing access to justice and enforcement of rights are minimised or removed. Each piece of EU law should, therefore, be considered individually on their merits,[57] and not rejected – or embraced – *en bloc.*

6. PROCEDURAL AUTONOMY AND MULTISPEED INTEGRATION

Despite the fact that justice affairs are not part of the EEA Agreement, and that EEA/EFTA states consequently have in theory only a limited obligation to implement EU civil procedural law, the procedural autonomy of EEA/EFTA states is far from complete. One reason is that efficiency and equivalence as well as the principle of effective judicial protection ensue from the EEA Agreement and the principle of homogeneity. Another reason is that the strong interconnections between procedural and substantive law make the two inseparable in practice. Thus, many procedural rules fall under the scope of the EEA Agreement. The most interesting factor is, however, that a single market with a level playing field requires approximation of procedural law. Hence, although EEA/EFTA States have limited formal obligations to implement EU law with a primarily procedural content, there is often a need to do so voluntarily to ensure effective and equivalent judicial protection of rights deriving from EU law. Therefore, it is hardly surprising that the room for manoeuvre is not diametrically different in Norway than in EU Member States, as Anna Nylund explains.[58]

John Sorabji argues in a similar manner on English law: maintaining regulatory alignment of substantive law could be desirable after Brexit. In these cases, EU procedural law could pose a *de facto* restriction of British procedural autonomy even after formal obligations of approximation of

[57] Krans, in this volume, Section 8.
[58] Nylund, in this volume, Section 6.

law have been abolished.[59] One could conclude that being outside of the EU does not equate to full procedural autonomy, and that a level playing field, ensuring efficient judicial protection through identical or equivalent rules, judicial cooperation and cross-border litigation all constrain procedural autonomy to some degree. Competition among (commercial) courts could intensify the push towards approximation.

Furthermore, the extent to which EU law puts limits on national law, or at least the perception of the extent, appears to vary across EU Member States. It could be a matter of specific doctrines or design of specific parts of the system, a willingness to continuously review the national system, openness towards innovations or the level of knowledge of and interest in EU civil procedural law. Regardless of variation in the level and form of interference from EU/EEA law, vigilance is required to avoid the potential adverse effects of a significant gap between EU/EEA (sectoral) procedural law and national (general) procedural rules. The case of Norway illustrates how a proactive stance serves to mitigate the problems.[60]

7. PROCEDURAL AUTONOMY: REDEFINING THE CONCEPT AND THE CONUNDRUM

Procedural autonomy is an ambiguous concept. Assessing the leeway is onerous considering the complexity and extent of relevant law. Sometimes EU law influencing civil procedure law is ignored in the legislative process. Although the reason for this is not entirely clear, lack of awareness of the relevant rules and principles is seemingly a significant factor in this process. Consequently, the perception of the leeway at the national level is exaggerated, and national law is – unintendedly – discordant with the requirements of EU law.[61]

Another source of ambiguity to procedural law is a matter of the nature of procedural autonomy. Is procedural autonomy an end in itself or a means?[62] Wolfgang Hau replies that procedural autonomy, or more precisely maximising procedural autonomy, is not an end in itself.

59 Sorabji, in this volume, Section 4.
60 Nylund, in this volume, Sections 4 and 5.
61 Taelman and Werbrouck, in this volume, Section 4; Nieva-Fenoll, in this volume, Section 4; Galič, in this volume, Section 1.
62 Ervo, in this volume, Sections 5 and 7.

Nevertheless, diversity is also valuable since it ensures competition and innovations.[63] Most, if not all, contributions in this book appear to be concordant with this balanced view of procedural autonomy and welcome more EU civil procedure law.

The extent of EU procedural law leads Aleš Galič to conclude that procedural autonomy is a myth: Member States have merely a margin of appreciation in a similar manner as in relation to the European Convention on Human Rights.[64] Bart Krans concludes the opposite: procedural autonomy still stands firmly as a starting point, but it has numerous exceptions.[65] Regardless of whether one concurs with Galič or Krans, the room for manoeuvre of EU Member States – and states with close ties to the EU – has been palpably reduced during recent decades. 'Autonomy' is therefore highly relative.

Perhaps more importantly, framing procedural autonomy primarily as a matter of the size or nature of national leeway is not as fertile as alternative approaches. All authors in this volume concur in welcoming more integration in civil justice.[66] However, they are equally univocal in their criticism of the quality of EU law and the quality of implementation of it.

Our attention should be directed at identifying traits in EU law that propels innovations across Europe and enhances the quality of national law, as well as access to justice, in particular for weaker parties and in cross-border cases.[67] Concurrently, it is imperative to improve the quality of EU civil procedure law. Both Hau and Krans pinpoint how the lack of basic tenets of EU civil procedure law reduces its quality and utility as a tool for benchmarking national law.[68] Creating a backbone for EU civil procedure law would also remedy the problem of incompatibilities and inconsistencies across EU hard law. Furthermore, a coherent core could ensue in more coherent regulation, where EU law would to a lesser extent fall back on national law. The question for further research is to create a blueprint for how this could be achieved. The forthcoming Model Rules of European Civil Procedure drafted in a joint ELI and UNIDROIT project could serve as a starting point.

---

63 Hau, in this volume, Section 4.

64 Galič, in this volume, Section 4.

65 Krans, in this volume, Section 8.

66 E.g. Nieva-Fenoll, in this volume, section 8.

67 See also Hau, in this volume, Section 4.

68 Hau, in this volume, Section 4, and Krans, in this volume, Section 3.

Additionally, the level of awareness of EU procedural law nationally must be increased, in general. Methods of implementation require particular attention, as does changing the perception of EU civil procedural law as merely 'technical' issues connected to cross-border cases. Spill-over implementation is an art in itself: the gain is increased efficiency through state-of-the-art proceedings. Poorly done over-implementation brings few, if any, benefits. Many of the authors in this book, however, regret that the potential of voluntary over-implementation of EU law remains untapped. The result is considerable differences among Member States and a slower pace of innovation and reforms.[69]

Finally, improving the quality of civil procedure law – be it national or European – is a matter of cross-fertilisation and collaboration between national law and European law. A continuous dialogue, starting early in the legislative process and continuing through implementation to stages where law is applied, between national and EU legislators, policymakers and courts is essential for improving the quality of civil justice and the access justice in Europe.

---

69 Ervo, in this volume, Section 2; Piszcz, in this volume, Sections 3 and 4; Taelman and Werbrouch, in this volume, Section 3.2.

INDEX

ABOUT THE EDITORS

Bart Krans is full professor of Private law and Civil Procedure law at Leiden Law School, the Netherlands. He has previously worked as a practicing lawyer and as a full professor at the University of Groningen. His main research areas are the Europeanisation of civil procedure law, civil procedure law in general, the law of evidence and contract law. He currently serves as an editor of inter alia a leading commentary to the Dutch Civil Code and of a Dutch book series on civil procedure law.

Anna Nylund is full professor at the Faculty of Law at the University of Tromsø – The Arctic University of Norway, where she leads the Research Group for Procedural Law and Dispute Resolution. Her specialist research areas are comparative and European civil procedure, alternative dispute resolution and child law. She is a member of the board of the Nordic Association of Procedural Law and also of the council of the International Association of Procedural Law.

Lightning Source UK Ltd.
Milton Keynes UK
UKHW021838270120
357688UK00002B/6

9 781780 689067